A Faith That Endures

Discovery House PUBLISHERS

BOX 3566 • GRAND RAPIDS, MI 49501

*PUBLISHING BOOKS THAT FEED
THE SOUL WITH THE WORD OF GOD.*

A Faith That Endures

The Book of Hebrews
Applied to the
Real Issues of Life

J. Dwight Pentecost

with notes by Ken Durham

A Faith That Endures
The Book of Hebrews Applied to the Real Issues of Life

Copyright © 1992 by J. Dwight Pentecost

Unless otherwise indicated, Scripture is taken from
The Holy Bible, New King James Version.
Copyright © 1979, 1980, 1982 by Thomas Nelson, Inc.
Used by permission of Thomas Nelson Publishers.

Library of Congress Cataloging-in-Publication Data

Pentecost, J. Dwight.
A faith that endures : the book of Hebrews applied to the
real issues of life / J. Dwight Pentecost.
p. cm.

ISBN 0-929239-66-0

1. Bible. N.T. Hebrews—Commentaries. I. Title.
BS2775.3.P337 1992
227'.8707—dc20   92-26390
                        CIP

Discovery House Publishers is affiliated with Radio Bible Class,
Grand Rapids, Michigan

Discovery House books are distributed to the trade by
Thomas Nelson Publishers, Nashville, Tennessee 37214.

Printed in the United States of America

92 93 94 95 96 / CHG / 10 9 8 7 6 5 4 3 2 1

Contents

Preface

The path of the godly person has never been easy. It is a way beset with trials, tests, difficulties, and opposition. Saints in the Old Testament found this to be true. Old Testament believers such as Noah, Abraham, Moses, Joseph, Joshua, David, Jeremiah, and Daniel all were called on to suffer for the sake of righteousness. The Lord Himself warned, "In the world you shall have tribulation" (John 16:33). He promised that those who belong to Him would experience the same opposition and rejection that He Himself endured (John 15:18-25). The book of Acts records the first fulfillment of the Lord's warning in the lives of His witnesses; as long as believers are in this world, we also may experience such suffering.

It becomes evident from a study of the epistle to the Hebrews that the recipients of this "word of exhortation" (Heb. 13:22) were undergoing serious testing. The author recognizes that this is not only the common lot of believers, but also that it is inescapable as long as we are in this world. Consequently, those who were suffering needed help to cope with these experiences; that help is what the author sought to give through this letter.

While it might have been expected that the writer would rebuke them for their fears and for the weakness of their faith, he instead exhorts his readers to patiently endure in the life of faith they had previously known. He does this by showing them the superiority of the revelation from God they had received through His Son. He shows that they have a merciful and faithful Priest who is ministering on their behalf, whose position is based on a covenant superior to the covenant on which the Old Testament priests ministered, whose ministry is based on a better sacrifice than those of the Levitical system, and who ministers in a better sanctuary than the one in which Aaron ministered.

Since the Old Testament saints lived by faith (Heb. 11), the readers of this letter are called on to live by faith in the midst of their circumstances and to exhibit patient endurance as their predecessors did. These exhortations are coupled with warnings about what they would forfeit if they did not continue to walk by faith in patient endurance—not the loss of salvation, but the loss of the blessings that flow from that salvation.

While the details of our lives may differ from those to whom this epistle was written, the general conditions under which we live are the same. We live in a hostile, unredeemed world, in an unredeemed body, with an unredeemed nature within us. Because we belong to Christ, we are targets of the enemy's attacks. The flesh can grow weary in the conflict. The confidence of faith may give way to weakening doubts. Therefore we need encouragement to fight the good fight of faith, to continue to walk by faith, to manifest patient endurance in every trial or test, to live in light of the hope set before us rather than in light of present circumstances.

The help the author of Hebrews gave to those in circumstances similar to ours will provide the help we need to live victoriously by faith. His exhortations to patiently endure and his warnings against moving backward in our spiritual experience are still valid. They show us the importance of walking by faith.

This book, then, is one of the most significant in all the New Testament for strengthening and guiding believers into a life of faith. We cannot seriously study this book and apply its truths without maturing both in a knowledge of the truth and in a walk that pleases the One who has called us to a life of faith.

—*J. Dwight Pentecost*

Outline

I.   God's Revelation Through Jesus Christ Is Superior to His Revelation Through Angels (1:1–2:18).

   A. God's revelation through the Son (1:1–2a)
   B. The position of the Son (1:2b–3)
   C. The Son's superiority to angels (1:4–14)
   D. A stern warning against neglect (2:1–4)
   E. Reasons for the incarnation of the Son (2:5–18)
      1. To fulfill God's purpose for man (2:5–9a)
      2. To taste death for all (2:9b)
      3. To bring many sons to glory (2:10–13)
      4. To destroy the devil (2:14)
      5. To deliver those in bondage (2:15)
      6. To become a priest for people (2:16–17a)
      7. To make propitiation for sins (2:17b)
      8. To provide help for those tested (2:18)

II. Jesus Christ the Redeemer and Ruler Is Superior to Moses (3:1–4:13).

   A. The faithfulness of Moses and Christ contrasted (3:1–6)
   B. The rebellion at Kadesh Barnea (3:7–11)
   C. The consequences of unbelief (3:12–19)
      1. A departure from God (3:12)
      2. A hardening of the heart (3:13–16)
      3. An act of rebellion (3:17)
      4. The loss of promised blessings (3:18–19)

INTRODUCTION

The Nature of Hebrews

Four books in the New Testament were written specifically to Jewish readers. And while all four writers address Jewish audiences, the specific recipients differ in each case, and the circumstances the writers address are quite different.

The first of these is the gospel of Matthew. Matthew was not writing to prove that Jesus was the prophesied Messiah, for the resurrection had already done that beyond question. Rather, Matthew wrote to explain *why*—since Jesus was the prophesied Messiah, as proven by His words and works—the kingdom He had come to establish on earth in fulfillment of the Old Testament covenants and promises was not established.

Matthew traced the leaders' response to Christ's offer of Himself as King and showed that because of their official rejection of Him (Matt. 12:24), the kingdom Christ had come to establish could not be established. Instead, Christ revealed a new form of theocracy in His prophetic discourse (Matthew 13), while a new entity—the church—was foretold in Matthew 16. Moreover, because of the nation's rejection of Messiah, that generation of Israel would fall under a physical and temporal judgment (Matt. 12:31–32; 23:38; 24:2). Thus Matthew explained why the kingdom was not instituted at Messiah's first advent.

The second book addressed to a Jewish audience was the epistle of James. James' letter was addressed ". . . to the twelve tribes which are scattered abroad" (James 1:1). It is recorded in Acts 8:1–4 that most of the Jewish believers in Jerusalem fled because of the great persecution against the church and were widely scattered. Consequently they were without the oversight or instruction of an apostle. James wrote to provide the instruction and oversight they needed.

These Jewish believers knew that a righteous God demands righteousness as a basis of fellowship with Himself. They had been brought up under the standards of the righteousness of the Law. And even though they had been delivered from bondage to the Law, they were concerned with matters of practical righteousness. So James wrote to show how faith could produce a righteousness that would please God in every area and situation of life. In short, if they lived by faith, they would produce the righteousness of the Law.

The third set of books specifically addressed to a Jewish audience was the two epistles of Peter. He wrote "to the pilgrims of the Dispersion in Pontus, Galatia, Cappadocia, Asia, and Bithynia" (1 Pet. 1:1). These people, like the recipients of James' epis-

tle, were Jewish believers who were widely scattered and were without the oversight or instruction of an apostle. And even though they were scattered, they were still undergoing persecution and great suffering.

Peter, in his first epistle, wrote to explain how faith related to the sufferings those believers were undergoing, and to encourage them on toward patient endurance. In his second letter, Peter went on to warn them of the dangers of false teachers and false doctrine lest they should be led away from the faith.

The fourth book addressed to a Jewish audience is the epistle to the Hebrews. This epistle, by an unnamed writer, was ad-dressed to Jewish believers in Palestine, perhaps even close to or inside Jerusalem itself. These believers, because of their identifi-

---

The relationship between faith and righteousness is as important today as ever. As believers we need to remember that our trust in the Lord Jesus Christ makes us righteous before God, which in turn produces obedience in our lives. Obedience from the flesh, on the other hand, can never make us righteous before a holy God.

cation with Christ by baptism, had left the established religious order and consequently were cut off from all the privileges that belonged to citizens in the commonwealth of Israel. As Jesus had foretold, the nation showed its ongoing hatred of Christ by hating those who identified themselves with Him. And while at first they perhaps had gladly welcomed persecution and isolation, because of its long duration they had grown weary in the conflict and were looking for some way of escape. It seems that some had suggested that if they were to observe certain feasts and rituals in the temple without giving up faith in Christ, the Jewish community might overlook the fact that they had renounced their identification

with the nation and had identified with Christ.

As we will see, the author of Hebrews will exhort these believers to exercise faith and patient endurance in their present circumstances. He will take the precious things in Judaism and show the superior worth of that which Christ has provided through His death, His resurrection, and His present intercession as their High Priest.

The Author of Hebrews

Unlike all other New Testament epistles except 1 John, there is no salutation in which the author identifies himself and those he is addressing. Thus it appears that the author desired to remain anonymous.

Clement, Bishop of Rome, made mention of the epistle

Although the culture we live in is not uniquely religious like the Jewish community of the first century, those who identify with Christ today may be cut off from former relationships and privileges because of their profession of faith. If you have experienced mistreatment because of your relationship with Christ, remember that the world system hates Jesus Christ, and it will hate you because you belong to Him. But remember, too, that the book of Hebrews has words of encouragement for you!

in A.D. 96, although he made no reference to its author. It was attributed to Paul by Clement of Alexandria about A.D. 180, but no evidence was given to support this view. It is even possible that this attribution was made so there would be no question concerning the authenticity and canonicity of the epistle.

Though the authorship of Hebrews is widely debated, there are many good reasons to accept the idea of Paul's authorship. These can best be grouped into two categories.

1. Similarities in circumstances.

The reference to Timothy in 13:23 is very similar to ref-

erences Paul makes to his young companion in his epistles, as when Timothy was with Paul in Rome. The author's expectation to be restored to those to whom the epistle is addressed (13:18–19) suggests that the author was in prison. The greetings in 13:24 from those from Italy suggest that the epistle may have been written from Rome. Thus, chronologically the epistle could have been written by Paul from Rome at the same time he wrote to the Ephesians, the Philippians, and the Colossians.

The reference in 10:34 to the help given to the author by the recipients of this epis-

Have you ever been tempted to give in or compromise in some areas of your life just to ease the pressure of taking a stand for Christ? Some believers would rather give up a biblical stand on God's creation of all things if it means they will not be ridiculed for their beliefs. Others would rather give in to social drinking than be laughed at for abstaining. Still others would prefer to remain in a liberal or apostate church rather than face the social (or family) consequences of leaving. Just as the original readers of Hebrews faced tremendous pressure to give in to their peers, most Christians today are pressured by those around them to give in to the popular way of thinking about issues like morality, divorce, abortion, even the natural world around us. Without fail, the toughest option always will be to remain faithful to God's Word and God's calling.

tle could refer to the two years Paul was imprisoned in Caesarea. It would have been entirely possible for these recipients to have given Paul help during that time. While in prison in Caesarea Paul would have had ample opportunity to know the state of the Christian community. Since he could not minister to them in person, it would be possible to do so through this epistle. So it seems very easy from references made in the epistle to fit this writing into the chronology of Paul's experiences as reported in the book of Acts.

2. Similarities in doctrine.

Upon careful examination, there are numerous similarities in doctrine between what is written in this epistle and what is found in Paul's letters, and no doctrine found in this epistle disagrees in any way with doctrine found in Paul's letters.

The author displays a very high regard for the Old Testament Scriptures. He shows high esteem for the Law itself, for the Aaronic priesthood, for the tabernacle, for the feasts, and for the sacrifices that were such an integral part of the Law. As Paul affirmed in Philippians 3:4–7, the author gave up what was good for what was superior, yet held the Old Testa-ment in highest esteem.

The writer to the Hebrews also shows that the blessings made possible through the coming of Jesus Christ are of greater benefit than any benefit found under the Law. While he does not despise the revealed Judaism of the Old Testament, the writer of

---

The real beauty of Hebrews is the way it shows how Jesus Christ is superior to the old system He came to fulfill. This contrast between that which was good and that which is best holds a lesson for us today. Many times we are pulled in several directions by causes and projects that are good—but which threaten to dominate our time at the expense of what would be best. As we study God's Word and understand His idea of what is most important in life, we may be able to set aside some good things for that which is best in His eyes.

Hebrews does show the superiority of Christianity over Judaism. This is very similar to Paul's attitude toward the Law and the superiority of Christianity over Judaism. Like Paul, the writer of Hebrews emphasizes faith over the attempts of the flesh to keep the Law.

In this letter great emphasis is placed on the person of Christ, who is certainly an essential theme in Paul's epistles. Specifically, great emphasis is placed on the death of Christ as a propitiatory sacrifice.

There is a strong similarity between this writer and Paul in the use of Scripture. Some eighteen times the writer, quoting Scripture, refers to it as the spoken word of God (1:5–7, 10, 13; 2:12–13; 3:7; 4:3; 5:5–6; 7:21; 8:8; 10:5, 15, 17; 13:5). Likewise, direct quotes from the Old Testament are found in every chapter. Some examples include:

Hebrews	Old Testament
1:5a	Ps. 2:7
1:5b	2 Sam. 7:14
1:7	Ps. 104:4
1:8–9	Ps. 45:6–7
1:10–12	Ps. 102:25–27
1:13	Ps. 110:1
2:6–8a	Ps. 8:4–6
2:12	Ps. 22:22
2:13a	Isa. 8:17
2:13b	Isa. 8:18
3:2, 5	Num. 12:7
3:7–11	Ps. 95:7b–11
4:4	Gen. 2:2
5:5	Ps. 2:7
5:6	Ps. 110:4

The writer of Hebrews obviously had a high regard for the entire revelation of God, including the Old Testament Scriptures. Do we Christians today share this preoccupation with the Word of God? While books about the principles and application of God's Word have a valid place in our lives, we should ask God to give us an insatiable hunger for His Word itself—to know it, to study it, and to live it. It appears from Hebrews that the only real basis for understanding the complexities of the Christian life is the living Word of God (Hebrews 4:12). That fact alone should motivate us to make a lifetime pursuit of studying its pages!

Hebrews	Old Testament
6:14	Gen. 22:17
7:1–2	Gen. 14:17–20
7:17, 21	Ps. 110:4
8:5	Ex. 25:40
8:8–12	Jer. 31:31–34
9:20	Ex. 24:8
10:5–7	Ps. 40:6–8
10:30a	Deut. 32:35a
10:30b	Deut. 32:36a; Ps. 135:14a
10:37–38	Isa. 26:20
11:18	Gen. 21:12
12:5–6	Prov. 3:11–12
12:20	Ex. 19:12–13
12:21	Deut. 9:19
12:26	Hag. 2:6
13:5	Deut. 31:6
13:6	Ps. 118:6

Thus we see the author's heavy dependence on Scripture to support his argument.

There is a similarity between this writer and Paul in the way they use the Old Testament Scriptures. In writing to the Hebrews, the author's illustrations are taken from Old Testament history, and his doctrine is based on Old Testament revelation. Likewise, the letter's exhortations are based on the Old Testament, and its warnings are taken from Israel's past failures. This is very similar to Paul's use of the Old Testament in teaching doctrine and in making application of doctrine to the conduct of believers.

A careful examination of the phraseology found in Hebrews reveal a multitude of parallels with the phraseology found in Paul's letters. In fact, many of the phrases that are essential to understanding Paul's writings are duplicated in the book of Hebrews. The following list offers a sampling of the similarities in words and allusions between the Epistle to the Hebrews and Paul's epistles:

Hebrews	Paul's Epistles
1:2	Eph. 3:9
1:3	Col. 1:15; Phil. 2:6; 2 Cor. 4:4
1:3	Col. 1:17
1:4	Eph. 1:21; Phil. 2:9
1:5	Acts 13:33
1:6	Rom. 8:29; Col. 1:15
2:2	Gal. 3:19
2:4	1 Cor. 12:4, 11;

Hebrews	Paul's Epistles
	Rom. 12:6
2:8	1 Cor. 15:27;
	Eph. 1:22;
	Phil 3:21
2:10	Rom. 11:36;
	Col. 1:16;
	1 Cor. 8:6
2:14	2 Tim. 1:10
2:16	Gal. 3:29; 3:7;
	Rom. 4:16
3:1	Phil. 3:14;
	Rom. 11:29
4:12	Eph. 6:17
5:8	Phil. 2:8
5:13	1 Cor. 3:1;
	Eph. 4:14;
	Rom. 2:20;
	Gal. 4:3
5:14	1 Cor. 14:20
6:1	1 Cor. 3:14
6:3	1 Cor. 16:7
6:10	2 Cor. 8:24
8:5	Col. 2:17
8:6	1 Tim. 2:5;
	Gal. 3:19–20
8:10	2 Cor. 6:16;
	Rom. 2:15;
	2 Cor. 3:3
9:15	Rom. 3:25
10:19	Rom. 5:2;
	Eph. 2:18; 3:12
10:28	2 Cor. 13:1;
	1 Tim. 5:19
10:30	Rom. 12:19

Hebrews	Paul's Epistles
10:32	Phil. 1:30;
	Col. 2:1;
	1 Thess. 2:2
10:33	1 Cor. 4:9;
	Phil 4:14
10:38	Rom. 1:17;
	Gal. 3:11
12:1	1 Cor. 9:24;
	Phil. 3:14
13:18	Acts 23:1;
	1 Thess. 5:25
13:20	Rom. 15:33;
	16:29;
	1 Cor. 14:33;
	2 Cor. 13:11;
	Phil. 4:9;
	1 Thess. 5:23

(cf. Moses Stuart, *Commentary on the Epistle to the Hebrews.* Andover, New York: 1833, 147–151)

There are, of course, some factors that argue against Paul's authorship of this letter, though a closer look provides reasonable answers for many of these.

Many who believe in Paul's authorship explain the absence of Paul's normal salutation by proposing that he was writing to a Hebrew nation that held him in low esteem because he had left his influential position in Judaism to devote himself to the ministry of Jesus Christ. This explanation would be valid only if Paul was addressing the Jewish nation, as a nation, to bring them from unbelief to faith in Jesus Christ. A careful examination of the epistle, however, shows that the writer was not addressing unbelievers to bring them to faith. Rather, he was addressing *believers,* exhorting them to walk by faith in the midst of their present sufferings and to demonstrate patient endurance. And since Paul was held in high esteem by believers, there would be no reason for anonymity.

A better explanation of the change from Paul's usual style is the compromise suggested by Tertullian, who attributed the epistle to Paul who wrote in Hebrew, which then was translated into Greek by Luke. Although this seems to suggest some doubt at that time about Paul's authorship in the form we have the book today, this explanation was offered because the style of the Greek text does not seem to be Pauline. Rather it seems to follow the rhetoric and logic of the Greeks as exemplified by the Christian writers in Alexandria. There is a consistency in style and rhetoric in Paul's recognized epistles, while the style in the epistle to the Hebrews differs.

Another objection to Paul's authorship is based on the use in this epistle of the Septuagint, the translation of the Hebrew text into Greek, whereas in his epistles Paul normally makes reference to the actual Hebrew text.

How comforting it is to know that first-century believers faced social pressures so great that they, too, were tempted to become discouraged and to return to their old way of life. Although some preachers today claim that the Christian life should be nothing but "sunshine and roses," the truth is that a profession of faith in Christ may be just the beginning of great hardships and challenges. The good news is that God has provided for us both the motivation and the means to walk by faith even in the face of present sufferings. That is what the book of Hebrews is all about.

Still another question often raised is why the apostle to the Gentiles would write to Hebrews. This suggests that if Paul wrote this letter, he was stepping outside his designated role and usurping the role given to another apostle such as Peter.

Regardless of arguments to the contrary, Paul's authorship of Hebrews was accepted in the Eastern church centered in Alexandria from the close of the second century onward. Through Jerome and Augustine, this dominant view also was adopted in the church in the West centered in Rome. And while they gave no support for that view apart from tradition, they did not question it.

There seems to be some merit to the suggestion that just as the gospel according to Mark was written under Peter's apostolic oversight, so the epistle to the Hebrews may have been written under Paul's oversight, so that the truth contained in it and the doctrine it propagates are Paul's.

However, from the time of the Reformation onward, serious questions have been raised concerning the authorship of this epistle. It has been variously attributed to Barnabas, to Luke, to Apollos, to Sylvanus, and to Aquila and Priscilla. In fact, nearly every individual who appears in the New Testament has been advocated by someone as a possible author. Still others have attributed this epistle to extra-apostolic authors, such as Clement of Rome.

So while the debate has gone on endlessly, there has been no consensus concerning the author's identity. And since the author chose to remain anonymous, it would seem the better part of wisdom for us to let him so remain. Doubts concerning the authorship of the epistle have never raised serious questions concerning its authority, canonicity, or trustworthiness.

The Recipients of the Epistle

A second important part of information normally included in a salutation but that is lacking in Hebrews is identification of its recipients. Therefore we are left to deduce from the epistle itself those to whom the author was writing, their spiritual condition, and the circumstances they faced. The title, The Epistle to the Hebrews, which we read in our modern versions, was not found in any ancient manuscripts. In A. D. 180, Clement of Alexandria did make reference to an epistle to the Hebrews, although this was not the title given by the author. That title, however, obviously became the epistle's accepted title.

Because of the book's theological presuppositions, some have supposed it was addressed to Gentiles. However, this idea arises from mistakenly transferring to the church those Old Testament covenants given to the nation of Israel. This view sees the church as the recipient of things that were promised and foreshadowed in the Old Testament. Yet, since all of the covenants were made with Abraham and Abraham's descendants, the church cannot supplant Israel as the entity in whom the covenants will be fulfilled.

There are others who suggest that the book is ad-dressed to a mixed audience composed of both Jews and Gentiles. This is certainly true in many of Paul's epistles addressing problems that arose practically and doctrinally between the two groups. But in this epistle there is no reference to conflict between Jews and Gentiles, either doctrinally or practically. Had this letter been addressed to a mixed congregation, the author could scarcely have avoided dealing with those issues.

The only reasonable conclusion we can reach based on a careful study of the epistle is that it was addressed to believers who were also Abraham's physical descendants known as Hebrews. This is supported by the author's frequent references to the Old Testament and to Old Testament history as the basis for his warnings and exhortations. The author also presupposes the recipients' detailed knowledge of the tabernacle, the priesthood, sacrifices, and the feasts that were an essential part of the Old Testament Levitical system.

The danger the author envisions is that the believing

Hebrew recipients of the letter were considering a return externally to the system they had left when, by baptism, they made their public confession of faith in Jesus Christ.

The believers in Corinth or Ephesus or Colosse could not possibly have been the recipients of this epistle (as some have suggested), for those churches established by Paul were first-generation believers. By contrast, those to whom this epistle was addressed were second-generation believers (Heb. 2:3).

In short, there has been little serious attention given to any interpretation other than the one that asserts that the epistle is addressed to Hebrews.

Another question to consider is the residence of those who first received this letter. At one time or another, almost every city in the Greco-Roman world where churches are known to have been established has been suggested. However, careful consideration of this book suggests that these Hebrew believers were living in Palestine. This is supported by a number of observations.

For example, the readers have an intimate knowledge of tabernacle and temple rituals, sacrifices, forms of worship, services, priesthood, and feasts. Such knowledge would come only from long exposure to these things and was something those dwelling elsewhere would not have had.

Further, the persecutions and privations that caused the kind of suffering discussed in the book (10:32–34) came from organized Judaism and from Jewish people devoted to that religious system, and we know that such persecution was confined to Palestine. Conversely, the Christian persecutions to which Paul referred in his letters did not come from Jewish sources but from those involved in pagan religious systems or from Roman political oppression.

Another important factor to consider is that the proposed solution to their sufferings—namely that they return outwardly to Jewish practices and observe certain Jewish feasts—would have been possible only for those living inside Palestine. It seems apparent that the recipients had ready access to Jerusalem and to the temple. Thus we can reasonably conclude that if they did not live in Jerusalem or in the immediate environs of Jerusalem, they were in sufficient proximity to be there for special observances.

The Date of the Epistle

The epistle was obviously penned before A.D. 96, since Clement of Rome mentions it. In addition, if the temple was not standing, there would have been no temptation for believers to seek relief from persecution by returning to its practices. Therefore this letter must have been written before A.D. 70, when the temple was destroyed by the Roman general, Titus. Such a momentous event could not have taken place without any mention of it in this letter, particularly since Jewish rituals and sacrifices play such an important part in the author's arguments. In fact, the author seems to have had that event in view when he made reference to an approaching calamity (10:25).

One more factor limiting the time frame of this epistle is an anticipation of the onset of the Jewish wars that culminated in the desolation of Jerusalem (Heb. 8:13). Since these military activities began in A.D. 67, this epistle must have been written before that date. If Paul was writing from prison in Caesarea (where he was confined by Felix who governed until A.D. 58) and was transferred to Rome by Festus (who governed until A.D. 61), the book would have been written around A.D. 60. And finally, if one acknowledges Paul's influence on the book, and we remember that Paul was martyred in A.D. 65, a date between A.D. 60 and 65 would seem to best fit the circumstances. If Paul had no influence on the book, a date around A.D. 65 would still fit the historical situation.

Historical Context

To understand the situation in which the original readers of this letter were living, we need to survey the historical background within the nation of Israel. A thorough survey of the historical background and contemporary situation of this letter and its recipients is essential to understanding much of what the apostle wrote.

Prior to the birth of Christ, angels announced to Mary the coming of David's Son to sit on David's throne and rule over David's kingdom (Luke 1:31–33). A similar announcement was delivered by an angel of the Lord to Joseph, announcing the coming of the One who would fulfill the messianic prophecy of Isaiah 7:14 (Matt. 1:20–23). At the time of the Christ's birth, angels again announced to shepherds that the Savior Messiah had arrived (Luke 2:9–11). Eight days later Simeon proclaimed publicly that he had seen the Lord Christ (Luke 2:26–35), and Simeon's announcement was corroborated by the prophetess Anna (Luke 2:36–38).

The God who gave His covenants to Israel promising the coming of a Messiah not only revealed through angels the coming of the King, He also sent the one the prophets had said would introduce the Messiah (Isa. 40:1–5; Mal. 3:1). As John the Baptist introduced Jesus Christ to the nation Israel as their Savior (John 1:29) and their King (Matt. 3:2), the knowledge of John's message was so widespread (Matt. 3:5) that the nation knew that Messiah had come and the messianic kingdom was at hand. Of course, a divinely revealed precondition for receiving the messianic kingdom and its covenanted blessings was the nation's repentance (Deut. 30:1–6; 2 Chron. 7:14; Matt. 3:2; 4:17).

To authenticate His offer of Himself as king and to substantiate the nearness of His messianic kingdom, Jesus performed many miracles. Israel as a nation was called on to evaluate the evidence He presented and to respond to Him in the light of that evidence. But while some of Israel's people were willing to accept the evidence as a valid authentication of Christ and His offered kingdom, the religious leaders of Israel publicly proclaimed their rejection. Acting as God's duly appointed representatives of the nation as a nation, they claimed that Christ did not receive His power from God but from Satan; that He had not come from heaven, but had come from hell; and that He was a blasphemous imposter (Matt. 12:24).

In spite of all the evidence, the leaders persisted in their rejection of Messiah. Therefore Christ gave a serious warning to the leaders and to the nation that if they continued in this formal rejection, that very generation of Israel (which rejected Christ as Savior and Sovereign) would suffer a severe physical and temporal judgment for which there would be no forgiveness (Matt. 12:31–32). And as the time for the leaders' final rejection of Christ—which would consummate in His crucifixion (John 19:15)—drew near, Jesus repeated His warning of the judgment that would fall on that generation if they continued to reject Him and His offer of the promised Davidic kingdom (Matt. 23:37–39; 24:2).

As we know from history, Christ's crucifixion indeed sealed God's judgment on that generation—a judgment the religious leaders of Israel accepted when they said "His blood be on us and on our children" (Matt. 27:25). That judgment was carried out by Titus who destroyed Jerusalem in A.D. 70.

This forthcoming judgment, which Christ had said

Today we are sometimes told that unbelievers can be led to faith in Christ by some kind of outward influence—the success of believers, miraculous events, or other evidences of God's work. Yet the Bible shows us that even when Jesus Christ proved His identity through miracles, He was rejected by those who refused to come to Him by faith. We need to remember that it is the simple gospel—salvation by grace through faith based on blood—by which people are saved. Yet those who reject the gospel would continue to reject Him even if He were to appear in person. In your witness for Christ, concentrate on verbally communicating the good news of the gospel, and allow God to draw people to Himself through it.

was inescapable (Matt. 12:31–32), loomed large in the apostles' thinking between Pentecost and the destruction of Jerusalem. As we read in Acts 2, Peter addressed the nation that had assumed responsibility for the crucifixion of Christ by exhorting them, "Be saved from this perverse generation" (Acts 2:40). As long as individuals were identified as citizens of the nation, they were still under the judgment God would bring on that generation of Israel.

It was possible, however, for those who accepted Peter's message to escape that coming judgment. Specifically, if they would disassociate themselves from the nation, they would no longer be under the judgment God had pronounced on it. Therefore Peter invited them to "repent, and let every one of you be baptized in the name of Jesus Christ" (Acts 2:38).

Because the resurrection was God's ultimate validation of both the person of Christ and the offer of His kingdom, Peter's proclamation of the resurrection of Jesus Christ convinced many of the nation's error in condemning Jesus to death. On the basis of this change in attitude toward Jesus Christ and their acknowledgment of the nation's sin in rejecting Him, these were invited to separate themselves from the nation and to identify themselves with Jesus Christ through the act of baptism. Water baptism, then, was a sign that those who had been identified

---

Some people mistakenly believe that Christ's word of judgment on that generation of Israel represented God's condemnation of Jews for all time. Tragically, this misconception has led to mistreatment of the Jews at different times and places throughout modern history. As we will see, God is not finished with Israel, nor does he love Jewish people any less than all the Gentiles for whom He came and offered Himself. If you have any Jewish friends or acquaintances, remember to treat them with Christian love and respect, understanding that God loves them dearly and desires that they come to faith in Messiah.

with the nation Israel—now under judgment—disavowed that relationship and now identified themselves with Jesus Christ.

This act of baptism is referred to by the writer of Hebrews as their profession (Heb. 3:1; 4:14; 10:23). Those Jews who were baptized in the name of Jesus Christ were "put out of the synagogue" (John 16:2). They were no longer considered Jews or members of the commonwealth of Israel. They were treated as Gentiles. They were no longer welcomed in the synagogue or in the temple. They also gave up any possibility of employment because they were considered unclean.

But if they, because of faith in Jesus Christ, publicly identified themselves with Him, they would be delivered from the judgment God had pronounced on that generation of Israel. Baptism, then, built a wall between those Jewish believers and the community in which they had previously lived. Before their separation from Israel, these people would attend the synagogue, sit at the feet of the rabbi, and be taught the Scriptures. But now, rather than gathering in the synagogue, they gathered together to be taught by the apostles (Acts 1:12–14; 2:42; 4:34–37; 9:26–27). The apostles assumed the role that had been fulfilled by the rabbis in the synagogue, as believers

In some parts of the world, public identification with Christ through baptism brings the same kind of persecution and suffering that Jewish believers faced in the first century. That should cause us to wonder if our profession of faith in Christ is really "public" in that our friends and acquaintances know we belong to Him—and whether it is so clear to some that we actually experience the same reaction Christ would experience if He were here today. While we should not intentionally invite persecution, the Bible seems to show us that if we are living godly lives, some of those around us will take exception to our identification with Christ. In that way, persecution will be a hallmark of a godly witness.

fellowshipped together from house to house rather than finding their fellowship in the synagogue. This separation from the synagogue and from the rabbis only further emphasized their departure from the nation of Israel, which faced an irrevocable coming judgment.

For those with true understanding, the Resurrection validated Jesus Christ and demonstrated that Israel's rejection of Him was a sin in God's sight. This in turn vindicated the judgment Jesus had announced to that generation of Israel. Therefore the separation of thousands of Hebrew believers from the synagogue produced a hatred for them and ultimately generated a prolonged and intense persecution at the hands of the remaining unconverted Jews.

The book of Acts provides many examples of this persecution, beginning with Peter's ministry and continuing through the conclusion of Paul's ministry (cf. Acts 4:1–3; 5:17–28; 7:57–60; 8:3–4; 9:2; 12:1–4; 19:8–9; 21:10–11, 20, 27–31; 22:4, 19; 23:12; 26:10–11). Since these persecutions originated in Jerusalem, believers who suffered this persecution must have been in the land of Palestine, if not even closer to the center of persecution.

While many believers suffered because of the famine

With all the talk about poverty and homelessness today, it is difficult for Christians to know just what their responsibilities are. Based on examples in both the Old and New Testaments, God's priority for true believers in relation to those in need is always first to take care of the family of faith, particularly those closest to us. While feeding the "anonymous poor" is genuinely compassionate and can provide wonderful evangelistic opportunities, both in the Mosaic Law and in New Testament history, believers were expected to help those in the family of faith living godly lives yet in material need. How wonderful it would be if more churches would take seriously this call to help out those in their own assembly and believers in other areas who are experiencing the trial of material need.

that swept through the land (Acts 11:27–30), other believers who were baptized in the name of Christ lost any opportunity for employment. So fellow believers, because of their concept of a family relationship, contributed what they could to meet one another's needs. We also know that these circumstances led believers elsewhere to contribute to the saints in Jerusalem (Acts 2:44–45; 4:32–37).

Roman law guaranteed freedom of religion, and Rome had previously made every effort not to hinder the religious practices of the peoples under their authority. Christianity was considered a sect of Judaism and therefore was tolerated. However, after the devastating fire that destroyed Rome in A.D. 64, for which Christians were held responsible, the Jewish wars that Rome waged against Palestine began. These military conflicts would eventually climax with the destruction of Jerusalem under Titus in A.D. 70, fulfilling Christ's prediction of judgment.

To the writer of Hebrews, those devastating days were fast approaching. Speaking of the Mosaic Covenant, the foundation of the temple services, he wrote: "What is becoming obsolete and growing old is ready to vanish away" (Heb. 8:13). The writer seemed to anticipate the desolation by Titus—in which one-and-a-half million Jews would lose their lives—when he wrote, "You have not yet resisted to bloodshed, striving against sin" (Heb. 12:4). He said again, "You see the Day approaching" (Heb. 10:25). Thus we can clearly see that readers of this letter were living in days just prior to the calamitous judgment that would fall on the nation Israel, on Jerusalem, and on the temple.

According to the book of Acts, one other thing is evident in a study of this epistle's historical background: While the believers distanced themselves from the synagogue, apparently they did not separate themselves from the temple. Since the synagogue was a human institution not divinely inaugurated, and since the rabbis in the synagogues had not been appointed by God, believers no doubt felt free to separate from the synagogue and its teachers. However, the tabernacle/temple was a divine institution and its services were obligatory.

In Acts we find frequent references to believers fellowshiping together in the temple (Acts 2:1; 3:1, 11; 5:12, 21, 42; 20:16; 21:26–28). Evidently they saw Christ as the fulfillment of that which was prophetic in the Old Testament feasts, and they continued to observe those rites as memorials to Christ (Acts 20:6; 1 Cor. 5:7–8; 16:8). The centrality of the tabernacle/temple in their thinking would have made it easy for some believers to conclude that since the apostle Paul desired to be in Jerusalem to observe feasts (Acts 20:16), it would be proper for them to observe feasts at appointed times in the appointed place. Most significant, many apparently hoped that doing this would erase from their persecutors' memories the fact that they had abandoned that sys-

tem when they identified themselves with Christ through baptism.

Through an overview of Hebrews, we can conclude certain facts about those who first received this epistle.

1. It is clear from the book that the author views the recipients as genuine believers. And this perspective influences the rest of what we know about the intended audience of this letter. Consider the following passages:

1:3—"He had by Himself purged our sin."

2:1–3—The author warns them about neglecting, not rejecting, the salvation that has been provided.

3:1—The apostle refers to them as holy brethren, partakers of the heavenly calling, and Jesus Christ as the Apostle and High Priest of our confession.

4:1—The apostle argues that the danger is not that they will fail to attain salvation, but that they will not experience the rest such salvation brings.

4:3—The apostle includes the recipients as fellow believers together with him.

4:14—Christ is assumed to be the High Priest interceding for these believers.

4:16—They have access to the throne of grace, not to obtain salvation, but to obtain help in their present circumstances.

5:12—They are sufficiently mature and have been taught so well themselves that they are qualified to teach others.

6:4–5—When the apostle refers to those who were once enlightened, have tasted the heavenly gift, have become partakers of the Holy Spirit, and have tasted the good Word of God and the powers of the age to come, he is referring to the actual spiritual experiences into which his original readers have entered.

6:9–10—Their works demonstrated the genuineness of their salvation.

7:26—8:1—The writer affirms again that Jesus Christ is their interceding High Priest.

9:14—They could serve the living God.

10:10—They have been sanctified.

10:15—They received a ministry of the Spirit.

10:19—They are called "brethren."

10:21—They have a High Priest.

10:22–25—Their hearts have been sprinkled from an evil conscience. They have

The wonderful benefits that come with a relationship with Christ are often called our "spiritual heritage." As we will see, the writer of Hebrews believed that our spiritual heritage should have a dramatic and lasting effect on our lives. But is this really true of believers today? Does being enlightened by the Word of God cause us to lose our appetite for the crude language and crass humor of the secular world around us? Does becoming partakers of the Holy Spirit cause us to conduct our marriages, our families, and our businesses differently from the way we did before we yielded to Him? Today—and every day—is a good time to review some aspects of our spiritual heritage and look for concrete ways in which its benefits have changed the way we live.

been cleansed. They had made public confession of their faith in Christ. They are identified with other believers.

10:34—They had made sacrifices for the writer.

10:36-39—Their need is not salvation but patient endurance, which is the product of a genuine faith.

12:2—Jesus Christ is the author and finisher of their faith.

12:7—They are called "sons."

12:28—They are inheriting a kingdom.

13:1-19—All of the exhortations delivered to the recipients are applicable only to believers.

In short, from a survey of the book we must conclude that the original recipients of this letter were genuine believers.

2. They had been baptized, publicly identifying themselves with Jesus Christ and renouncing their old associations with Israel's religious system that had rejected Messiah. The confession referred to in 3:1; 4:14; and 10:23 is baptism.

3. They were undergoing intense persecution (10:34; 12:4; 13:3, 5).

4. If not wealthy, they at least had not been poor (6:10), but now they had become impoverished.

5. Because of hardship and persecution, serious spiritual regression had taken place (5:11-14). Instead of growing under discipline, they had fallen away.

6. They needed encouragement to live by faith so that faith might produce patient endurance (11:39-40).

7. They obviously were neither first-generation believers (2:3), nor were they new believers (5:11-12). Much of their disappointment may have come through their failure to realize the eager expectation that Jesus Christ would return to subjugate all to Himself, establish His kingdom, and deliver them from persecution. Therefore they were in danger of losing hope. Because of this, the apostle would encourage them to a steadfast confidence based on the hope that had been laid before them.

The Nature of the Epistle

For generations there has been much disagreement concerning the essential nature of this book. Because of the strong emphasis on doctrine, some have concluded that it is a theological treatise. This is supported by the fact that there is no salutation and no address to a particular group. Others have suggested that it is a theological treatise with a letter appended. Observing that there is a closing salutation in 13:24, proponents of this view would see chapter 13 as a personal letter the writer added to the thesis contained in chapters 1–12.

The nature of this letter, however, argues against these conclusions. A treatise is quite general, with no specific audience in view, and is essentially impersonal throughout. By contrast, there are many personal references throughout the book of Hebrews (2:1; 3:1, 12; 4:1, 14; 5:11; 6:19; 10:19; 13:7, 22–25). The writer obviously was well acquainted with the background and the present circumstances of a specific group to whom he addressed this epistle. Further, the writer identified himself with those to whom he was writing as one who shared in all their experiences (1:2; 2:1, 3;

"Losing hope," or becoming discouraged because of the corruption of the world around us, is as real a problem for Christians today as it was in the first century. Unfortunately, many believers simply give in to discouragement, disobedience, or even depression in the face of overwhelming opposition to the things of God and the Bible. One simple solution—or at least a start—would be to begin spending as much time receiving God's perspective on the world as we spend receiving the world's perspective on God. For example, perhaps you could spend as much time in devotional Bible reading as you spend watching television each day. Or you could commit yourself to be as faithful to spending a daily "quiet time" in the Word of God as you are to reading the daily newspaper. Once you try it, you'll likely find that no day is complete without your "appointment" with God.

3:19; 4:1–2, 11, 14–16; 6:1, 6, 18–20; 7:26; 8:1; 9:24; 10:10; 11:3, 40).

These observations show that the epistle to the Hebrews is one of the most personal of all the New Testament letters. Perhaps the author himself best defined the nature of the book when he referred to it in 13:22 as a "word of exhortation." This statement, in fact, may give us our most valuable clue to a correct interpretation of Hebrews. It is easy to concentrate on the great body of doctrine contained in this book and overlook this one fact: The author uses doctrine as a basis for exhorting believers.

Understanding that, a list of exhortations will prove quite helpful.

2:1—Pay attention to the things you have heard.

3:1—Consider the Apostle and High Priest of our confession, Christ Jesus.

3:8—Do not harden your hearts.

3:12—Beware, lest there be in any of you an evil heart of unbelief.

3:13—Exhort one another daily.

3:15—Do not harden your hearts.

4:1—Do not fall short of the promise of God's rest.

4:11—Be diligent to enter that rest.

Not too many years ago, many Christians became consumed with doctrine to the exclusion of its practical applications. More recently, much Christian literature has concentrated on the Christian experience, to the exclusion of Bible truth behind it. As we will see in the book of Hebrews, God wants His children to know what His Word says—and to respond to it appropriately. Is this your commitment to His Word? One Bible study process encourages Christians to ask three logical questions when reading or studying the Bible. They are: (1) what does it say? (2) what does it mean? and (3) what does it mean to me? By carefully asking and answering these questions each time you approach God's Word, you may find that your personal interaction with the Bible will become much more meaningful and life-changing.

4:14—Hold fast your confession.

4:16—Come boldly to the throne of grace.

6:1—Go on to perfection.

6:11—Show the same diligence to the full assurance of hope until the end.

6:12—Do not become sluggish.

10:22—Draw near with a true heart in full assurance of faith.

10:23—Hold fast the confession of your hope without wavering.

10:24—Consider how to spur one another to love and good works.

10:25—Do not forsake the assembling of yourselves together, but exhort one another.

10:32—Recall the former days.

10:35—Do not cast away your confidence.

12:1—Lay aside every weight and run with endurance the race that is set before you.

12:3—Consider Him who endured hostility from sinners.

12:12—Strengthen the hands that hang down.

12:14—Pursue peace with everyone.

12:15—Look diligently lest anyone fall short of God's grace.

12:25—Do not refuse Him who speaks.

12:28—Worship God with reverence and godly fear.

13:1—Let brotherly love continue.

13:2—Do not forget to entertain strangers.

13:3—Remember the prisoners.

13:5—Conduct yourselves without covetousness, and be content with such things as you have.

13:7—Remember those who rule over you.

13:9—Do not be carried away by various and strange doctrines.

13:13—Go forth to Him, outside the camp.

13:15—Continually offer the sacrifice of praise to God.

13:17—Obey those who rule over you.

13:18—Pray for us.

13:22—Bear with the word of exhortation.

13:24—Greet all those who rule over you, and all the saints.

As we can see, doctrine is the basis for the writer's exhortations to faith and patient endurance in this epistle.

The Purpose of the Epistle

The author seems to have had several purposes in mind as he wrote this epistle.

First, he wanted to warn his readers of the dangers they faced. There was the danger they would neglect God's revelation through Christ, which superseded His revelation given through Moses. The writer deals with this danger in 1:1–2:18. There also was the danger that, just as those redeemed under Moses had failed under that redeemer, so those he is addressing might fail under a greater Redeemer, Jesus Christ. This is developed in 3:1–18.

Another danger is discussed in 4:1–13. This section warned that just as their forefathers through unbelief at Kadesh Barnea had failed to enter the rest that God provided in the promised land, so this generation might not appropriate by faith the rest God had provided, consequently missing the promised blessings.

And there was the danger explained in 4:14–10:39, that the recipients might fail to appropriate the fullness of Christ's priestly work. Within this section we find the added danger that these believers might retrogress and not continue on the path to maturity, as discussed in 5:12–6:20.

It is the writer's purpose, then, to acquaint his readers with these dangers so that

Although we do yet not face the same kind of physical attacks the original readers of Hebrews faced, our beliefs are under attack daily in our culture. The New Age movement, atheistic humanism, popular liberalism, and a compromising, watered-down form of "Churchianity" threaten to undermine our trust in the absolute truth of God's Word. This letter's exhortations to faith and perseverance, then, are as relevant to us today as they were in the first century. And according to this biblical book, our enjoyment of God's "rest"—a victorious Christian life—depends on how we respond to those exhortations.

their spiritual development might not be hindered.

The writer's second purpose was to bring these believers to maturity in Christ. This is seen in 5:11–14 and in the exhortation of 6:1.

Third, it was the author's purpose to prepare these believers for the coming persecution. Although they had experienced persecution from the Jews throughout their generation, their sufferings would intensify as the Roman suppression drew near. It is this increased intensity of afflictions to which the author makes reference in 8:13, 10:25, and 12:3–15.

Fourth, it was the writer's purpose to warn his readers about false doctrines (13:9). Thus the body of truth presented in this epistle would become a test of any doctrine.

Fifth, it was the author's purpose to prevent believers from "forsaking the assembling of ourselves together as is the manner of some" (Heb. 10:25). Some of these Christians had become weak in faith and had given up hope that Jesus Christ would return to deliver the oppressed and establish His kingdom. Therefore they had broken fellowship with their fellow believers and were seeking refuge in a return to the external rituals of temple service. Still others considered doing the same. Therefore it was the

---

Our society thrives on things that are quick or "instant." Microwave ovens make possible instant meals; telephones give us instant contact with friends and business associates; fax machines provide us with instant correspondence; contests and lotteries offer the phantom hope of instant riches. To our detriment, we sometimes erroneously believe that one bit of knowledge or some type of experience can provide us with instant spiritual maturity. The Bible is clear, however, that maturity in Christ is a long, steady process of growth in the knowledge of His Word and in obedient submission to Him. Like athletic conditioning or physical growth from childhood to adulthood, there are no shortcuts to spiritual maturity. That was true for the original readers of Hebrews, just as it is true for us today.

writer's desire that they should not forsake the assembling of themselves together, because their help did not lie in the temple or in fellowship with those in the temple. Rather, they were encouraged to seek the support that could be found only in fellowship with other true believers.

To accomplish his purposes, the writer sounded some very serious and sober warnings. In our subsequent study, it will be necessary to consider each of these warnings in greater detail. For now, however, a brief mention of some of these warnings will be helpful.

In 2:3 we find the warning, "How shall we escape if we neglect so great a salvation?" This was a warning against neglecting the revelation God had given through Jesus Christ. In 4:11–13 is the warning, "Lest anyone fall after the same example of disobedience." As we will see, this was a warning against repeating a sin similar to Israel's at Kadesh Barnea, where a redeemed generation lost the blessings God had provided. In 6:4–6 is the warning against regressing from their present spiritual experiences, which would confirm them in a state of immaturity. There is a warning in 10:26–31 that would involve these believers in "a certain fearful expectation of judgment and fiery indignation which will devour the adversaries." That is, if to escape persecution these

Over the past 20 years, the priority of worship has all but disappeared from our culture. Although movies and even television shows of the previous generation occasionally portrayed families in worship or religious practice, the only mentions of religious worship in the media today are derogatory or derisive. Even among professing Christians, faithfulness to weekly worship is easily pushed aside by recreation, Sunday sports, or matters of scheduling and convenience. Yet God's Word places a high priority on the practice of corporate worship, especially in the midst of adverse circumstances. If God considers worship to be this important, shouldn't we?

believers identified themselves again with the temple and the nation, then they would again become subject to the physical judgment Christ had decreed on that generation.

In 10:31, the author pointed out the results of neglecting these warnings. He says it is a fearful thing to fall into the hands of the living God. In 10:38 he writes, "If anyone draws back, My soul has no pleasure in him." In 12:14–15 he states, "Pursue peace . . . and holiness . . . looking carefully lest anyone fall short of the grace of God; lest any root of bitterness springing up cause trouble, and by this many become defiled." In 12:16–17 he warns them that if they ignore these warnings they might, like Esau, be confirmed in a state in which the promised blessings are forfeited. In 12:25–27 by referring to prophecy he reminds them that at the coming of Christ, this earth will be shaken and the very institutions in which they were tempted to take refuge will be removed. Therefore they would be returning to the temple only to come under its judgment.

These serious warnings were designed to arrest the attention of the hearers, to warn them of the consequences of not living by faith, so that they might exercise patient endurance. Again, the period in which these believ-

---

Too many times we think of disobedience or spiritual apathy in terms of the "hereafter" rather than in terms of "the here and now." If we understand Scripture correctly, however, we realize that there are present, temporal, physical consequences to our disobedience or neglect. The Bible frequently links spiritual obedience (such as faithfulness to worship, honoring one's parents, and marital fidelity) to temporal benefits like physical preservation, longevity of life, and the answering of one's prayers. If our lives are beset with perpetual difficulties, the first place we should look for help is in our own faithfulness to God and His Word. Only when we know that our suffering is not self-inflicted can we begin to look for the greater purposes God may be working in our lives.

ers were living was one of transition that began with the momentous event of Pentecost. It was a transition from God's covenanted program with Israel to a new program to be developed in the church. It was a transition from Jew to Gentile. It was a transition from Law to grace. It was a transition in which God formerly dwelt in a tabernacle/temple and now would indwell a new temple, the body of believers. It was a transition from the expectation of an earthly Davidic kingdom to the inauguration of a new form of theocratic administration outlined in Matthew 13.

This transition period that began in Acts 2 would continue until the destruction of Jerusalem in A.D. 70. Certain practices that would have been perfectly normal at the beginning of the transition no longer could be considered normative as the end of that transition period approached. While the doctrine of these new believers and the person to whom they had joined themselves were hated by the nation they had left, in the beginning the individuals themselves were tolerated. But as the period progressed, the breach be-tween Judaism and Christianity widened. That which was tolerated by the nation at the beginning of the transition was no longer tolerated at the end. An intensified

---

With all of the cults, movements, philosophies, and "isms" that face us today, we might well wonder how we can best safeguard ourselves from deception. According to the writer of Hebrews, the best defense is a good offense. That is, the best way to remain safe from deception is to be involved in steady growth toward maturity. And the best way to move steadily toward maturity is by diligently practicing what the Word of God reveals. This gives new meaning to the importance of Sunday sermons, home Bible studies, and Sunday school classes, since these are probably our best sources of food for spiritual growth. We should do all we can to ensure that these practices provide us with what we need to grow—and that we grow according to the spiritual "food" we receive!

persecution of believers by the nation made it impossible for believers ever to be accepted again into that community.

By the time Hebrews was written, sufficient time had passed for those who were immature at the beginning of the transition to have become mature (5:11 ff.). Therefore any continuation of, or return to, the practices associated with their immaturity would be a serious step backward.

Therefore the doctrines the epistle presents, the warnings it delivers, and the exhortations it gives all were intended to prevent regression and to encourage continuous dynamic development toward spiritual maturity.

TEXT AND COMMENTARY

I. God's Revelation Through Jesus Christ is Superior to His Revelation Through Angels (1:1–2:18).

When God placed Adam and Eve in the Garden of Eden, there was no barrier to their fellowship with Him. While all creation bore testimony to God's existence and to the exceeding greatness of His power, Adam and Eve grew in their knowledge of God through intimate fellowship with Him. God's daily walk with them in the garden (Gen. 3:8) involved a continuous revelation of Himself to them. Thus as they enjoyed fellowship with Him, they grew in their knowledge of Him.

However, after Adam and Eve's willful act of disobedience (Gen. 3:1–6), it was no longer possible for God to come to walk with them and reveal Himself to them. Therefore their knowledge of the Creator became dependent on His revelation of Himself through nature. The light of God's personal presence gave way to spiritual darkness, and the knowledge of God they had gained through intimate fellowship with Him gave way to progressive spiritual ignorance.

This is why Paul testified that people are characterized not by light, but by darkness (Rom. 1:21–23; Eph. 4:17–18). This darkness is ignorance of God. Paul further testified that "the natural man does not receive the things of the Spirit of God, for they are foolishness to him; nor can he know them because they are spiritually discerned" (1 Cor. 2:14). And again, "The world through wisdom did not know God" (1 Cor. 1:21). In other words, if people come to any knowledge of God, it is not by the exercise of their fallen intellects. Rather, it comes through divine revelation. Fortunately for us, our God has not chosen to hide Himself from the human race, but has acted to reveal Himself through special revelation, that we might come to know Him.

A. God's Revelation Through the Son (1:1–2a).

1 God, who at various times and in various ways spoke in time past to the fathers by the prophets,

2a has in these last days spoken to us by His Son,

In the introduction to his epistle, the writer of Hebrews affirms the great fact that God has indeed revealed Himself to us. Reviewing all of human history, the author declares that in time past God has spoken to the fathers by the prophets. That revelation was not given directly, but indirectly; for while the fathers were recipients of direct revelation, that revelation came to them through the prophets. Moreover, that revelation was given at various times and in different ways. While the author affirms that throughout the Old Testament there was a progressive revelation from God through the prophets to people, he also views this revelation as incomplete. Old Testament revelation anticipated a fuller revelation yet to come. Specifically, Old Testament revelation looked forward to New Testament revelation. And as we well know, there are notable contrasts between the two concerning

Anyone who has ever worked with tools or kitchen utensils knows that each one was designed for a specific purpose or task. If we try to use them for something other than that specific purpose, we will face frustration and possibly even damage the instrument. This reference to the early chapters of Genesis reminds us that God created human life for a specific purpose—to know Him and to enjoy fellowship with Him. And to employ that life—our own lives—for anything other than that overriding purpose will only result in frustration, possibly even a broken life. Although knowing Christ certainly equips us to pursue pleasure, wealth, success, or other tempting goals better than we ever could before, let's not forget that our purpose for existence today is the same as it's always been: to know Him.

the time of revelation, the agents in revelation, and the methods of revelation.

The Old Testament prophet was unique in that he was the one through whom God was revealing Himself to His people. Therefore there were various methods by which God gave revelation to the prophets. On frequent occasions, God gave revelation directly to the recipients. Abraham, for example, received direct revelation from God as God appeared to him (Gen. 12:1; Acts 7:2). Moses also received direct communication from God (Ex. 33:9, 11; 34:1). Isaiah received a word from the Lord (Isa. 8:11; 31:4). Jeremiah received direct communication from God (Jer. 1:4–10). On countless occasions the word of the Lord came directly to Jeremiah, and Ezekiel likewise received word directly from the Lord (Ezek. 1:3; 2:1; 3:22). Whenever it pleased Him, then, God could give direct revelation to the prophets, who then communicated His word to the people.

In Numbers 12:6 God revealed that He would speak to the prophets through dreams and through visions. In revelation through a dream, the recipient was asleep and in the dream received direct revelation. Such was the experience of

Many modern "gurus" claim to know a lot about God, yet they have nothing more upon which to base their assumptions than their own opinions or the ideas of others. The Bible, on the other hand, claims to be the one source of God's own revelation about Himself to mankind. This makes it unique above all other books and holy writings of history—and unique in our world today. Although using the Bible to witness to unbelievers and to counter false teachers is not as popular today as it once was, it still is the only source for final, definitive, authoritative, supernatural truth. Dedicate yourself to studying it and committing it to memory, and you will never be without an answer for the one who asks.

Jacob (Gen. 28:11–16), Joseph (Gen. 37:5–9), Pharaoh (Gen. 41), the Midianite (Judg. 7:13–15), Solomon (1 Kings 3:5–15), Nebuchadnezzar (Dan. 2:1; 4:5), and Daniel (Dan. 7:1). As with all true revelation, that which was delivered to the recipient through a dream was trustworthy and authenticated; it revealed God's infallible plan or purpose to the people through the one who received that revelation.

In revelation through a vision, the recipient was wide awake and often became an actual participant in the event that was being revealed. Such was the experience of Abraham (Gen. 15:1) and Samuel (1 Sam. 3:11–15). Ezekiel frequently was given revelation through visions (Ezek. 1:1; 8:3; 40:2; 44:3). Daniel received revelation through visions (Dan. 8:1; 9:24–27; 10:1–7). Hosea likewise received revelation in this way (Hos. 12:10), as did Nahum (Nah. 1:1). Such also was the experience of Habakkuk (Hab. 2:2–3), while Zechariah received details of the prophetic program for Israel through eight night visions (Zech. 1:7–6:15). Again, revelation given

---

How do we know whether someone has really received direct revelation when they say, "God told me this," or "Thus says the Lord"? First, in the Old Testament, God's revelation was authenticated by infallibility (never being wrong or unfulfilled) and by verifiable miracles. In other words, God's message through His messenger always was confirmed by events that could not be refuted or "debunked." No tricks, no gimmicks, no counterfeits. Second, these first few verses of Hebrews seem to indicate that the revealing God did in the Old Testament through prophets, dreams, and visions has been replaced by a superior revelation through His Son, Jesus Christ. Therefore we should be extremely wary today of anyone who claims to receive direct revelation from God. And if what they claim is not consistent with what God has revealed in Scripture, we should stay as far away as possible!

through visions was considered authoritative and trustworthy, and it was viewed as God's revelation to His people.

Sometimes God's revelation was accompanied by storm and fire, as in the experience of Moses (Ex. 19:19; Deut. 5:22). In other instances revelation came through a still, small voice, as in the experience of Elijah (1 Kings 19:12). But even though God's revelation to man spanned all of Old Testament history—from the time of Abraham to the days of Malachi—and even though God gave His revelation sometimes directly, sometimes through dreams, and sometimes through visions, it all was God's revelation of Himself, His plan, and His program. It all was considered authoritative and trustworthy, and through that revelation people could come to a personal, intimate knowledge of God and of God's program.

However, all of that revelation also was considered temporary. Because it anticipated a full and complete revelation to come (Deut. 18:15), it was incomplete. Thus the writer of Hebrews declares, "God . . . has in these last days spoken to us by His Son."

This reference to "last days" puts God's new revelation in sharp contrast to the revelation He had previously given through the prophets. This later revelation is complete rather than incomplete, permanent rather than temporary, and is the realization of all that was anticipated in His former revelation. The great fact the author presents here

How much do we really know about the Son, Jesus Christ? How much do we study Him and His nature in our churches and Sunday school classes? If someone asks us about Jesus, how much can we tell them? The Bible tells us that Jesus is the fullest, most complete, most accurate, and convincing revelation of God ever given. To know more about Him is to know more about the Father. To understand Christ and His ministry is to understand God and to understand what He is doing in our lives today.

is that this new revelation does not follow a pattern of former revelation. Rather, it is God's revelation through a new method, the Incarnation.

In our English translation, we read that God has spoken to us "by His Son." Notice, however, that in some versions the word His is in italics, signifying that it was not in the original Greek text. The English reading "by His Son" puts emphasis on the Person through whom revelation is made; however, if we read the text literally, without that insertion, it tells us that God "has spoken to us by Son." This emphasizes the method rather than the person. And while it is certainly true that God's revelation was made through the person of the Son, here the writer wants to emphasize the new method by which the revelation was made—the great fact of Christ's incarnation.

John, in the introduction to his gospel, points out that the world was in darkness (John 1:5), which to John meant ignorance of God. In that darkness, men did not and could not know God (1 Cor. 1:21). The only way men could know God was through revelation. Therefore this revelation was given as "the Word became flesh and dwelt among us, and we beheld His glory, the glory as of the only begotten of the Father, full of grace and truth" (John 1:14).

This revelation through the Son is not viewed by the writer of Hebrews as simply another in progressive forms of revelation; rather, it is

> If it is true that Jesus Christ is God's ultimate revelation of Himself to people, then any so-called understanding of God that is inconsistent with all that we know about Jesus Christ is incomplete or in error. This leaves religions like the New Age movement, Eastern mysticism, humanism and the various cults far short of the truth they profess to teach. Remember, the Bible teaches that Jesus Christ is not just another form of revelation; He is God's final and ultimate revelation of Himself to people.

God's ultimate and climactic revelation of Himself in the Son.

B. The Position of the Son (1:2b–3).

2b whom He has appointed heir of all things, through whom also He made the worlds;
3 who being the brightness of His glory and the express image of His person, and upholding all things by the word of His power, when He had by Himself purged our sins, sat down at the right hand of the Majesty on high,

Since God's new and ultimate revelation is Son-revelation, emphasis is placed not so much on what the Son said as upon who He is. Because through the incarnation God became flesh, and because the Son is God, the Son—apart from anything He said—is the revelation of God to people. Therefore the writer of Hebrews shows the Son's eligibility to be Son-revelation by stating seven significant facts concerning Him who became incarnate Deity.

The first stated fact is that God has appointed the Son as heir of all things (1:2b). This appointment as heir specifically concerns an appointment to authority. When Jacob gave Joseph the coat of many colors (Gen. 37:3), he was assigning administrative authority in the family to Joseph and was designating him as his heir. It was because of this appointment that Joseph was to rule over his brothers.

In the same way, God the Father has designated the Son as His heir and has placed Him in a position of authority over "all things." This

Since Jesus Christ is the ultimate heir of all things—including us—it seems ridiculous to think that we can rebel against His authority or hide from our accountability to Him! One way to cultivate our submission to Him is by spending time in His Word daily and consciously practicing Christian obedience. Remember, one day all things—either willingly or unwillingly—will be subject to His authority.

encompasses the entire universe and all that will ever develop in that realm. And because God is the Creator and He alone has the right to rule, the One to whom rulership is assigned can be nothing less than God Himself. Moreover, this appointment to an inheritance was not temporary; it is timeless. It is because of this appointment that eventually "at the name of Jesus every knee should bow, of those in heaven, and of those on earth, and of those under the earth, and that every tongue should confess that Jesus Christ is Lord, to the glory of God the Father" (Phil. 2:10–11).

The second statement is: ". . . through whom also He made the worlds" (Heb. 1:2c). A better translation of this phrase would be "He ordered the ages." Although the English word "world" seemingly refers to the creation of the physical universe—which is certainly true (John 1:3; Col. 1:16)—the specific word used here actually refers to all the ages of time that will ever unfold within the universe. Because the Son ordered and controls all history throughout its successive time periods, all that develops within history follows a divinely ordered arrangement over which the Son is sovereign administrator.

The third statement affirms that the Son is "the brightness of His glory" (1:3a). Because it does not say that the Son became the brightness of His glory, but rather states that the Son has existed eternally in continuous unbroken fellowship with the

---

If the turmoil, uncertainty, and increasing evil of today's world troubles us, we can take comfort that Jesus Christ Himself has created all the ages of time that will ever pass on this earth, and He is in perfect control of the events that take place within them. This outlook is quite different from the environmentalist philosophy that proposes that human beings have it within themselves to destroy or "save" the earth. According to Scripture, human history is unfolding just as our Lord has known from eternity past that it would.

Father, this emphasizes the eternality of the Son. The word brightness means to radiate, to flash forth, or to cause to shine, stressing here that the Father's glory which Christ revealed was not a mere reflected glory. Rather, it was the shining forth of Christ's inherent glory, which itself was the glory of His Father. This emphasizes the oneness of the Son with His Father.

God's glory refers to that in Himself in which He can take justifiable pride, in which He can find delight. God glories in the perfections of His person, in the attributes that are a manifestation of His character. Therefore we learn that God the Father can find delight in God the Son, because everything in Himself in which He delights is in His Son as well.

The fourth statement is that the Son is "the express image of His person" (1:3b). This emphasizes that the Son in Himself is a full and perfect revelation of what is in the Father. Even though we have not seen the Father, we know the Father because all that is in the Father is in the Son.

In the Greco-Roman world, coins bore the image of the emperor. Because the image of the emperor had been impressed on the coin by a die, by looking at a coin one could recognize the emperor. And though the likeness of the emperor on the coin was only a representative likeness, if the die were cast away, one could determine exactly what was in the die by studying the coin. Why? Because the die reproduced itself in every detail on the coin.

Throughout the Old Testament, one of the characteristics of God's glory was that no manifestation of evil could stand before it. Similarly, the greater our understanding of the Son—who is the brightness of God's glory—the greater will be our distress before Him regarding our sin and uncleanness. Anyone hungry for a cleansed life will continually cultivate a greater understanding of Him and a closer relationship with Him.

This is the essence of the word the author chose here to show the relationship between the Son and the Father. While we do not see the Father, all that is in the Father is in the Son. By studying the Son we learn of the Father. Just as an impression on a coin becomes an expression of the die, so what was in Christ is a revelation of the Father.

The fifth statement affirms that the Son is "upholding all things by the word of His power" (1:3c). This statement implies first that this creation is sustained and kept in its creative order by the power that belongs to the Son. But the statement implies far more. The word *upholding* has in it the idea of carrying something along to a designated end. Not only is the Son the One who was the architect of the ages, He is also the One who through the ages has been carrying creation to its designated end. He does this not by the exertion of physical strength but rather "by the word of His power." This word has in it the idea of an authoritative command that is consequently executed, implying the exercise of His will that is carrying all things to their predetermined end.

Through the sixth statement, "He had by Himself purged our sins" (1:3d), the author is looking at the redemptive work of the Son.

In today's world of pseudo-spirituality, God-talk, and generic mysticism, the true measure of anyone's relationship to God is their response to Jesus Christ as the Bible reveals Him. Though some cults and liberal churches will give lip service to a few of Christ's statements or the "Jesus" they have defined in their own doctrine, once they are faced with Christ's statements concerning sin, righteousness, and judgment, they begin to compromise their acceptance of Him as God in the flesh. Today, more than ever, the true test of a person's view of God is the question, "What do you think of Jesus?" According to Hebrews, to reject Jesus Christ as the Bible reveals Him is to reject the one true God!

Through this work the Son has made a revelation of God's unprecedented love, grace, justice, holiness, and righteousness. This in fact will become a main theme of the epistle—the Son's work to provide purification from sin. In His work He deals not only with personal sins, but with cleansing all creation from sin itself. This is viewed as a once-for-all purification which is adequate and complete, a work in which the Son alone was involved. It was a work He accomplished "by Himself."

The seventh statement affirms that He "sat down at the right hand of the Majesty on high" (1:3e). The fact that He "sat down" signifies more than taking rest after labor. It is a solemn enthronement, the taking of a seat of honor and authority after the work He had come to do had been finished. Having completed the work of revelation and the work of redemption that were to have been accomplished during the Incarnation, He could then assume the position of honor and authority that was His from eternity past (John 17:5). And the fact that He is enthroned at the right hand does not so much signify geographical location as it does the dignity, the honor, and the glory that have been given to Him.

In these seven statements the writer makes it clear that

Although we are reminded daily of the celebrity and status of people who possess a certain amount of "power" in our society (politicians, stars, professional athletes), we are amazingly unimpressed with the sheer power of Jesus Christ. Anyone who has ever witnessed the unharnessed natural power of a hurricane, earthquake, volcano, or other natural catastrophe knows that the sensation is overwhelming; yet Jesus Christ holds together the entire universe in which those events are tiny details! Is this the kind of power in which we consciously place our trust during times of crisis? The scope of His power is far greater than any problem we might ever face.

the One whom God has sent to give ultimate revelation concerning Himself is fully qualified, not only to *give* revelation but to *be* revelation from God to people, so that anyone who is in darkness and ignorance of God might come to the light, the true knowledge of God.

In summary, the author of Hebrews teaches that throughout the course of Old Testament history God revealed Himself to the prophets—either directly or through dreams and visions— who in turn communicated that revelation to people. But to give the climactic and complete revelation of Himself, God devised a new method of revelation. That revelation was the incarnation of the Son, who came to reveal the Father. The Son revealed the Father not only by what He said, which also was revelation, but by *what He is.* Because He is one with the Father, the Lord could say of this revelation, "He who has seen Me has seen the Father" (John 14:9). People therefore are held responsible for this revelation in the Son.

C. The Son's Superiority to Angels (1:4–14)

4 having become so much better than the angels, as He has by inheritance obtained a more excellent name than they.

5 For to which of the angels did He ever say: "You are My Son, Today I have begotten You"? And again: "I will be to Him a Father, And He shall be to Me a Son"?

An interesting prophetic sidenote: When Jesus Christ returns to establish His millennial kingdom on this earth, he will redeem the creation itself from the effects of man's sin at the Fall. In other words, He will bring environmental harmony to the earth for the first and only time since the fall. Yet, before Christ does return, Satan will attempt to counterfeit this messianic miracle by convincing the human race that it can "save the earth" through its own collective efforts. This is just one of many uniquely messianic feats Satan will attempt to counterfeit as Christ's return draws near.

6 But when He again brings the firstborn into the world, He says: "Let all the angels of God worship Him."

7 And of the angels He says: "Who makes His angels spirits And His ministers a flame of fire."

8 But to the Son He says: "Your throne, O God, is forever and ever; A scepter of righteousness is the scepter of Your Kingdom.

9 You have loved righteousness and hated lawlessness; Therefore God, Your God, has anointed You With the oil of gladness more than Your companions."

10 And: "You, Lord, in the beginning laid the foundation of the earth, And the heavens are the work of Your hands.

11 They will perish, but You remain; And they will all grow old like a garment;

12 Like a cloak You will fold them up, And they will be changed. But You are the same, And Your years will not fail."

13 But to which of the angels has He ever said: "Sit at My right hand, Till I make Your enemies Your footstool"?

14 Are they not all ministering spirits sent forth to minister for those who will inherit salvation?

Throughout the Old Testament, God's revelation to mankind was frequently communicated through angels. Hagar received revelation from God through angels (Gen. 16), as did Abraham (Gen. 22:11–18). Jacob was visited by angels who brought revelation to him (Gen. 31:11–13), and the Angel of Jehovah brought revelation to Moses (Ex. 3:1–2). Balaam (Num. 22), Gideon (Judg. 6), and Manoah (Judg. 13) all received revela-

---

Of all the furniture in the temple, one item that was not present was a chair or couch on which the priests could sit. This was because their work of offering sacrifice for sin was never finished. In contrast, because the sacrifice Christ offered was perfect and complete, when His work was finished, He sat down at the right hand of God. Not only does this vividly show us that His work is complete, it also shows that when His sacrifice is applied to our sins, that payment is complete and perfect. We cannot add to it, we cannot improve on it, and we cannot lose it.

tion through angels. The prophet Elijah received a message from God through angels (1 Kings 17:2–4). Gabriel brought revelation to Daniel (Dan. 10:11–12), and angels communicated revelation to Zechariah, the prophet (Zech. 1:9; 4:1–6).

What was true in the Old Testament was also true in the New Testament. Joseph received an announcement concerning the birth of Jesus from an angelic messenger (Matt. 1:20). The announcement concerning the birth of the promised forerunner, John the Baptist, was given by an angel to Zechariah (Luke 1:11–17). And the announcement of the conception of the promised Messiah was given to Mary through an angel (Luke 1:28–32).

While all of these revelations given to individuals were significant, the greatest revelation given to people through angels was the Law, which was revealed by angels to Moses at Sinai. Paul wrote concerning the Law, "It was appointed through angels by the hand of a mediator" (Gal. 3:19). Israel considered all revelation given through angels to be authentic, trustworthy, and binding. However, special heed was paid to the Mosaic Law, because it was revealed directly by God to Moses, the mediator. For countless generations, the nation to whom the Law had been given held that Law in highest esteem and considered itself to be bound by the Law. If God's people, then, were to put themselves under a new revelation from God, they would have to be shown that the new is superior to the old. The writer does this by show-

> How much time do you spend studying the person of Jesus Christ? How much time does your church or Bible study spend teaching about the person, the work, the attributes, and the nature of Jesus Christ? If we truly want to draw near to God, and if Jesus Christ is the ultimate revelation of God, we will do well to spend our time learning about Him, talking to Him, walking with Him, obeying Him, and drawing ever closer to Him.

ing that the new revelation came through a Person superior to the angels and to Moses, through whom the old revelation came.

In verses 4–14 the writer presents what could be viewed as a summary of Old Testament doctrine concerning angels. Rather than appealing to the innumerable Jewish traditions that had arisen concerning the nature and function of angels, the apostle reviews the Old Testament Scriptures' teachings about the nature and ministry of angels. He does this to contrast angels with the Son, the authoritative administrator in the universe, the Architect of the ages, the One who carries all human history to its God-designed end.

While verse 3 emphasizes the eternal relationship of the Son to the Father, verse 4 now emphasizes the exalted position to which the God-man was appointed, evidently at the time of His resurrection. As we will see later in the epistle (5:5–6), at the time of the resurrection, the One who from eternity past had been appointed as heir now actively engaged in the administration of that inheritance. Because the administration given to the Son includes not only the physical universe but all created beings within God's creation, and because angels are a part of creation,

From the fall of man on, God communicated with humankind through mediators because of His holiness in contrast to man's sinfulness. God's separateness from sin is something we should never forget nor make light of in our relationship with Him. God is holy, which means He is entirely without sin and separate from sin. Just because He has allowed us to draw near to Him through the blood of Christ does not mean that He has changed his mind about sin—or that we can make light of sin in our lives. His desire for us is that we share His holiness as Jesus Christ conforms us to His image. Let's get serious about sin in our lives, and strive to live holy lives, because He is holy.

the One in authority must be superior to all those over whom He exercises rule. Therefore the eternal Son clearly is superior to the angels.

To support his assertion that the Son is superior to angels, the writer of Hebrews appeals to seven passages from the Old Testament.

The first quotation (1:5a) is from Psalm 2:7, where a covenant given by the Father to the Son declares, "You are My Son, today I have begotten You." Without doubt, the day referred to is the day of resurrection. The "begetting" does refer to the inception of the Son's existence, as though there was a time when the Son did not exist and then was brought into existence. Just as Jacob appointed Joseph to an authoritative position and Joseph became "the son" or "the heir" at that specific time, so at the specific time of the resurrection, God the Father established the positional right of the Son to rule. That is why Paul declared in Acts 13:33 that Psalm 2:7 was fulfilled by the resurrection of Jesus Christ. While some angels were appointed as "principalities and powers" (Eph. 1:21) and were assigned to rule in the angelic realm,

Because at least one cult today insists that Jesus Christ is not co-eternal with the Father but was brought into existence at a point in time, it is important to understand this legal language of the ancient Near East. The bestowal or "begetting" of sonship rights as legal heir to all things possessed by one's father was a legal pronouncement, much like the naming of an heir or a legal successor in a will. It was at the point of the Resurrection that this prophetic pronouncement concerning the "son" of David was fulfilled—the point at which there was no further barrier to Messiah's legal right to inherit from the Father possession of all creation. Although we know from biblical prophecy that He will take possession of that inheritance in the future, His legal right to that inheritance was made sure by His victory over Satan at the Resurrection.

none were ever called "sons." This authority belongs exclusively to the resurrected One, Jesus Christ.

The second quotation (1:5b) is from 2 Samuel 7:14, a passage in which God makes a covenant with David. Here God affirms that there will be a continuing relationship between Himself and David's descendant, and that through this descendant the covenant God made with David would be fulfilled. The emphasis in this passage is on the verb "I will be," indicating a continual position of authority that will be given to that descendant. This positional authority is based on the relationship between the ultimate Son of David and His Father who gave the covenant. We see, then, that Jesus Christ, David's greater Son, is the One through whom all of the Messianic promises concerning a kingdom, redemption, and blessing would be fulfilled.

In verse 6 the writer anticipates the second advent of Jesus Christ into this world

By now it has become obvious that much of Hebrews deals with the fulfillment of things God promised throughout the Old Testament. The Bible—and God's plan for humankind—is like that. Nothing He has begun will remain unfinished. No promise will remain unrealized, and no prophecy will remain unfulfilled. There is not a "God of the Old Testament" and a "God of the New Testament." There is one God, who initiated in the Old Testament many, many things that have been fulfilled in the New Testament or will be fulfilled in the prophetic future. That is why it is so important that we, as Christians, understand the full scope of God's Word, from Genesis to Revelation. While the popular emphasis on "practical application" is helpful, without careful study of the Bible from cover to cover, we will have precious little in our hearts to practically apply! If you are not involved in a weekly study of the Scriptures, do your best to find a Bible study group that will help you understand more of God's Word and His wonderful plan for the ages.

subsequent to His resurrection by quoting a third Old Testament passage. In Deuteronomy 32:43 (quoted in the Septuagint version), it is foreseen that at Messiah's return the angels of God will worship Him. The scene here is of the millennial reign of Christ on the earth in fulfillment of God's Old Testament covenants. According to Hebrews 12:22–24, when Christ's kingdom is instituted here on the earth, the unfallen angels will be a part of that kingdom dwelling with the Father and the Son. And along with the Old Testament saints and redeemed saints of this present age, they will be in the heavenly city, New Jerusalem, as worshipers. Certainly, therefore, He who is worshiped is superior to those who worship Him! This quotation, then, emphasizes the future position of authority and dignity of the Son in His 1,000-year reign on the earth.

The fourth quotation, from Psalm 104:4, is found in verse 7. There the angels are referred to as spirits, and in ministry they are likened to flames of fire. Because angels are spirits, their ministry cannot be observed; and just as a flame is temporary and transitory, so the ministry of angels is periodic and temporal. Most important, here the author contrasts the unseen and temporary ministry of angels with the eternal character and ministry of the Son.

In the fifth quotation (1:8–9), another contrast between Christ and the angels is based on Psalm 45:6–7. Here the writer affirms the eternality of the Son and shows that every exercise of His administrative authority is in keeping with God's perfect righteousness. According to the Jewish tradition of that day, angels were created new every morning, and after they completed their

---

Another book by Dr. Pentecost can prove extremely helpful in understanding the continuous unfolding of God's perfect plan. That book is titled "Thy Kingdom Come" and is published by Victor Books.

daily ministry, they returned to the stream of fire from which they had been taken. This concept may have arisen from an interpretation of Psalm 104:4. Regardless, it is with stark contrast that the author emphasizes the eternality and the deity of the Son. Further, this anointing has set Him apart to the position of an administrator, since anointing in the Old Testament always had in view empowerment by the Holy Spirit to discharge a special office or appointment. In Psalm 45, then, the Son is shown as anointed by the Father with the Spirit for the discharge of His office as earthly king. As we know from the gospels, at His baptism the Son was anointed and empowered by the Holy Spirit to fill His messianic office in His earthly kingdom (Acts 10:38).

The sixth quotation is from Psalm 102:25–27 and is found in verses 10–12. Here the eternality of the One who is addressed as "Lord" is affirmed. He is the Creator of the universe, and while the universe is destined to pass away, the Creator remains. He is the eternal uncreated Son of the Father, in contrast to the angels who are created beings.

The seventh and final quotation, found in verse 13, is from Psalm 110:1. Again reference is made to the time of the resurrection when Christ was officially enthroned at His Father's right hand. This enthronement was the Father's answer to the Son's petition on the eve of the crucifixion: "O Father, glorify Me together with Yourself, with the glory which I had with You before the world was" (John 17:5). Christ's

---

If the existence and ministry of angels is something you would like to study further, ask your local bookstore for a copy of "Angels, Elect and Evil," by C. Fred Dickason. A study of all the Bible has to say about angels can help you understand more about your place in God's plan.

enthronement was the Father's declaration of His acceptance of the Son and His satisfaction with the Son's work. Moreover, Christ's enthronement at the Father's right hand anticipates His enthronement here on the earth following His second coming, when all the enemies of the enthroned One will become subject to Him. The right to rule given by the Father to the Son will be exercised here on earth in the Son's millennial kingdom.

Throughout these seven quotations the writer of Hebrews has emphasized the sovereignty and authority of the Son, in contrast to the role of angels who are "all ministering spirits" (Heb. 1:14). Angels who minister under the authority of an administrator are certainly inferior to the one they serve. Thus by that which the Old Testament reveals about the nature and work of angels, the author clearly demonstrates that the One who has come as Son and Revealer is superior to the angels. Consequently, His revelation should take precedence over any and all revelation given through angels.

Understandably, it has been difficult for many recipients of this epistle to sever their ties from the order originally established by God's revelation given to Moses through angels. But the apostle desired that those who were still bound to that old revelation would realize they were following an inferior revelation, and that they

Some people who trust Christ for salvation have trouble believing they are completely forgiven, either because of the nature of their sins, or because they come from churches that teach that we must "help" God by making up for our sins. However, God the Father's total satisfaction with the work of Christ shows us that nothing can be added to what He has done for us. God considered Christ's work perfect and complete—who are we, therefore, to think that anything could ever be added to it?

should submit themselves to the revelation given through the superior Revealer, Jesus Christ.

D. A Stern Warning Against Neglect (2:1–4)

1 Therefore we must give the more earnest heed to the things we have heard, lest we drift away.

2 For if the word spoken through angels proved steadfast, and every transgression and disobedience received a just reward,

3 how shall we escape if we neglect so great a salvation, which at the first began to be spoken by the Lord, and was confirmed to us by those who heard Him,

4 God also bearing witness both with signs and wonders, with various miracles, and gifts of the Holy Spirit, according to His own will?

As the writer of Hebrews will do throughout this epistle, after presenting a doctrinal truth, he makes a direct application of that truth to the experience of his readers. This passage presents the first of those many applications.

First of all, the writer voices an exhortation to "give the more earnest heed to the things we have heard," followed by a solemn warning of inescapable discipline. "The things we have heard" can

For several generations of Christianity in our culture, much emphasis was placed on the responsibilities of being a Christian, without much talk about its privileges and blessings. Today, much is made of the privileges and blessings of knowing Christ, perhaps to the neglect of understanding its responsibilities. The point of Hebrews—and one we should take seriously—is that each of us who enjoys the privileges and blessings of knowing Christ should realize that there also are responsibilities. Neglecting to take these responsibilities seriously will not cause us to forfeit our salvation but can cause us to forfeit the privileges and blessings we would otherwise enjoy. Conversely, properly understanding the two-sided coin of privilege and responsibility can set our feet on the path to spiritual maturity and a fulfilled Christian life.

only refer to the superior revelation given through the Son. The recipients' responsibility is to respond appropriately to this superior revelation. But there is a danger that the recipients might "drift away." The Authorized Version renders this phrase, "lest we should let them slip." Compared to the reading in the New King James, these are two quite different concepts. In the Authorized Version, the recipient of the revelation is viewed as immobile and the revelation, like a river, drifts past him. In a more accurate translation, however, it is God's revelation that stands secure, while the one who has received that revelation could, through neglect, fail to attach himself to that revelation—thus carelessly drifting past the secure mooring. In short, God's revelation is the safe haven for the recipient, and exhortation is given lest through carelessness the recipients should drift away from that revelation.

Each and every revelation from God carries with it a responsibility. God's revelation given through angels at Sinai carried with it a penalty for disobedience (Lev. 26:1–46; Deut. 28:15–68). Even this now-inferior revelation had serious consequences if it was neglected. And so the writer asks, "how shall we escape if we [that is, we who have received God's superior revelation in the Son] neglect so great a salvation?"

Here the author is using the word salvation to summarize the entire scope of revelation given through the Son. This was the revelation "spoken by the Lord." Remember, the author was writing to second-generation believers who had not heard that revelation directly from the Lord Himself. Rather, they had heard it conveyed to them by apostles who themselves had heard and seen the revelation given in and through the Son, and whose testimony to that revelation was authenticated by "signs and wonders, with various miracles, and gifts of the Holy Spirit."

Throughout Scripture various valid signs, wonders, and miracles were God's authentication of His messenger with His message. Signs first occurred in the days of Moses, when Moses was sent to Israel with God's message of redemption. That message and God's deliverer, Moses, were both authenticated by the signs he was given to perform before Israel (Ex. 4:1–9). He was also sent as God's messenger with God's message to Pharaoh. The message was to let God's people leave Egypt, and those miracles that we call the ten plagues were signs given to authenticate Moses' message to Pharaoh. Elisha and Elijah were sent with a message of God's judgment that would come unless God's people repented. The prophets and their message were authenticated by the miracles they performed.

Miracles did not occur again in Israel until Jesus Christ came to offer Himself as Messiah and to announce the establishment of His covenanted kingdom, conditioned on Israel's repentance (Matt. 3:2; 4:17). Through the miracles He performed, Christ was authenticated as God's messenger and His message concerning the kingdom authenticated as God's message. Finally, in the book of Acts the apostles were sent with a new message: salvation by grace through faith based upon blood. Again, they were authenticated as God's messengers by the miracles that they performed.

What the writer of Hebrews is arguing here, then, is that even though this generation of believers had not personally heard and seen the revelation given in the Son, the truth He revealed had been transmitted to them by the apostles who had heard and seen Christ. Further, the

To understand God's discipline of believers, we should never lose sight of parents' loving discipline of their children. If God is disciplining you through trials or hardships, remember that He loves you far more than anyone else can ever love you, and He wants the best for you. His discipline is always designed to bring you back into fellowship with Him, and into the experience of His varied blessings.

miracles the apostles performed had already authenticated them as God's messengers with God's message to this new generation.

Because the revelation given through the Son was authenticated by God in this way, the readers of Hebrews were accountable for that revelation—and any neglect of that revelation would certainly bring discipline. This is indeed an equally serious warning for us today, for even though we are far removed from the revelation God gave through His Son, it still stands as authenticated by God, and we are just as responsible to respond to it. And any failure to respond will certainly bring discipline.

E. Reasons for the Incarnation of the Son (2:5–18)

5 For He has not put the world to come, of which we speak, in subjection to angels.

6 But one testified in a certain place, saying: "What is man that You are mindful of him, Or the son of man that You take care of him?

7 You have made him a little lower than the angels; You have crowned him with glory and honor, And set him over the works of Your hands.

8 You have put all things in subjection under his feet." For in that He put all in subjection under him, He left nothing that is not put under him. But now we do not yet see all things put under him.

9 But we see Jesus, who was made a little lower than the angels, for the suffering of death crowned with glory and honor, that He, by the grace of God, might taste death for everyone.

10 For it was fitting for Him, for whom are all things and by whom are all things, in bringing many sons to glory, to make the captain of their salvation perfect through sufferings.

11 For both He who sanctifies and those who are being sanctified are all of one, for which reason He is not ashamed to call them brethren,

12 saying: "I will declare Your name to My brethren; In the midst of the assembly I will sing praise to You."

13 And again: "I will put My trust in Him." And again: "Here am I and the children whom God has given Me."

14 Inasmuch then as the children have partaken of flesh and blood, He Himself likewise shared in the same, that through death He might

destroy him who had the power of death, that is, the devil,

15 and release those who through fear of death were all their lifetime subject to bondage.

16 For indeed He does not give aid to angels, but He does give aid to the seed of Abraham.

17 Therefore, in all things He had to be made like His brethren, that He might be a merciful and faithful High Priest in things pertaining to God, to make propitiation for the sins of the people.

18 For in that He Himself has suffered, being tempted, He is able to aid those who are tempted.

Because the exhortation and warning in 2:1–4 is really a parenthesis in the development of the writer's thought, he returns to the theme of the superiority of Christ to angels. In verse 5 he anticipates the subjection of all things to the authority of Jesus Christ as Messiah. This will occur at His second advent when He returns to this earth to sit as David's Son on David's throne and rule over David's kingdom in fulfillment of God's covenants and promises.

When the writer refers to "the world to come," he is speaking in light of the accepted Old Testament eschatology, which divided God's program into two ages. The first age was this present age, or the age of expectation, in which the covenanted people were looking forward to the coming of the Messiah who would fulfill all of God's covenants made with the nation. That present age would then terminate with the appearance of Messiah and the establishment of the Messianic kingdom, and it would be followed by the age to come. This second age, or "world to come," was the age Messiah would introduce at His advent, the age in which all of Israel's hopes would be realized. So when the apostle speaks here of "the world (or better, the age) to come," he is anticipating the millennial glory that belongs to Jesus Christ.

Since the Son has been presented as eternal, coexistent with the Father, and the One to whom the right to rule has been assigned, a question inevitably arises: Why did such a One become incarnate? This is the question the apostle will deal with in the extended section of 2:6–18 as he presents eight reasons for the incarnation of the Son.

1. To fulfill God's purpose for man (2:5–9a).

The first reason for the Incarnation is so that God's purpose for man might be finally realized by the One who would take the title, "The Son of Man."

Answering the question, "What is man," the writer quotes from Psalm 8:4–6, where the psalmist asked the same question. The psalmist's real question was, "What is Your divine purpose for man as man?" The answer from Scripture is that man as man is lower in time and order of creation than the angels. But while angels have no greater destiny than that which they now possess, man is destined to be crowned "with glory and honor." Man is destined to rule over all of creation. And all created things eventually will be put in "subjection under his [man's] feet."

Actually, this is the psalmist's own commentary on Genesis 1:26, where God's purpose for the creation of man is clearly stated. As Creator, God is sovereign over all creation. And God has chosen to assign the administrative authority over creation to man as man. It was man's responsibility to exercise dominion over the fish of the sea, over the birds of the air, over the cattle over all the earth, over every creeping thing that creeps on the earth. And in bringing all created things under his authority as

God's purpose for humankind is quite different from the present-day philosophy that proposes that people are a blight on the earth and should not exercise any dominion over it! While various movements in our world might seem harmless on the surface, as believers we should be careful to look for areas in which they clearly contradict the Word of God. In this way we will "test the spirits" and be "wise as serpents," able to discern between those things that are consistent with the Bible and those that are not.

God's administrator, man would bring all creation into subjection to God's authority.

After the creation of humankind, God charged them to "be fruitful and multiply; fill the earth and subdue it; have dominion over the fish of the sea, over the birds of the air, and over every living thing that moves on the earth" (Gen. 1:28). Because divine administrative authority was assigned to man as man, God's rule on the earth would be established by and administered through man. This original purpose is reaffirmed in Psalm 8. The psalmist shows that God's original purpose continues even in spite of man's rebellion against God and his failure to subjugate all things to the authority of God.

What the writer of Hebrews affirms in verse 8 is that although God's original purpose has not been terminated, it has not yet been realized. That is why he states, "We do not yet see all things put under him." The "him" in this passage refers to man as man. When he says we do not yet see, he is affirming that God's purpose must be realized in the future—for God's purposes are unchanging and unchangeable.

While the multiplication of people on the earth certainly has brought about the multiplication of sin, nowhere does God ever revoke or disparage His command to "be fruitful and multiply." There are few movements afoot today that demean humankind as much as does the overpopulation myth. While it is true that many cities are grossly overpopulated, many evil governments economically abuse their populations, and many countries fail to do whatever is necessary to provide first for their masses, the problem in every case is man's sin, not humankind itself. While greed, false religion, and atheistic governments can and do create horrible hardships for millions of unfortunate people, God still loves all people and desires that His kingdom be populated with as many as will come to Him.

But then in verse 9 the author goes on to point out that Jesus took the position of man, a little lower than the angels, so that He might be crowned with glory and honor. The "glory and honor" of verse 9 is the fulfillment of the same "glory and honor" referred to in verse 7—which would be the fulfillment of God's original purpose to subject all things to man! In other words, if the eternal Son did not take to Himself a true and complete humanity, it would have been impossible for Him to fulfill God's purpose for man. However, by becoming flesh and identifying Himself with the human race, He alone is able to fulfill the original purpose God stated for man in Genesis 1:26–28.

The title Christ used for Himself in the gospels more frequently than any other was "the Son of Man." This title emphasizes that because of the incarnation—whereby Christ took to Himself true humanity—He was not only eligible but also able to fulfill God's original purpose for man. And because that purpose (subjecting all things to

Himself as Son of Man) was not accomplished during His first advent, the second advent of Messiah is a necessity. As the writer of Hebrews has stated, even after Christ's first advent "we do not yet see all things put under him" (2:8). But he also assures his readers that God's original purpose for man will be fulfilled, and that Jesus Christ, as the Son of Man, will be crowned with glory and honor when He returns.

Notice that our attention is focused not on humankind in general, but on Jesus specifically, through whom God's purpose for man as man ultimately will be fulfilled. And it is through "the suffering of death" that He will be crowned with glory and honor, emphasizing Christ's obedience to the will of His Father even to the point of death. This stands in stark contrast to the disobedience of the first man, Adam, to whom administrative authority was given, but who became disobedient and who consequently fell into disgrace and death. But through the obedience of Jesus, even unto death, he will be brought to glory and honor.

Thus the first reason given for the Incarnation is that God's purpose for man as man might be fulfilled.

2. To taste death for all (2:9b).

The second reason for the Incarnation is given in the latter part of verse 9. Jesus Christ became incarnate that He "might taste death for everyone."

The penalty for man's disobedience to God was spiritual death; that is, the separation of the soul from God. And before one who is dead can be restored to life, to fellowship with God, the penalty for his disobedience must be paid. Jesus Christ came to offer a payment to God on behalf of the sin of the human race. He came to offer Himself as the sinner's substitute in death. And to be man's substitute, He must be identified with man. Thus the Incarnation was necessary that Jesus might offer Himself as an acceptable sacrifice to God on man's behalf, as humankind's substitute. Jesus Christ came into the world specifically that He might die.

3. To bring many sons to glory (2:10–13).

The third reason for the Incarnation is stated in verses

Our society seems to be consumed with hate, especially in respect to securing retribution for wrongs suffered. Nearly every accident—no matter how "accidental"—must be blamed on someone, who then is sued for as much cash as possible. Even in the so-called "Christian community," punishment and revenge is sought through lawsuits for wrongs ranging from lost jobs to photocopied songsheets. What a contrast Christ provides! Though we wronged Him, though we are sinners by nature as well as by choice, He took our penalty upon Himself. Shouldn't that attitude, that "mind" that was in Christ, be in us as well? And while we diligently hold the line against willful evil and lawlessness, shouldn't our hearts of compassion, understanding, and forgiveness set us apart from the society around us?

10-13. He came that He might bring many sons to glory.

Christ was not content to be crowned alone with glory and honor; He desired to bring many to share His glory with Him. And those who will share that glory will share it as sons. In verse 10 the writer affirms that all that has been created was created by Him, and that all that has been created was created for Him, to serve His purposes. And one of His ultimate goals was to identify many with Him in His glory.

The perfection the author refers to in verse 10 does not imply that there was a pro-gression from imperfection to perfection in the person of Christ. Rather, the word perfect deals with the accomplishment of a divine purpose. It was God's eternal purpose to identify many as sons with His Son in glory; and through the incarnation Jesus Christ so identified Himself with the human race that He could look upon men and women as brothers and sisters.

Because this wonderful union between the saved and the Savior was anticipated in the Old Testament, the writer quotes Psalm 22:22 and Isaiah 8:17; and he quotes Isaiah 8:18 to show that the Old Testament foretold an identi-

In the world of celebrities, those who tag along after the famous are derisively called "groupies." With no merit of their own, they latch onto the coattails of famous stars, athletes, and politicians, hoping to share in their glory. And usually, of course, they are shunned by those they so fervently admire, because they are not wanted, needed, or useful. What a contrast we have in our wonderful Savior! Though He was "crowned with glory and honor" by God Himself, He desires that we share that glory and honor with Him. He willingly elevates us to share His exalted position, and takes pleasure in our identification with Him. How can we possibly think we need to grope for meaning outside of Christ, when we obviously are of such great value in His eyes?

fication between the incarnate Son and mankind. The quotation from Psalm 22 is a direct reference to the Messiah, while the two references from the Septuagint version of Isaiah are indirect references. In the passage from Isaiah, the prophet identifies himself with a people who have rejected the Lord and have rejected him as the Lord's messenger. He chooses this identification in spite of their rejection. In this, then, he foreshadows Messiah's identification with a people who are in rejection.

But even more than stressing Christ's identification with men, the writer of Hebrews is stressing that this identification was the means by which God's purpose to bring many sons into glory was to be accomplished.

4. To destroy the devil (2:14).

The fourth reason for the Incarnation is given in verse 14. Jesus Christ partook of flesh and blood; that is, He took to Himself a true and complete humanity so that on man's behalf "He might destroy him who had the power of death, that is, the devil."

Christ's death was a divine judgment on Satan, the being through whom man experienced spiritual death, the separation of the soul from God. It is because of this judgment that Satan can be bound for the thousand years

It is not often that we are reminded that we dwell on Satan's "turf." Ever since the fall, this world and the world system has been his territory; he is the prince of the power of the air, the god of this age, the ruler of this world. That is why any and every world view, taken to its logical conclusion, will ultimately oppose the plan and purpose of Jesus Christ. And that is why when we belong to Him, we are out of place here on this earth. In short, as Christians we are foreigners in a land that is under hostile rule. And sometimes that can be very difficult. The good news, however, is that when the time is right, Jesus will finish God's plan to destroy the enemy forever. That is certain, and that is our "hope" in the midst of difficulty.

in which Jesus Christ will be crowned with glory and honor on earth (Rev. 20:2–3). It is also the basis for Satan's consignment to the lake of fire and brimstone for all eternity (Rev. 20:10). Significantly, the word destroy does not mean to annihilate, but rather to render inoperative. As man's representative, Jesus went into conflict with Satan at the cross in order that He might break Satan's rule over the human race.

5. To deliver those in bondage (2:15).

The fifth reason for the Incarnation is found in verse 15. Through the Incarnation, which included the death of Christ, people could be delivered from bondage to the fear of death.

The fear of death that grips the sinful race comes from an intuitive consciousness of the judgment that will follow death. But by delivering people from all judgment (Rom. 8:1; John 5:24), Christ can remove the dread of death. Those who experience life in Christ have an assurance that at the moment of physical death they will go immediately into the presence of the Savior (2 Cor. 5:1–8). Thus, our fear of death is removed.

6. To become a priest for men (2:16–17a).

The sixth reason for the Incarnation is found in verses 16–17a, namely, that He might become a merciful and faithful High Priest on man's behalf.

A priest is a mediator between God and man. He

Apart from knowing Christ, virtually every person is fearful of death and its uncertainty. That is why Christians often can effectively witness to unbelievers by sensitively but forthrightly bringing up the subject of death and what will follow. Of course, the purpose is not to use "scare tactics" to frighten someone into the kingdom; but we cannot ignore the fact that death and judgment hover over anyone who does not know Him. Remember—the fear and uncertainty in their lives is real, and we can offer them the good news of a cure. Jesus can deliver those in bondage to that fear.

represents God before men and represents men before God. Since Jesus Christ is the Son of God, He is qualified to represent God before men. And to represent men before God, it was necessary for Him to become man through incarnation.

Because of the Incarnation, He is able to be a faithful High Priest on man's behalf before God. A merciful priest must understand the miseries of those whom He represents; to understand, He must identify with men in their sufferings. To be a faithful priest to those in need, to manifest God's perfect faithfulness, He must be God Himself. Therefore the Incar-nation was necessary to provide the kind of priest we needed to represent us in our need before God.

7. To make propitiation for sins (2:17b).

The seventh reason for the Incarnation is stated at the end of verse 17. The Son became man "to make propitiation for the sins of the people." The writer has in mind the fulfillment of that which was anticipated by every Day of Atonement throughout Israel's history. The most significant day in all of Israel's annual religious calendar was the one day in which the high priest stood on behalf of a guilty people and covered the broken Law by sprinkling blood on the Mercy Seat. This provided a substitute in death for the guilty people so God could view the penalty of the Law as having been carried out. Not only was blood-covered sin forgiven, it was also

How would you feel if you had a personal representative in the White House, someone who—in response to a simple phone call—would immediately bring your every problem or concern to the attention of the president? Amazingly, if you are a Christian, you have such a representative before God—only better! Jesus is our personal High Priest before the Father, representing us with a perfect understanding of our weaknesses and failures.

removed from the congregation, as typified in the act of
confessing the nation's sin
over the scapegoat that was
then led away into the
wilderness. This act provided
a basis upon which God
could deal with the sin of a
guilty nation and could dwell
in their midst, accessible to
the people in any time of
need. This satisfaction of
God's wrath is what the Bible
refers to as "propitiation."

Since the writer of
Hebrews will go into great
detail later to show how
Christ's death fulfills that
which was foreshadowed in
the Day of Atonement, we
will not develop this theme
further here. However, we
need to recognize that the
incarnation was that which
made Christ's propitiatory
sacrifice possible.

8. *To provide help for those*
tested (2:18).

The eighth reason for the
Incarnation is given in verse
18. Since God Himself cannot
be tempted with evil (James
1:13), nor can He be put to a
test (Deut. 6:16; Matt. 4:7), it
was necessary for Jesus Christ

by incarnation to identify
Himself with people to faith-
fully represent those who are
tempted and tested.

Only through this identification was He able to suffer,
and apart from His suffering
that which people suffer, He
could not have been an understanding priest. Christ's sufferings and testings did not
come from a fallen sin nature
such as men experience, but
rather were from the world
and from Satan. But that
which He suffered has
become the foundation for
His compassion. In having
experienced, apart from a fall-
en sin nature, that which
men experience, He is able to
aid those who are tested.

One question that might
arise here is how Jesus,
because He was sinless, could
really understand and respond
to our testings and temptations. We must recognize that
Jesus, who is indeed sinless,
does not identify Himself
with us in our solicitation to
sin. As 1 John 3:4 points out,
sin is lawlessness, which is
the tendency to declare one-
self independent of God. This
temptation can come from

the sin nature within or from Satan without. Whatever the source, however, the testing is essentially the same.

At His temptation in the wilderness, Jesus was enticed to lawlessness. The temptation did not come from a sin nature within Him, but from Satan without. Therefore Christ understood the nature of temptation. We suffer because we live in an unredeemed body in an unredeemed world with an unredeemed sin nature within us. Jesus Christ did not have a fallen sin nature within Him but He did live in a corruptible body in this unredeemed world. He therefore was subject to the same sufferings to which we are subject, even without that fallen sin nature. As a consequence He can be sympathetic with us, a compassionate, merciful, and faithful High Priest. His sympathy is related to our testings, not to our sin. His sympathy does not depend on personal experience of sin, but upon the experience of the strength of sin as He did in His temptation, again in Gethsemane, and finally at the cross.

The sufferings Christ endured from the world and Satan were far greater than any of our individual experiences. Satan conserves his energy and exerts no more pressure on any individual than it takes to conform that individual to his desire. Because of our weakness, we conform to Satan's will when

---

For many Christians, defeat begins with simply experiencing temptation. At the point we face temptation, we think that Christ has abandoned us or, just as wrong, that we cannot turn to Him for strength. Nothing could be further from the truth! Though our temptations may be coming from our own sin nature within as well as from the adversary without, Jesus understands our weakness, understands the full power of temptation, and is able to respond to any plea for help we direct to Him. So the next time you face temptation, turn to Him immediately, knowing that He understands, cares, and can deliver you.

we experience only a small portion of the pressure he has available to bring to bear on us. By contrast, in his attempt to conform Jesus to his will, Satan exerted all available pressure—and found that Jesus could not be made to sin.

Jesus Christ therefore has endured a far greater weight of testing than any individual has experienced. And because He has endured the full weight of Satan's testings, He understands our weakness, our need, and is able to respond. This testing from Satan was possible only because of Christ's true humanity, and because of this He is able to respond to any cry of help that comes from those He represents as a merciful and faithful High Priest.

In summary, then, verses 5–18 list all of the work Jesus Christ accomplished because of and during the time of His incarnation. He has done what no angel could possibly do. He is superior to angels in His person and superior to angels in His work. The obvious conclusion is that revelation from such a superior Person must take precedence over any revelation given from an inferior person. As great as was the revelation through angels given at Sinai, far greater is the revelation given through the Son/Revealer. And just as Israel was held responsible for the revelation given through angels, so we are held responsible for the superior revelation God has given in the superior person, Jesus Christ.

II. Jesus Christ the Redeemer and Ruler Is Superior to Moses (3:1–4:13).

The foundation of Israel's hope as a nation was the covenant God gave to Abraham (Gen. 15:18–19) in which the land—occupied at that time by the Canaanites—was given as a perpetual inheritance to Abraham and Abraham's descendants. God gave to this covenant people the promise that One would come who would bless not only that nation but all the nations of the earth (Gen. 12:3). God revealed to Abraham that his descendants would be strangers in a land that was not their own, and that they would serve as slaves and be afflicted for four hundred years. God also promised to judge the nation they would serve, and that afterward the children of Israel would come out with great possessions (Gen. 15:13–14).

In fulfillment of this revelation, the family of Jacob settled in Egypt where, under Joseph as their benefactor, they enjoyed many privileges.

But with the passage of time they were reduced to insufferable bondage (Ex. 1:8–14). Faithful to His covenants and promises, God "heard their groaning, and God remembered His covenant with Abraham, with Isaac, and with Jacob. And God looked upon the children of Israel, and God acknowledged them" (Ex. 2:24–25). God reached into the recesses of the wilderness and took Moses, a refugee from the wrath of Pharaoh, and set him apart to become His people's redeemer/deliverer from bondage (Ex. 3:10–12). As a redeemer/deliverer from bondage in Egypt, Moses foreshadowed the work of the promised Blesser who would become a Redeemer/Deliverer —not from physical bondage in Egypt, but from bondage to sin.

The one who was appointed as Israel's redeemer was also set apart as ruler and judge. And while the nation accepted the redemption God provided through Moses, they rebelled against Moses as God's ruler over them (Acts 7:34–35). In being set apart as ruler over God's redeemed people, Moses foreshadowed the right to rule that would be vested in the Redeemer to come.

The work Moses accomplished and the position in which he was placed anticipated the coming of a new Moses who would redeem and rule over God's covenant people. But in addition to being set apart as redeemer and ruler, Moses also was the appointed one through whom God would give revelation to His redeemed covenant people. And while God's covenant given to Abraham was the foundation of Israel's hope, His covenant given through Moses at Sinai—the Law—was the foundation of Israel's daily life.

The Law revealed the kind of life God expected of a redeemed people if they were to live in fellowship with Him and please Him. God's revelation in the Law provided for acceptable worship. It also provided for sacrifices through which one who violated the Law might be restored to fellowship with God. In short, the Law ruled over every aspect of the life of those who had been redeemed and had received the revelation of the Law. Because of this all-perva-

A good summary of the Old Testament Law is that it was not given to redeem people, rather it was given to a redeemed people. Those who had been redeemed by God would display their faith in God's promises by living in submission to the Law. Although the Mosaic law has been supplanted by the superiority of Jesus Christ, the believer's relationship to the Word of God is much the same today. We cannot be saved—or "keep" our salvation—by living in obedience to the Bible's commands. But those who are saved should display their saving faith by willfully living in submission to God's Word. Those who fail to submit to God's Word are either not truly His, or they know Him but are willfully forfeiting the blessings that would otherwise be theirs.

siveness of the Law, Moses was held in the highest esteem by the people of Israel.

But as seen in Israel's history, the children of Israel murmured and rebelled against the one who had been set apart as their redeemer, ruler, and channel of revelation. Because of this fact, the author of Hebrews recognizes the possibility that those who now have received a superior revelation might be guilty of a similar rebellion against the Redeemer and Ruler through whom it has come.

A. The Faithfulness of Moses and Christ Contrasted (3:1–6).

1 Therefore, holy brethren, partakers of the heavenly calling, consider the Apostle and High Priest of our confession, Christ Jesus,
2 who was faithful to Him who appointed Him, as Moses also was faithful in all His house.
3 For this One has been counted worthy of more glory than Moses, inasmuch as He who built the house has more honor than the house.
4 For every house is built by someone, but He who built all things is God.
5 And Moses indeed was faithful in all His house as a servant, for a testimony of those things which would be spoken afterward,
6 but Christ as a Son over His own house, whose house we are if we hold fast the confidence and the rejoicing of the hope firm to the end.

The word *therefore* in 3:1 connects back to 2:10–18 the writer's exhortation to his readers, with particular reference to verses 17–18. While the faithfulness of Christ as a priest will be developed beginning in 4:14, here the contrast between the faithfulness of Christ and Moses is developed.

Because the writer refers to the recipients of this epistle as "holy brethren," it is obvious that he does not consider them to be unbelievers. They are partakers of the heavenly calling, and the word *partaker* emphasizes the genuineness of their experience. Therefore, without detracting from the preeminence of Moses as a redeemer, ruler, and revealer in the Old Testament, the author wants his readers to focus their attention on Christ Jesus. The word *consider* is an intensive verb, meaning to concentrate carefully or to fasten the mind on Christ Jesus to the exclusion of all else. The word *confession* refers to each believer's testimony of faith in Christ and identification with Him at the point of baptism. By referring to Christ as "the Apostle," the writer is emphasizing that Jesus had been sent by God, while referring to Him as a "High Priest" calls attention to His role as our representative before God. What the writer is particularly stressing here is the perfect faithfulness that characterizes Jesus Christ.

In spite of his reluctance to assume the role to which he was appointed by God (Ex. 3:11–4:1), Moses was found faithful once he accepted that role. In spite of all of the testings, opposition, and obstacles he faced, Moses never wavered in his belief that God would accomplish that for which he had been set apart. That faithfulness of Moses is called to our attention in 3:2; but that which characterized Moses also characterizes the

new Redeemer, Ruler, and Revealer—Jesus Christ.

While parallels exist between the faithfulness of Moses and the faithfulness of Christ, there also are contrasts. Christ was faithful as the architect of the house, while Moses was faithful as the "house" the architect designed and built. Further, while Moses was faithful as a servant in God's house, Christ was faithful as the administrator over His house. The writer's thinking here is based on the relationship between Creator and creature, thus emphasizing the superiority of Christ over Moses. Christ is the builder; Moses was a part of the house being built. Christ is over the house; Moses is in the house. Christ is a Son; Moses is a servant. While the previous chapter related Christ to the seed of Adam as Son of Man, this chapter relates Christ to the seed of Abraham and the house of Israel.

In verse 5 the author stresses that all that was revealed to Israel through Moses anticipated things that were yet to come. God's revelation through Moses was "a testimony of those things which would be spoken afterward," indicating that the Law was temporary and anticipatory.

In verse 6 the writer again assumes the genuineness of his readers' faith as he writes, ". . . whose house we are." The evidence of their faith is reflected in the writer's assumption that they will "hold fast the confidence and rejoicing of the hope firm unto the end." Clearly, obedience to revelation is an evidence of the genuineness of anyone's salvation. By faith the children of Israel accepted the plan of redemption that was delivered to them by Moses. In obedience they sacrificed the lamb, placed the blood of the sacrifice on the lintel and doorposts of their houses, and entered through blood into safety from the judgment of death. There was no rebellion against the redemption that a faithful Redeemer had provided.

However, even after experiencing redemption, God's redeemed people continually rebelled against Moses, God's appointed ruler. In fact, that redeemed generation was characterized by continual murmuring (Ex. 15:24). The words translated *to murmur* carry the thought "to be discontented," which reveals their inward attitude, and "to grumble," which was the outward expression of their inner attitude. From the time of

---

The biblical answer to today's "easy believe-ism" is not adjusting our doctrine to incorrectly suggest that only those who are perpetually, completely submissive to Christ as Lord are saved; rather, it is to recognize (1) that knowing Christ involves more than simply mouthing the words; and (2) that those who genuinely know Christ but ignore their responsibility to obey Him are in danger of forfeiting His blessings in their lives, perhaps even life itself. Living life as a carnal, apathetic, uncommitted Christian is indeed possible—but it is far from desirable!

their redemption from Egypt, the people were characterized as murmurers (Ex. 16:2, 7–8; 17:3; Num. 14:2, 27–36; 16:41; 17:5; Deut. 1:27). The history of the nation and the relationship between murmuring and disobedience is summarized in Psalm 106:23–25, where we read that they "murmured in their tents, and did not heed the voice of the Lord."

B. The Rebellion at Kadesh Barnea (3:7–11).

7 Therefore, as the Holy Spirit says: "Today, if you will hear His voice,

8 Do not harden your hearts as in the rebellion, In the day of trial in the wilderness,

9 Where your fathers tested Me, tried Me, And saw My works forty years.

10 Therefore I was angry with that generation, And said, 'They always go astray in their heart, And they have not known My ways.'

11 So I swore in My wrath, 'They shall not enter My rest.'"

Next, the writer of Hebrews passes over the long history of Israel's murmuring and focuses his readers' attention on the climactic rebellion that took place at Kadesh Barnea. The reason he focuses on this episode is that he sees the possibility that the recipients of this letter are in danger of repeating the sin of their forefathers in the wilderness, and he fears that his generation might suffer the same consequences their ancestors suffered in the wilderness. Therefore it is essential that we consider and understand Israel's experience at Kadesh Barnea, as recorded in Numbers 14.

God had said to Moses "I have come down to deliver them out of the hand of the Egyptians, and to bring them up from that land to a good and large land, to a land flowing with milk and honey, to the place of the Canaanites" (Ex. 3:8). The first part of that promise was fulfilled through the redemption of Israel from Egypt on the night of the first Passover. By faith that nation had become a redeemed nation (Isa. 43:1). Therefore it would be reasonable to expect that the other portion of what God had told Moses was His purpose for His people would likewise be fulfilled.

After their journey from Egypt to Sinai, and after their sojourn there (during which time they received God's revelation of the Law through Moses), the people were led to the border of the land God had promised to give them. Before them lay the prospect of enjoyment of the land and a life of peace and rest in fulfillment of God's covenant with Abraham. In obedience to God's command, Moses set apart representatives of the twelve tribes. These were to enter in and survey the land, which, because of the obstacles that lay before them, could only be possessed by faith (Num. 13:1–2). These spies brought back a very realistic report concerning both the obstacles to their occupation of the land and the wealth the land offered. Even though they knew the difficulties ahead in occupying the land, Joshua and Caleb called on the people to believe God, saying, "The land we passed through to spy out is an exceedingly good land. If the Lord delights in us, then

He will bring us into this land and give it to us, a land which flows with milk and honey" (Num. 14:7–8).

However, the people refused to believe either Joshua and Caleb or God Himself. They responded in unbelief to this call to faith (Num. 14:11; Heb. 4:6). This unbelief led to overt rebellion (Num. 14:9), and it was only through the intervention of Moses that the unbelieving nation was not judged with immediate physical death (Num. 14:11–12). Because of the faithfulness of Moses, the intercessor, the people were delivered from death—but they were deprived of enjoyment of the privileges in the land that had been promised to them. That generation was turned back to wander in the wilderness until there arose a new generation that, in response to faith in God, would possess the land and occupy the land of rest and enjoy a life of rest.

In Acts 7:35, Stephen made it clear that this rebellion was not only a rebellion against God, it was a rebellion against Moses as well. While they

had followed Him as
redeemer, they were unwill-
ing to follow Him as ruler.
Therefore the author of this
epistle quotes Psalm 95:7–11
to give the same exhortation
to his generation that the
psalmist gave to his. The
psalmist invited his generation to acknowledge that as
Creator, God is worthy to be
worshiped. But he also realized that some might not
respond appropriately to that
fact, and that his people could
repeat the rebellion of their
fathers in the wilderness. As a
result, they would suffer a
similar loss of privileges.
Using that passage, then, the
writer of Hebrews appeals to
his recipients not to become
discontented because of their

suffering, and not to let dis-
contentment give way to
open rebellion—lest they, like
their forefathers, lose the
blessings of the privileges that
now were available to them
as believers.

C. The Consequences of Unbelief (3:12–19).

12 Beware, brethren, lest there be
in any of you an evil heart of unbelief in departing from the living
God;

13 but exhort one another daily,
while it is called "Today," lest any of
you be hardened through the
deceitfulness of sin.

14 For we have become partakers
of Christ if we hold the beginning
of our confidence steadfast to the
end,

15 while it is said: "Today, if you

Have you faced—or are you facing now—a crossroads in
life in which the risks of trusting God seem too great to take
that route? Are you standing at your own Kadesh Barnea
thinking that moving ahead with a steadfast commitment to
God is too chancy, too dangerous, too different? Before you
decide to turn your back on Him and settle for a lifetime in
the wilderness, consider the nation of Israel and all they
missed out on. In other words, consider the difference
between peace and rest in the "land of promise," and death
in the wilderness.

will hear His voice, Do not harden your hearts as in the rebellion."

16 For who, having heard, rebelled? Indeed, was it not all who came out of Egypt, led by Moses?

17 Now with whom was He angry forty years? Was it not with those who sinned, whose corpses fell in the wilderness?

18 And to whom did He swear that they would not enter His rest, but to those who did not obey?

19 So we see that they could not enter in because of unbelief.

After reviewing the historical precedent in verses 7–11, the writer now shows the consequences of unbelief leading to rebellion, to inform his readers of the serious consequences they face if, like their forefathers, they do not walk by faith and claim God's promises concerning a life of peace and rest. These consequences are:

1. A departure from God (3:12).

In verse 12 the warning is sounded, "Beware, brethren, lest there be in any of you an evil heart of unbelief in departing from the living God." Once again, the author views his recipients as believers, referring to them as "brethren." He recognizes that even though they have been saved by faith, they might not choose to live by faith, but instead may have "an evil heart of unbelief." Such unbelief would cause them to depart experientially from the living God, and they would lose their fellowship with Him.

2. A hardening of the heart (3:13–16).

If they broke fellowship with God, their hearts would become calloused and insensitive to Him. While they did not renounce their salvation, neither did they laying hold of the help God provides for those who are going through difficult circumstances. In verse 12 the apostle placed responsibility on each believer for his or her own conduct. In verse 13, however, he also placed responsibility on believers for the brother who may be weak in faith and who may not be availing himself of God's support in the experiences of life. Believers are to "exhort one another daily."

This exhortation is based on the truth that "we have become partakers of Christ." Frequently in this epistle the writer will emphasize the responsibility of one believer to another lest the weak should stumble and fall. Once again, then, holding steadfast confidence is evidence of the genuineness of our faith.

3. An act of rebellion (3:17).

Their hardness of heart toward God could result in open rebellion against Him. Referring to Psalm 95:7–8 and stressing the word *today* in verse 15 (as in verse 7), the apostle saw that his generation was in a similar situation to that of their forefathers at Kadesh Barnea. That is, it would be possible for a redeemed people to respond in unbelief to God's promises and thus lose the blessings God provides for those who walk by faith.

4. The loss of promised blessings (3:18–19).

Rebellion causes the loss of promised blessings. The Jews of the Exodus generation responded in unbelief to the promises of God. That unbelief led to disobedience (3:18),

Notice the downward spiral that begins with simple doubt concerning God, brought on by hardships or uncertainty. Doubt leads to complaining. Complaining leads to a departure from fellowship with God, which in turn leads to a hardening of the heart against Him. Next follow open acts of rebellion, which can result in a permanent loss of promised temporal blessings. Somewhere at the beginning of our troubles, we all face the temptation to think that God has abandoned us, that He doesn't really care about us, that "He has brought us into the wilderness to die." According to Hebrews, this is a far more dangerous situation than we may realize! It is at this time that we should return to His certain promises of blessing and listen to them rather than listening to our own murmuring and complaining.

and that disobedience was sin (3:17). The consequence of that sin was "they could not enter in because of unbelief" (3:19). Please notice that the people who had been redeemed by faith on the night of the first Passover did *not* lose their status as a redeemed nation—but they *did* forfeit the blessings and the privileges that were to have been theirs in the land, and they forfeited a life of peace and rest.

D. The warning from Israel's experience (4:1–13)

1 Therefore, since a promise remains of entering His rest, let us fear lest any of you seem to have come short of it.

2 For indeed the gospel was preached to us as well as to them; but the word which they heard did not profit them, not being mixed with faith in those who heard it.

3 For we who have believed do enter that rest, as He has said: "So I swore in My wrath, 'They shall not enter My rest,'" although the works were finished from the foundation of the world.

4 For He has spoken in a certain place of the seventh day in this way: "And God rested on the seventh day from all His works";

5 and again in this place: "They shall not enter My rest."

6 Since therefore it remains that some must enter it, and those to whom it was first preached did not enter because of disobedience,

7 again He designates a certain day, saying in David, "Today," after such a long time, as it has been said: "Today, if you will hear His voice, Do not harden your hearts."

8 For if Joshua had given them rest, then He would not afterward have spoken of another day.

9 There remains therefore a rest for the people of God.

10 For he who has entered His rest has himself also ceased from his works as God did from His.

11 Let us therefore be diligent to enter that rest, lest anyone fall according to the same example of disobedience.

12 For the word of God is living and powerful, and sharper than any two-edged sword, piercing even to the division of soul and spirit, and of joints and marrow, and is a discerner of the thoughts and intents of the heart.

13 And there is no creature hidden from His sight, but all things are naked and open to the eyes of Him to whom we must give account.

1. The possibility of rest (4:1–10)

a. The promise of rest (4:1–2)

The word *therefore* in 4:1 draws a conclusion to the truth the apostle has just presented. He had said in verse 16 that the people who had been redeemed by God provoked God by their unbelief. In verse 17 their unbelief led to overt sin, and they suffered the consequences. In verse 18 their disobedience caused God to reject them and to withhold the promised blessings. And in verse 19, although they had started for the land of promise by faith, they could not enter that land and life of rest because of their unbelief. Since it was possible that the recipients of this letter might fall into a similar pattern of unbelief and disobedience, he gives an exhortation in light of the promises given in the Son/Revelation: "Let us fear lest any of you seem to come short of it."

In these first two verses the author points out that the promises of a life of rest are given to us just as it was given to the redeemed generation that left Egypt. The gospel that had been delivered to the readers was not only the good news of salvation; it also included the good news (literally, *gospel*) that God has also provided a life of rest that can be appropriated by faith, even in the midst of difficult circumstances.

Different interpretations have been given to the "rest" promised in verses 1–2. Some, believing this letter was addressed to unbelievers, interpret the "rest" as salvation rest or eternal rest; that is, they believe "rest" refers to the eventual result of salvation. However, as has been clearly demonstrated, this epistle was addressed to believers, not to unbelievers. Moreover, after the writer has drawn a lesson from the experience of the redeemed nation Israel in the Old Testament, it would be most strange for him to suddenly turn from addressing believers to giving an exhortation to unbelievers.

A second interpretation is that the "rest" here refers to the millennial rest—that rest which the nation Israel will eventually enter when the Messiah promised to Abraham delivers His people from bondage to Gentiles, and institutes His kingdom of peace and righteousness here on earth. Based on the covenants God had given to the Hebrew forefathers, this certainly was the nation's expectation. However, the rest into which the generation at Kadesh Barnea could have entered was not the millennial rest, for Messiah had not come, nor had He exercised His authority to subdue all nations to Himself and institute His millennial kingdom. While millennial rest is indeed the expectation of God's covenant people, that was not the rest that was before Israel at Kadesh Barnea, nor the rest into which the next generation would enter under Joshua.

That leads us to the logical conclusion that the "rest" in this passage must refer to what we would call a faith/life rest, a rest appropriated by faith and enjoyed even in the midst of the conflicts, obstacles, and opposition of life. Such was the rest missed by the exodus generation; and the rest entered into by Joshua's generation when by faith they possessed the land and enjoyed its blessings.

During the closing days of Christ's life on the earth, the immediate fulfillment of God's millennial kingdom

Even within the Christian sphere, many people are looking for "rest" elsewhere, not in the knowledge of Christ and the assurances of His Word. To be sure, even the Christian life, apart from submission and obedience to Him, will be filled with dissatisfaction and inward turmoil. And no amount of material success, physical comfort, psychological counseling, or religious duty will provide the peace and rest He has promised. It can only be appropriated by faith in the promises of God, regardless of adversity and the circumstances around us.

promise was withheld from the nation Israel because of its unbelief as a nation (Matt. 19:11; 21:43). Because of the religious leaders' rejection of Christ as King, that generation of Israel fell under divine judgment (Matt. 21:41; 23:37–24:2; Luke 21:24). Jesus made it clear that the promised Davidic kingdom could not be established on earth until after that physical/temporal judgment had been executed, the nation comes to repentance, and the King—then absent—returns physically, visibly, and bodily to the earth.

Thus the establishment of the earthly millennial kingdom was not the expectation of the readers of this epistle. The writer does say, however, that the good news preached to us (4:2) is that by faith we may enter into the blessings of a faith/life rest. In fact, the apostle is so confident of the faith of the recipients that he can declare, "We who have believed do enter that rest." This can be literally translated, "We who have believed are now entering into the rest of God." Note that the faith/life rest is not viewed as static, but progressive. It is a dynamic process in which the believer goes from faith to faith, and from victory to victory.

b. The pattern of rest (4:3–5).

In verses 3–5 the rest into which God entered following His work of creation is presented as the pattern of the rest into which a believer may enter. Referring back to the creation account of Genesis 2:2, the writer shows that God entered into rest.

How interesting that God Himself is the author of rest! And the divine rest God instituted following creation is still continuing today. That means that although we live in one of the most hurried, tense, tumultuous societies that has ever existed, we can experience His perfect rest by maintaining and cultivating our relationship with Him. But we must take time out from our own busy lives to do that.

Because the work of creation was completed in six days, it was not necessary for God to resume work after a temporary rest. Instead, with the completion of creation, God entered into a permanent state of rest. While God worked in six days to bring creation to its desired conclusion, once that work was completed, no additional work was necessary. The author's application of this principle is that when we—by faith —enter into a life of rest, it is no longer necessary to *attain*, but only to *maintain* that rest into which we have entered by faith.

c. The perpetuity of the promise (4:6–10).

Because the sinning generation in the wilderness for-
feited its rest, some might incorrectly conclude that the promise of entering into rest was permanently withdrawn. By referring to Psalm 95:11, however, the author points out that generations later, during the days of David, an invitation could be given to that generation to enter into the faith/life rest. David's generation lived in the midst of conflict. There was political strife within the nation, and the royal house was divided. There were conflicts between Israel and the nations. Even so, David could assure those living in the midst of conflict that God still extended the privilege of entering into rest by faith.

Jesus once said that if all those who are weary and burdened with the weight of sin and religious duty would come to Him, He would give them "rest." Are you hungry for the rest of a life of faith, regardless of circumstances? Are you willing to trust God and His promises for every area of your life? Are you willing to be obedient to His authority as you experience that life of faith-rest? If anything is standing between you and Him, between you and the rest He offers you, why not go to Him in humble submission and turn it over to Him . . . today?

Again, it might have been erroneously concluded that the generation that entered the land and life of rest under Joshua had fulfilled God's promises, and therefore those promises were not available to later generations. But since David promised rest long after Joshua had completed the conquest, it is evident that this promise is a continuing promise that may always be realized by faith. The conclusion we can draw, then, is that "there remains therefore a rest for the people of God" (4:9). And the writer makes it very clear that this rest is not realized by human effort, but by faith (4:10).

2. The exhortation to enter that rest (4:11–13).

After clearly demonstrating that a faith/life rest is available to believers today, the author concludes by an exhortation to enter into that rest (4:11–13). This type of life is not one into which a believer passively drifts, suddenly awakening to a realization of blessings. Rather, it is realized only by giving diligent attention to enter that rest. Faith is never passive; it is always active. And if one does not give careful attention to the exercise of faith, he or she will not enter that promised rest. It is sad but true that apart from such diligent attention to the exercise of faith, any believer can disobey and fail to enter that rest.

In verse 12, the word *for* explains why we should be diligent to enter the promised rest. Not only may we fall short of the promised blessings, but through our neglect we might also come under God's discipline. The believer who is called upon to exercise faith and thus enter into rest is judged by the revelation God has given. In the Old Testament, Israel was judged by revelation of the Law given through Moses. In the same way, believers today are judged by the revelation given through the One greater than Moses. Specifically, the believer is judged by the Word of God.

In this passage, five things are said about the Word of God:

First, it is living. The Scripture is given by inspiration of God (2 Tim. 3:16). Because it is God-breathed, it partakes of the character of God Himself. Because God lives, the Word He has breathed is a living Word.

Second, the Word of God is powerful; or, as it could be rendered, it is active. It does something to those who hear it and heed it. It not only enlightens the mind, it also alters conduct. It not only reveals what is within man, it also sits as the judge of all conduct.

Third, the Word is sharper than any two-edged sword. Using as an illustration the sharpest weapon a Roman soldier had available, the author speaks of the penetrating quality of the Word of God. It is able to distinguish between what is godly and what is ungodly, what is right and what is wrong.

Fourth, the Word of God pierces. And while some have understood this as saying the Word of God can "separate" soul from spirit, it seems better to understand it as saying that God's Word is able to penetrate to the depths of the soul and the spirit.

This seems supported by the fifth statement, that the Word of God is a discerner of the thoughts and intents of the heart. Nothing can be hidden from exposure by the Word of God. Consequently, "there is no creature hidden from His sight, but all things are naked and open to the eyes of Him to whom we must give account" (4:13). Thus the author says that we should give careful attention

Whatever we do, we cannot miss the vital connection between the Word of God and the life of faith-rest God offers us. Without a careful, ongoing study of the Bible, we are completely unequipped to diligently pursue the rest He provides. Bible study is the key to spiritual growth and maturity. We cannot trust what we do not know, and we cannot act upon what we do not trust.

to enter into a life of rest; for if we fail because of doubts, unbelief, fear, or weariness in the conflict, those motives will be revealed.

In summary, we have seen that God gave Israel one who was to be a Redeemer, a Ruler, one through whom revelation would come. But the people who accepted redemption also rebelled against the ruler. That rebellion consummated in the unbelief and sin at Kadesh Barnea, which caused the redeemed generation to lose the blessings and privileges that were to be theirs in the Promised Land. Now a greater Redeemer, Ruler, and Revealer has come, and the writer of Hebrews points out the present danger that the readers may repeat the sin of their forefathers. This would again cause the loss of promised privileges and blessings.

The promise of a faith/life rest is before the recipients of this letter. They can enter into that faith/life rest, but to do that they must give careful attention to the exercise of faith. Their every thought and action will be judged by the Word of God. Thus, the author exhorts, "Let us fear lest any of you seem to come short" of that rest (4:1). And again, "Let us therefore be diligent to enter that rest" (4:11).

No matter how much we have been helped by the plethora of Christian books offered in bookstores today, we should always remember that the Word of God is the only living book in the world. Further, it is the only book about which any of the statements in Hebrews 4:12 is true. Therefore we would do well to spend at least as much time in the Word of God as we spend reading all other books combined.

III. Jesus Christ the Priest Is Superior to Aaron (4:14–10:18).

After his parenthetical warning that disobedience would bring about the loss of blessings, the writer returns to the theme of the high priesthood of Christ, which he will continue to 10:18. The mention of the High Priest in 4:14 refers us back to 2:17 and 3:1, while the confession hearkens back to 3:1, and the boldness in 4:16 looks back to 3:6. Thus we can see that the author will now develop in detail what he has already introduced in a previous section.

The phrase seeing then in verse 14 infers that we are responsible, and that it is necessary to take advantage of the High Priest we have and to appropriate the blessings He provides. The author is emphasizing the continuing availability of our High Priest when he says, "We have a great High Priest." In other words, He is our present and perpetual possession.

A. Christ in a Superior Position (4:14–16).

14 Seeing then that we have a great High Priest who has passed through the heavens, Jesus the Son of God, let us hold fast our confession.

15 For we do not have a High Priest who cannot sympathize with our weaknesses, but was in all points tempted as we are, yet without sin.

16 Let us therefore come boldly to the throne of grace, that we may obtain mercy and find grace to help in time of need.

On the Day of Atonement, Aaron went into the earthly tabernacle to minister in the presence of God on behalf of the people. And at the conclusion of his ministry he emerged from God's presence to mingle among the people again. But this is not the experience of our great High Priest, because He has passed through the heavens—that is, He has passed out of this earthly sphere, through the lower heavens, and into the very presence of God to appear on our behalf. He did not come into the presence of

God to minister briefly and then to return to this earthly sphere. Rather, He ministers continuously in God's presence on our behalf. And though Aaron could not bring into God's presence those on whose behalf he ministered, our High Priest brings us into the very presence of God.

In referring to our High Priest by the name of Jesus, the author emphasizes Christ's true humanity, through which He understands our need and can be a sympathetic priest. In referring to Him as Son of God, he emphasizes His deity and stresses the omniscience and omnipotence He exercises as

a priest on our behalf. Consequently the exhortation can be given, "Let us hold fast our confession." And, just as in 3:1, the "confession" is one's public testimony of faith in Jesus Christ as Son of God and Savior, given at the time of identification with Him in baptism.

The *for* in verse 15 gives the reason we should hold fast our confession of faith. He is not a high priest like Aaron, who cannot sympathize with weakness, ignorance, and immaturity. Instead He is a High Priest who was in all points tempted as we are, yet without sin. According to 1 John 2:16

While the Aaronic priesthood might not mean much to us today, prior to the advent of Christ it was God's divinely ordained means of worship and access to Him. Obviously, then, it was superior to all the pagan religions, all the mystical practices, and all the idolatry found elsewhere in the world. Since the book of Hebrews tells us that Jesus Christ is superior to Aaron's priesthood, it stands to reason that He, too, is far superior to all the other religious practices in the world today. That means, then, that the soft-spoken theological liberal who tries to reason that "there are many ways to God" or "Jesus was just one in a long line of spiritual lights" is offering a gross error in place of the truth.

there are three channels through which one may be tested: the lust of the flesh, the lust of the eyes, and the pride of life. These are the only three gates through which Satan can assault the citadel of the soul. And from the gospel records of Satan's temptation of Christ, we discover that He was tested in these three specific areas. When He hungered, Satan suggested that He exercise His divine creative power and turn stones to bread. This was an appeal to the lust of the flesh. When Satan offered Him the kingdoms of the world, this was an appeal to the lust of the eyes. And when Satan suggested that He demonstrate His confidence in God by leaping from the pinnacle of the temple, it was a solicitation to the pride of life. Having resisted testing in these three areas, there were no other avenues by which Satan could assault His soul. Thus Jesus was indeed tempted in all points the same way we are. Human beings can be tempted, and since Christ possessed true humanness, He could be tempted just as we are; yet He did not succumb to that temptation.

In fact, Christ bore a greater weight of temptation than any man has borne. Satan exerts only that pressure necessary to conform us to his will. It is not necessary for him to exert the full weight of temptation on us—for in our weakness, we submit. But Satan exerted on Christ the full weight of his ability to tempt, and yet

Under which categories do your most problematic temptations fit? Just recognizing the area(s) in which Satan regularly attacks you is a giant step toward realizing victory. Remember—Jesus had victory over the full force of Satan's temptations in every area, and He can provide victory for you, too. But we must go to Him first; waiting to turn to Him until after we've tried to solve the problem ourselves will almost always end in disaster.

could not cause Him to submit. Hence Christ bore a greater weight of testing than any man has known. In being thus tempted He knows what temptation is and He is able to suffer along with us when we are tempted. And it is because He endured temptation that He is able to be a merciful, faithful, sympathetic, understanding priest.

I recall my younger daughter's prayer when she had chicken pox at the age of seven. We were praying together before she was put to bed. She said, "Thank You for coming from Your beautiful home in heaven to earth. And thank You for having measles and chicken pox so You know how much I want to scratch." In her own childlike way, she was confident she had an understanding High Priest.

The word *therefore* in verse 16 draws another inference: Since our High Priest is both understanding and perfect, let us take advantage of His availability! We may come freely to the throne of grace. His throne, which would have been a throne of judgment, has been trans-formed into a throne from which grace flows like a river. We come not with fear or doubt, but with boldness, because our High Priest has made us acceptable and has accompanied us into the very presence of God. And when we come to that throne of grace, we come first to obtain mercy, which is love's response to any misery. And second, we come to find grace to help. Grace may be used in two senses. There is the grace that characterizes God in His dealing with sinners and with His children, because of the work of Jesus Christ. But there is also that grace that provides divine enablement to meet any need. Both these ideas of grace are used in this verse, so that we come to the throne of grace to find the needed help our High Priest alone can provide.

B. Christ a Superior Priest (5:1–7:28).

5:1 For every high priest taken from among men is appointed for men in things pertaining to God, that he may offer both gifts and sacrifices for sins.

2 He can have compassion on those who are ignorant and going astray, since he himself is also subject to weakness.

3 Because of this he is required as for the people, so also for himself, to offer sacrifices for sins.

4 And no man takes this honor to himself, but he who is called by God, just as Aaron was.

5 So also Christ did not glorify Himself to become High Priest, but it was He who said to Him: "You are My Son, Today I have begotten You."

6 As He also says in another place: "You are a priest forever According to the order of Melchizedek";

7 who, in the days of His flesh, when He had offered up prayers and supplications, with vehement cries and tears to Him who was able to save Him from death, and was heard because of His godly fear,

8 though He was a Son, yet He learned obedience by the things which He suffered.

9 And having been perfected, He became the author of eternal salvation to all who obey Him,

10 called by God as High Priest "according to the order of Melchizedek,"

11 of whom we have much to say, and hard to explain, since you have become dull of hearing.

12 For though by this time you ought to be teachers, you need someone to teach you again the first principles of the oracles of God; and you have come to need milk and not solid food.

13 For everyone who partakes only of milk is unskilled in the word of righteousness, for he is a babe.

14 But solid food belongs to those who are of full age, that is, those who by reason of use have their senses exercised to discern both good and evil.

6:1 Therefore, leaving the discussion of the elementary principles of Christ, let us go on to perfection, not laying again the foundation of repentance from dead works and of faith toward God,

2 of the doctrine of baptisms, of laying on of hands, of resurrection of the dead, and of eternal judgment.

3 And this we will do if God permits.

4 For it is impossible for those who were once enlightened, and have tasted the heavenly gift, and have become partakers of the Holy Spirit,

5 and have tasted the good word of God and the powers of the age to come,

6 if they fall away, to renew them again to repentance, since they crucify again for themselves the Son of God, and put Him to an open shame.

7 For the earth which drinks in the rain that often comes upon it, and bears herbs useful for those by whom it is cultivated, receives blessing from God;

8 but if it bears thorns and briars, it is rejected and near to being cursed, whose end is to be burned.

9 But, beloved, we are confident of better things concerning you, yes, things that accompany salvation, though we speak in this manner.

10 For God is not unjust to forget your work and labor of love which you have shown toward His name, in that you have ministered to the saints, and do minister.

11 And we desire that each one of you show the same diligence to the full assurance of hope until the end,

12 that you do not become sluggish, but imitate those who through faith and patience inherit the promises.

13 For when God made a promise to Abraham, because He could swear by no one greater, He swore by Himself,

14 saying, "Surely blessing I will bless you, and multiplying I will multiply you."

15 And so, after he had patiently endured, he obtained the promise.

16 For men indeed swear by the greater, and an oath for confirmation is for them an end of all dispute.

17 Thus God, determining to show more abundantly to the heirs of promise the immutability of His counsel, confirmed it by an oath,

18 that by two immutable things, in which it is impossible for God to lie, we might have strong consolation, who have fled for refuge to lay hold of the hope set before us.

19 This hope we have as an anchor of the soul, both sure and steadfast, and which enters the Presence behind the veil,

20 where the forerunner has entered for us, even Jesus, having become High Priest forever according to the order of Melchizedek.

7:1 For this Melchizedek, king of Salem, priest of the Most High God, who met Abraham returning from the slaughter of the kings and blessed him,

2 to whom also Abraham gave a tenth part of all, first being translated "king of righteousness," and then also king of Salem, meaning "king of peace,"

3 without father, without mother, without genealogy, having neither

beginning of days nor end of life, but made like the Son of God, remains a priest continually.

4 Now consider how great this man was, to whom even the patriarch Abraham gave a tenth of the spoils.

5 And indeed those who are of the sons of Levi, who receive the priesthood, have a commandment to receive tithes from the people according to the law, that is, from their brethren, though they have come from the loins of Abraham;

6 but he whose genealogy is not derived from them received tithes from Abraham and blessed him who had the promises.

7 Now beyond all contradiction the lesser is blessed by the better.

8 Here mortal men receive tithes, but there he receives them, of whom it is witnessed that he lives.

9 Even Levi, who receives tithes, paid tithes through Abraham, so to speak,

10 for he was still in the loins of his father when Melchizedek met him.

11 Therefore, if perfection were through the Levitical priesthood (for under it the people received the law), what further need was there that another priest should rise according to the order of Melchizedek, and not be called according to the order of Aaron?

12 For the priesthood being changed, of necessity there is also a change of the law.

13 For He of whom these things are spoken belongs to another tribe, from which no man has officiated at the altar.

14 For it is evident that our Lord arose from Judah, of which tribe Moses spoke nothing concerning priesthood.

15 And it is yet far more evident if, in the likeness of Melchizedek, there arises another priest

16 who has come, not according to the law of a fleshly commandment, but according to the power of an endless life.

17 For He testifies: "You are a priest forever according to the order of Melchizedek."

18 For on the one hand there is an annulling of the former commandment because of its weakness and unprofitableness,

19 for the law made nothing perfect; on the other hand, there is the bringing in of a better hope, through which we draw near to God.

20 And inasmuch as He was not made priest without an oath

21 (for they have become priests without an oath, but He with an oath by Him who said to Him: "The Lord has sworn and will not relent,

'You are a priest forever according to the order of Melchizedek'"),

22 by so much more Jesus has become a surety of a better covenant.

23 Also there were many priests, because they were prevented by death from continuing.

24 But He, because He continues forever, has an unchangeable priesthood.

25 Therefore He is also able to save to the uttermost those who come to God through Him, since He always lives to make intercession for them.

26 For such a High Priest was fitting for us, who is holy, harmless, undefiled, separate from sinners, and has become higher than the heavens;

27 who does not need daily, as those high priests, to offer up sacrifices, first for His own sins and then for the people's, for this He did once for all when He offered up Himself.

28 For the law appoints as high priests men who have weakness, but the word of the oath, which came after the law, appoints the Son who has been perfected forever.

1. Prerequisites for a priest (5:1–4).

Just as Jesus Christ was a Redeemer, Ruler, and Revealer superior to Moses, so is He a High Priest superior to Aaron. And the system in which He functions as Priest is superior to the Levitical order which Aaron administered.

To establish this truth, the writer, in the first four verses of chapter 5, reviews the two essential prerequisites for the priesthood that would apply to any priest in any priestly order. First, the high priest must be genuinely human (5:1–3). And second, he must be called by God (5:4). Since the High Priest was to represent men before God (5:1), he must be truly human so he could be the kind of priest we need. If he were not human and had not experienced all that men experience, he could not have had compassion on the weak and the erring. It was necessary for priests in the Aaronic order to offer sacrifices for their own sins, demonstrating their true humanity.

Since the priest was not only to represent men before God, but also to represent God before men, it was necessary that the priest be appointed by God. God was under no obligation to accept the ministry of priests appointed by men as their representatives. Since all offense was against God, and God's wrath was to be satisfied through the ministry of human priests, it was necessary that God appoint those whom He would accept as His representatives.

2. The prerequisites fully met (5:5–10).

The writer goes on in verses 5–10 to show that because Christ meets these requirements, He is fully qualified to be our High Priest. The proof for this is given in reverse order. In verse 5 the apostle states that "Christ did not glorify Himself to become High Priest." By quoting Psalm 2:7 he shows instead that, at the resurrection, Jesus Christ was *appointed* by His Father to the role of High Priest. Then, to have a second witness to the Father's appointment of His resurrected Son as High Priest, the writer quotes Psalm 110:4. There is no question that Christ was divinely appointed to the office of High Priest.

Christ's true humanity and His eligibility to represent people before God is stated in verses 7–9. Nowhere is the perfect humanity of Christ more clearly evidenced than in

Why does the author of Hebrews go into such painstaking detail to show that Christ is qualified to be our High Priest? Let's remember what our first temptation is in many of our crises: it is the temptation to think that God does not understand us, that He does not understand our situation, or that He does not really care. Taken further, these thoughts can lead us into rebellion, disobedience, even a long-term loss of blessings. But the characteristics of our High Priest as Hebrews reveals them show that thoughts like these are simply not true! Jesus does understand us, He does sympathize with us, He does care, and He is there before the Father to intercede for us continually.

that awesome scene in Gethsemane to which the author
makes reference in verse 7.
"The days of His flesh" refers
to the time of His life on earth
in a mortal body. The word
prayers refers to a specific
request that was made. Suppli-
cation refers to the petition of
one in need of protection or
help in some overwhelming
calamity. The weight of all
that lay before Him produced
"vehement cries and tears."
These indicate not the physical stress, but rather the *emotional stress* under which
Jesus was suffering. In this
time of need He presented His
petitions to "Him who was
able to save Him from death."
He in fact was coming boldly
to the throne of grace that He
might obtain mercy and find
grace to help in this time of
need. Jesus in His time of need
was demonstrating that which
the author had offered as help
to his readers.

The question arises, then,
concerning that for which
Jesus was praying when He
petitioned to be saved from
death. A number of different
explanations have been given.
Some have suggested that in
light of the physical sufferings
involved in death by crucifixion, Jesus was praying that He
might be spared that kind of
death. However, because
Christ frequently predicted
He would be crucified, this
explanation seems unlikely.

Many solutions are offered today for the great emotional
stress we might face. Some "experts" tell us that we cannot
escape it until we lay the blame for it on our parents or
some other outside influence. Others propose that we simply let ourselves go and express whatever feelings might
erupt. Still others suggest that we practice mystical medita-
tion, or take group therapy, or tell our troubles to a bar-
tender. What Jesus Christ Himself practiced, however, was
communion with the Father, blind submission to His will,
and trusting dependence on Him for the grace to see Him
through.

There are others who suggest that Satan was there in Gethsemane, making a final attempt to prevent Christ from offering Himself as a sacrifice on the cross. A premature death in the Garden would not have been accepted by God as a satisfactory substitute in death for sinners. But because Christ had already stated that He was sovereign over His own death (John 10:18), and His authority over His death could not be usurped by Satan, this could not have been the source of such agony in the Garden.

Yet another explanation is that He was praying not to be delivered *from* death, but *out of* death. That is, He was praying for resurrection. Christ seems to do this in His petition to His Father in John 17:1. However, Christ frequently predicted not only His death, but His resurrection as well. Even so, it is true that Christ depended on His Father to fulfill that which He knew was certain, so this is not an entirely unreasonable explanation.

Another explanation is that Christ was praying not concerning physical death, but spiritual death. The penalty for disobedience to God was death (Gen. 2:17). This death was the separation of the sinner from God—that is, spiritual death—and physical death was the result of prior spiritual death. Therefore if Jesus Christ was to satisfy the demands of God's holiness, righteousness, and justice to provide salvation for people who are dead, He would have to experience the same death that separated them from God. He must enter into spiritual death, as anticipated in the prophetic 22nd Psalm where the sufferer cried, "My God, My God, why have You forsaken Me?" (22:1). Here is a mystery deeper than any human mind can comprehend: How could God the Father and God the Son—who are One—be separated one from the other? Yet Christ realized that such separation was involved in providing salvation for sinners.

Since only that kind of separation or spiritual death could satisfy the demands of a holy, just God, Christ could not have been praying that He would be spared that which was essential. But the penalty for disobedience was *eternal* separation from God, and it may be that Jesus was facing the prospect that in offering Himself for spiritual death, the Father might require that the Son be separated from Him for all eternity.

The fact that in facing this prospect Jesus prayed "not My will but Yours be done" reveals His immeasurable love for sinners and the extent of His willingness to obey the Father. In the light of this, Christ may indeed be praying that He will be brought out of the spiritual death He was about to enter, and be restored to fellowship with His Father. This seems to be the content of the Son's prayer to the Father in John 17:5, "O Father, glorify Me together with Yourself, with the glory which I had with You before the world was."

The writer's confirmation that this petition was heard signifies not just that the Father was aware of what the Son prayed, but also that the petition was granted. Because the Son did not impose His will on the will of the Father, His prayer was fulfilled. Although Christ was not spared from physical death by crucifixion, He was brought out of the realm of physical death, as seen in His resurrection. He also was brought out

---

How many of our crises would all but disappear if we could instantly respond to God with the statement, "Not my will but Yours be done"? This, of course, runs contrary to our willful human nature, and often we struggle for days—or longer—with all the possibilities God's will might include before we reach a point of submission to Him. Based on Christ's example, however, there is no more secure position for the believer than resignation to the will of God, trusting Him to do what He has promised: to work all things together for good to those who love Him and who are called according to His purpose.

of the realm of spiritual death, as seen in His ascension to His position at the Father's right hand.

As the Son of God, He could not be tempted, because God cannot be tempted with evil. Yet in His true humanity He could be tested. In these testings Jesus did not learn to obey; rather, He learned all that obedience entails. He endured suffering beyond that which any mortal man has experienced. The words *having been perfected* do not imply that there was a progression from incompleteness to completeness, or from imperfection to perfection. Rather, when in His humanity His sufferings were completed, He—because of His obedience—"became the author of eternal salvation to all whom obey Him." Thus, in this graphic reference to the climactic sufferings in the Garden of Gethsemane, which could only have been experienced by one who is truly human, the author has shown that Christ met the second requirement. As a consequence He is "called by God as High Priest" (5:10).

As the writer will develop later, it is significant that Jesus Christ was not inducted as one of Aaron's sons from the tribe of Levi into the Levitical priesthood. Instead He was inducted into a different order of priests to minister on God's behalf to men and to represent men before God.

3. Exhortation to move forward to maturity (5:11–6:20).

a. They already have moved backward (5:11–14).

Having stated in verses 5 and 6 and 10 that Christ at the time of His resurrection was officially inducted into the office of high priest in the order of Melchizedek, the author will now show the superiority of the order of Melchizedek over the Aaronic order. This is not a concept he can cover briefly, so he will have much to say concerning it. He appears to recognize that this truth will be hard to explain to them so that they understand it, just as it is for us today.

Any truth may be difficult to convey for several reasons. One reason may be the complexity of the truth. A second reason may be that the person conveying the truth does not fully understand it. Neither of these reasons, however, is the cause for the difficulty the writer of Hebrews faced. Rather, the obstacle he faced is explained in verse 11: his readers "have become dull of hearing." The word *become* indicates that they were now in a state that previously had not characterized them. There was a time when they had not been dull of hearing, but now they have entered that undesirable spiritual state. His readers, then, are characterized by regression, by moving backward, and this state makes it difficult for the writer to convey the concept of the superiority of Melchizedek's priestly order over Aaron's. To correct this situation and make it possible for his readers to understand this truth, the writer pauses in his development of the priesthood of Melchizedek to give an extended exhortation. This is a warning that must be heeded before their regression can be reversed and they can understand, appropriate, and respond to the truth.

In verse 11 the writer made a categorical statement, "You have become dull of hearing." He then proceeds in verses 12–14 to validate his evalua-

---

Although we may not realize it, the longer we persist in spiritual lukewarmness, the more "dull of hearing" we can become. Even those who have studied the Scriptures for many years can become thick-skulled concerning spiritual things if they cease to move forward toward spiritual maturity. In simplest terms, when we cease to progress spiritually, we begin to move backward. And once we begin to move backward spiritually, our sensitivity to God begins to lessen, and our understanding of the Bible becomes more difficult. This is just one more reason why we should bolster our commitment to steadily, consistently grow in our relationship with Christ.

tion of their spiritual condition. There are several things the writer presents: first, they have been believers for an extended period of time. That is shown by the phrase *by this time.* Second, they have been taught sound doctrine in the past. This is seen in his observation that they "ought to be teachers." Third, they have not retained or used the truth they had been taught, so that they need someone to teach them again "the first principles of the oracles of God." And fourth, they have reverted from adulthood back to infancy in spiritual things, or have lapsed from maturity back to immaturity. This is illustrated through the analo-gy of food. Milk is suited to infancy, but solid food is suited to maturity. Therefore the writer concludes that their need is not the need of adults (solid food), but milk (the food of babies).

In verses 13 and 14 the apostle defines his concept of that which characterizes a baby and an adult. Spiritual babies are "unskilled in the word of righteousness," while spiritual adults are those "who by reason of use have their senses exercised to discern both good and evil." What he is indicating is that while both the spiritual baby and the spiritual adult have the Word, the baby is unable to use the Word to determine

Wouldn't it be interesting if God would somehow dress believers according to their progress in spiritual growth? How many of us would be dressed like infants, or perhaps like toddlers—after many, many years of knowing Him? How many of us would be dressed according to where we really should be "by this time" in our walk with Christ? Perhaps this would be a good time for you to take inventory, to count the number of years you have known Christ personally, and to determine where you should be "by this time." If that is not where you are, don't despair—but do begin to move forward!

what is right and wrong, to use the Word to guide in his decisions, or to use the Word as his standard of life. On the other hand, the spiritual adult is able to use the Word to determine what is right and wrong. While the baby *has* the Word, he does not *use* the Word. The adult, on the other hand, not only *has* the Word, he *uses* the Word. It is this continued use of the Word that causes a believer to progress from infancy to maturity. The opposite is also true. If a believer has used the Word in the past but now *no longer uses the Word*, he will move backward spiritually from maturity to immaturity.

b. A warning concerning failure to move forward to maturity (6:1–6).

Because either ignoring or neglecting truth will produce regression, the apostle in 6:1–6 draws his conclusion and sounds a sobering warn-

Mental retardation—the failure of the human brain to develop in accordance with the rest of the person—is one of the most heartbreaking realities of life. Anyone with a friend or loved one handicapped in this way knows the incongruity of an adult body coupled with a juvenile, or even infantile, mind. But for these special people, no choice was involved. In most cases it was a seeming accident of birth, a genetic miscue ordained by God for His own purposes. In tragic contrast, however, there are many thousands of Christians for whom spiritual retardation has been a willful choice. Though they are "adult" in the number of years they have known Christ, they are juvenile, or even infantile, in their spiritual maturity because of their failure to pursue energetically their relationship with Him. This, of course, is not God's ideal plan for them, or for us. And these characteristics listed in Hebrews, even more than convicting us, should motivate us to progress out of our spiritually retarded state toward maturity.

ing about the danger of not progressing toward maturity, as introduced by the word *therefore* in 6:1. The writer begins with an exhortation, "Let us go on to perfection." Perfection here is defined as the "full age" of 5:14, that is, spiritual maturity. This exhortation implies that they are babies, and also that they would not be considered babies unless they had evidenced life. In other words, they are saved. They are genuine believers. Thus their need is not knowledge; rather, they need to use the knowledge they possess. Their neglect of the Word has caused them to lapse into dullness or to regress into a state of spiritual infancy, and the "perfection" to which he exhorts them is not salvation, but progression toward maturity in Christ.

If they are to "go on to perfection" or maturity, then, there are certain things they must leave. The root meaning of the verb "to leave" is to go from one thing to another, and it can include the idea of building a superstructure upon a foundation. There

Since this is the focus of Hebrews, we can assume that it is one of God's greatest concerns for all Christians—that we "go on" to spiritual maturity. Unfortunately, everyday pressures and hassles often cause us to focus on simple survival rather than real growth. This is one area in which the tongue-in-cheek axiom, "Aim at nothing and you're sure to hit it!" definitely applies. If you have never taken time to list your spiritual goals, today is as good a time as any. Based on the admonition, "Let us go on to perfection," write down some specific things you would like to be true of you spiritually a year from now. Put the list in your Bible, or someplace where you will see it often. Then, pray, study God's Word diligently, and walk in submission to Him, trusting Him to move you in the direction of true spiritual maturity.

were certain truths the new Son/Revelation had in common with what had been revealed in the Old Testament. In that sense Christianity was built on the foundation laid by the revelation given through the prophets (Heb. 1:1). It might have been reasoned, therefore, that because Christianity was built on that foundation, it would be legitimate for Christians to continue to identify themselves with the old order as represented by the temple.

But the apostle was not asking them to build a new superstructure on an old foundation. Rather, they were to abandon the old foundation—the old order—completely. Without the freedom to make decisions for themselves, those under the old order of the Law were considered children (Gal. 4:1–3) and were kept in that state of infancy. The truth revealed

through the prophets was not final. It anticipated a fuller revelation that would come through Jesus Christ. And if his readers were content to build on that which was only a shadow of that which was to come, the writer warns that they will continue in a state of infancy and never progress to maturity. They are not asked to abandon the *truths* Christianity had in common with Old Testament revelation; rather, they were to move on from the shadow to the full reality of the truth revealed through Jesus Christ.

The six areas the apostle asks them to leave in verses 1–2 were all doctrines stressed in Pharisaic Judaism. These certainly were not wrong; but they were elementary and were not the foundation for maturity. The "dead works" for which they were to repent were those described in Romans 8:5–8.

Throughout Scripture, drawing near to God always entails leaving behind those things that would hinder us in our progress. Is there anything in your life today that would hold you back spiritually? If so, make your decision here and now to leave it behind and move on with Christ.

Faith has always been a prerequisite for a relationship with God (Gen. 15:6). The "baptisms" had to do with the necessity of removing external contamination from defilement and of being cleansed before one could have fellowship with God (Mark 7:2–5). "Laying on of hands" was the sign of identification with another and emphasized the unity between the one laying on hands and the one on whom hands were laid. The "resurrection of the dead" was a fundamental Old Testament doctrine (John 11:23–24). Those who lived under the old order had a concept of a coming "judgment" (Ps. 1:5–6). And while there was truth in all of these doctrines, they were truths that kept in infancy those who built life upon them. Those who would go on to maturity must leave behind those fundamental doctrines and move on.

The confidence the writer has in his readers is expressed in verse 3: "and this we will do." While some make the antecedent (or reference point) of "this" the leaving of elementary principles, it seems better to consider as the antecedent the phrase, "let us go on to perfection." It is the author's conviction that the dullness has not yet settled into an irreversible state. They may yet go on to maturity. There is no question that God desires that these believers progress to maturity, but the author does recognize the possibility that one may have regressed so far that it is impossible to again make progress toward matu-

---

Notice that there is a direct correlation between correct doctrine and spiritual vitality. Although the emphasis in recent years has been on the practicalities of Christian faith, the Bible is clear that a proper foundation in correct doctrine is absolutely essential. While not all of us can pursue a thorough education in Christian doctrine, each of us can and should be diligent to study God's Word carefully and to know why we believe what we believe.

rity. He therefore states in verses 4–6 that it may be impossible to renew certain believers so that they can progress toward maturity. This is a serious, sobering warning the apostle brings to all those who have regressed to a state of infancy!

To fully understand this, we must first recognize that the apostle views his hearers as saved individuals. He refers to them as having been "once enlightened." This enlightenment is not a reference to a light that was perceived and then rejected, but a to light that was actually appropriated and possessed (Eph. 5:8). Such people "have tasted the heavenly gift," the gift of eternal life (Rom. 6:23). They "have become partakers of the Holy Spirit" (Rom. 8:9–11). They "have tasted the good word of God." The word here does not refer to the entire revelation contained in the Bible, but rather to a specific answer God had given to them individually, possibly His direction through the written word in a specific circumstance.

Finally, they have tasted "the powers of the age to come." This refers to the Old Testament promise that during the coming millennial age the Holy spirit would indwell believers and empower those in the kingdom to obedience (Ezek. 36:27; Joel 2:28–29). Since all believers in this age are indwelt by the Holy Spirit, they have experienced the Spirit's empowerment that those who live in the coming millennial age will experience. All the words the writer uses—*enlightenment, tasted, become partakers*—are never used in the New Testament of empty profession, but always of an actual experience. Thus there can be no question that

---

The writer's optimistic outlook is something that should characterize us as believers. Unfortunately, the cumulative effects of sin our lives can prevent us from recognizing the "fresh start" He offers us if we are just willing to forsake ourselves and live for Him. The "will do" optimism of Hebrews 6:3 is only one decision away!

the apostle viewed the recipients as believers.

But now in verse 6 he introduces a condition: "if they fall away." To say that the "falling away" is the believer's loss of his salvation would contradict the great body of New Testament teaching that the life God imparts to a believer is his own eternal kind of life. The believer can no more forfeit that life than God can cease to exist. The question of salvation is nowhere in this context. Thus he is not warning about the possible loss of salvation. Rather, the writer is viewing a believer's experience as a journey from infancy to maturity. It was God's design that there should be steady, uninterrupted progress from immaturity to maturity. It is possible, however, that the journey might be interrupted, that the nature of the interruption might be such that their progress toward maturity would be permanently hindered, and that the

believer would revert to a state of infancy from which there would be no deliverance. Thus the "falling away" is a believer's failure to progress to maturity.

This can well be illustrated by that experience in Israel's history to which the author had referred in chapter 3. At the time of the redemption of the nation from bondage in Egypt, God's redeemed people began a journey that would bring them eventually into the Promised Land where they would enjoy a life of peace and rest. After a few months' journey they came to the very border of that land. But because of unbelief at Kadesh Barnea, they rebelled against God, and God did not permit them to enter the land. Instead He turned that generation back into the wilderness until a new generation could arise.

It was God who said, "How long shall I bear with this evil congregation who murmur against Me? I have heard the

---

For even more understanding of our spiritual heritage as Christians, take time to read Ephesians 1:3–2:10.

murmurings which the children of Israel murmur against Me. Say to them, 'As I live,' says the Lord, 'just as you have spoken in My hearing, so I will do to you: the carcasses of you who have murmured against Me shall fall in this wilderness, all of you who were numbered, according to your entire number, from twenty years old and above. Except for Caleb the son of Jephunneh and Joshua the son of Nun, you shall by no means enter the land which I swore I would make you dwell in. But your little ones, whom you said would be victims, I will bring in, and they shall know the land which you have despised. But as for you, your carcasses shall fall in this wilderness' " (Num. 14:27–32).

Because of their willful, deliberate disobedience, God would not permit that generation to enter the land of promise.

When the rebels heard the announcement of judgment, they changed their minds and were determined that they would occupy the land in spite of what God had said.

They said, "Here we are, and we will go up to the place which the Lord has promised, for we have sinned!" (Num. 14:40). The people did repent. They acknowledged their sin, and they thought that their acknowledgment would reverse God's judgment. And in spite of Moses' warning, they departed for the Promised Land. However, "Then the Amalekites and the Canaanites who dwelt in that mountain came down and attacked them, and drove them back as far as Hormah" (Num. 14:45). Thus God made it impossible for those who had rebelled—even though they repented—to proceed into the land to enjoy its blessings. Their loss of privilege, in other words, was irreversible.

Another illustration of this principle is found in Esau's experience in Genesis 25:29–34, where Esau bartered away his birthright for a vegetable stew. Esau had no faith in the promises of God's covenants and deemed the stew of more value to him than anything God's promises could bring. Thus Jacob became heir of the covenant promises. Later, when it came time for Isaac to pronounce blessing upon his son, the blessing was given to Jacob. And when Esau realized that the blessing which might have been his had been given to another, he repented and he said to his father, "'Have you only one blessing, my father? Bless me, even me also, O my father!' And Esau lifted up his voice and wept" (Gen. 27:38). However, neither Esau's plea nor his tears could bring Isaac's blessing to him. By his earlier willful act, the privileges and blessings that might have belonged to Esau were forever lost. And while we would view Esau in these circumstances as an unbeliever, the principle nevertheless is clearly illustrated. Continual willful acts of unbelief or disobedience may result in the loss of the privi-leges and blessings for which God has made one eligible. Only God can determine when an individual or a people has reached that state where, because they have interrupted their progress to maturity, it has become impossible to renew them again to progress toward maturity. God is gracious and does not, upon our every act of disobedience, consign us to an irreversible state of spiritual infancy. But the serious warning the apostle gives his readers is that by some decision that they might make, or by some neglect of the Word, their progress toward maturity might be barred, and they will remain in that immature imperfect state the rest of their lives.

This "falling away" is not accidental. It is deliberate. It is not a sin of ignorance, but a willful turning back from the

---

Because of the security and prosperity we enjoy in our society, the devastating effects of sin in our lives often are softened by the good things we can do for ourselves in spite of our guilt. These fleeting "quick fix" solutions, however, do not cure the real problem or prevent sin from robbing us of the blessings of spiritual growth and maturity.

journey toward maturity. If these Hebrew believers should willfully return to the old outward forms of Judaism, they would be identifying themselves with the generation of Israel that condemned Christ to crucifixion, and they would take part in God's decreed physical, temporal judgment for that rejection (Matt. 23:38; 24:2). Through their identification they would be condoning the decision of the nation, and thus they would "crucify again for themselves the Son of God, and put Him to an open shame."

To better understand this, we might visual a skier poised at the top of a steep ski jump. That skier is under no compulsion to propel himself down that slope to be launched out into space. But if by an act of his will he plants his poles and pushes himself over the brow of that slope, there is no way he can reverse his downward course, no matter how much he might desire to do so. By that decision he must eventually land at the bottom of the slope. Such is the warning the author of Hebrews makes against misuse of the Word or willful disobedience to the Word.

Their progress toward maturity had been interrupted, and if that became their static state, God could intervene and make it impossible for them to progress further toward maturity. They would remain perpetually in that immature state. History is replete with illustrations of men who seem to be mature, but who by a willful act were set aside and consigned to a state of uselessness from which there could be no return.

c. The illustration (6:7–8).

In verses 7 and 8, the writer turns to nature to illustrate the truth he has been presenting. Throughout Scripture, rain is an evidence of the Creator's provision for creation. Here the author envisions

> Notice that a love for Jesus Christ and obedience to Him always manifests itself in love for fellow believers.

two fields upon which the blessing of rain falls. One field uses God's provision to produce herbs useful for those by whom it is cultivated. The adjacent field, however, receives the same blessing from God, but produces thorns and briers.

The point here is that blessings from God may be *used* or *misused*. Blessings that are *used* produce that which is useful, while blessings *misused* produce that which is useless. So the warning concludes with the observation that while all who believe God receive blessing from God, some will use those blessings to produce that which is good, while others may use those blessings to produce that which is useless.

d. The assurance (6:9–12).

In verses 9–12 the apostle again states his confidence (as in verse 3) that his readers will continue or resume their progress toward maturity. He says, "We are confident of better things concerning you." These "better things" refer back to the illustration in verses 7–8. He is confident that they who receive God's blessings will use those blessings to produce that which is useful. This confidence is consistent with His assurance of their salvation. Even though it might seem that he is addressing them as unbelievers, he is sure of their salvation and is confident that their salvation will produce good fruit. The good fruit he has already seen in them is

It is unfortunate that some believers struggle and agonize under the misconception that, although they desire to walk with God, they have regressed beyond some "point of no return" and can never again walk in fellowship with Him. If you have a heartfelt longing to live for Jesus Christ, that desire alone shows that your heart has not been hardened to Him! All that remains is for you to turn to Him in commitment and submission, and to resume your progress toward maturity.

the work and labor of love that they have carried on in Christ's name. This was not merely love for Christ; it was love for the saints because of their love for Christ. It may be that their ministry to the saints was necessary because of the severity of persecution some of their fellow believers had endured. It is entirely possible that they had identified themselves with those who were suffering for Christ's sake, and he is confident that just as he remembers their good works as evidence of their salvation, so God will not forget their work and labor of love. Eventually they will be rewarded.

In verses 11–12 the apostle expresses his desire for these believers. In the same way he had exhorted them in 4:11 to be diligent to enter the rest God had provided, here he exhorts them to show that same diligence in pressing on to maturity. The goal he has in view is maturity in Christ, and this assured hope of progress toward maturity will support them so that they do not become sluggish. The writer

does not view them as having already become sluggish; but he sees that as an everpresent danger.

e. The reasons for assurance (6:13–20).

In light of the promise of God's enablement to journey from immaturity to maturity, they are called upon to exercise faith and patience as they trust God to bring them toward maturity and continue patiently on that journey. Using Abraham as an illustration, verses 13–20 give the reason for the author's assurance that they will reach that goal through the exercise of faith and patience. As early as Genesis 12:2, God had promised Abraham that he would have a son through whom a great nation would arise. That promise was reaffirmed in 12:7, and again in 13:15–16, 15:2–5, 17:6–7, and 17:16–19. But it was not until years later, as recorded in Genesis 21:2, that the expected child of promise was born. Abraham had exercised faith in the God who gave the promise (Gen. 15:6), but he also was called upon to exercise patient endurance while he waited for that promise to be fulfilled. The promise was not *completed* in Isaac, but was a continuing promise, as stated in Genesis 22:17–18. So even after its initial fulfillment, there was need for faith and patience before the promise would come to its final fulfillment. This is what the writer calls to his readers' attention concerning Abraham: "After he had patiently endured, he obtained the promise" (Heb. 6:15).

It may be that discouragement had come to some of this letter's readers because of the delay in Christ's promise, "I will come again and receive you to Myself; that where I am, there you may be also" (John 14:3). Or perhaps they were disheartened because of the delay in realizing their expectation that Jesus Christ would return in power and glory to institute the covenanted Davidic kingdom for Israel (Matt. 24:30; 25:31). While they believed God's promises, they found it difficult to be patient. Therefore the writer uses Abraham as an example of the relationship between faith and patience, so that his readers might not become discouraged, which would produce spiritual sluggishness.

Even though God's promises may be delayed so that patience is necessary, they are sure. When two men enter into a covenant agreement, they can argue the terms up until the moment the covenant is ratified. At that point, there is no further room for dispute. What has been ratified is confirmed. The promises of God concerning His program for Israel have been confirmed by a covenant. Therefore the author makes reference to that significant

---

One interesting aspect of the Christian life is that none of us is ever exempt from spiritual apathy or sluggishness. There is no point in our lives here on earth at which we can say, "I have arrived. I don't need to grow spiritually any more." The truth is that the only way to keep from moving backward spiritually is to diligently, patiently move forward.

event recorded in Genesis 15.

It appears that Abraham (Abram) was becoming impatient because of the long delay in God's fulfillment of His promise that Abraham would have a son. Therefore he offered Eliezer of Damascus, a servant in his house, as the one in whom that promise might be fulfilled. In his impatience he offered God an alternative to the birth of Isaac so that he would no longer need to exercise patience. But God rejected Eliezer and promised "one who will come from your own body shall be your heir" (15:4). Abraham responded to the promise of God in faith: "He believed in the Lord, and He accounted it to him for righteousness" (15:6). In response to Abraham's request for a sign (which would be the basis not for his faith, but for his patient endurance while he was waiting for the fulfillment of the promise), God told Abraham to prepare animals for a blood sacrifice. This was a ritual with which Abraham was very familiar. Two people entering into a blood covenant after sacrificing an animal would place the divided pieces of the carcass on the ground, join hands, recite the terms of the covenant, and then pass hand-in-hand between the pieces of the sacrifices. Thus the two were bound by blood. This covenant ritual signified that if either party failed to fulfill his part of the covenant, his blood would be poured out like the blood of the slain animal that bound them in covenant. It was a covenant, then, that carried the death penalty for failure to fulfill its terms.

Further, that animal was viewed as a substitute in death for those entering into the covenant. While the two were alive, they could alter the terms of the covenant. But after their death—as symbolized by the sacrificed animal—it was impossible for them to change the terms of the covenant. So the covenant was unchangeable and irrevocable.

To show that this covenant was dependent on God alone, God rendered Abraham incapable of participating in the ritual of ratification. While Abraham slept (15:12), he saw the Shekinah of God pass between the pieces of the sacrificed animals (15:17). In this way, God showed Abraham that He was binding Himself in a unilateral, unchangeable, irrevocable covenant, the terms of which were stated in Genesis 15:1: "To your descendants I have given this land." Abraham believed the God who gave this covenant; but Abraham also would be called on to exercise patience until that which God had covenanted would be fulfilled.

The writer of Hebrews, referring to this incident, points out that Abraham's faith rested on two things: the promise of God and the oath of God. From Genesis 12:1–15:6 Abraham put faith in God's *promises;* but now in Genesis 15:7–21, that which he had believed based on God's promise is confirmed by an *oath,* or covenant. Both the promise of God and the covenant of God are immutable, and their fulfillment rests entirely upon the character of God. Since God cannot lie, that which He promised and that which He covenanted are assured. Even though the fulfillment of the promise would be delayed, because of the official covenant, Abraham had an additional basis upon which he could exercise patience. The application the writer makes, then, is that we not only believe God, but we can—when necessary—exer-

---

There is a wonderful relationship in the Christian life between those things that are our responsibility before God, and those things that are God's responsibility to do for us. Just as the oath God swore to Abraham was dependent on God alone, and all Abraham had to do was trust God and patiently endure, so our spiritual progress is dependent on God alone, thus all we have to do is trust God and patiently endure. It is our responsibility to follow Him; it is His responsibility to move us on toward spiritual maturity.

cise patient endurance while we wait for the fulfillment of His promises. Why? Because God cannot lie to us any more than He could lie to Abraham.

When the author refers to the "hope set before us," he is looking back to verse 11, and ultimately back to the expectation in 6:1, that we will go on to maturity. In Scripture, "hope" is never merely a wish or a dream. Hope in Scripture is the settled confidence that comes to the child of God who rests by faith in the promises of the Word of God.

We have been promised that we can be brought to a state of maturity in Christ. This settled confidence, we are told, is to us what an anchor is to a ship. The harbors around the Mediterranean Sea were small and very shallow and could not provide a safe haven for more than a few vessels at a time. Moreover, the floor of the Mediterranean was sand and could not hold an anchor to keep a ship from drifting in a storm. So to secure a vessel, its anchor would be placed in a small boat and carried into the harbor where it would be secured to a safe mooring.

Outside the harbor the ship might be battered by storms, but because its anchor had been placed securely within the harbor, it remained safe. In the same way, even though we might be battered by storms as we progress on the path toward maturity, Christ's promises that we will be brought to maturity are to us what that anchor was to its ship.

We have a high priest who has entered on our behalf into the very presence of God. Our high priest is Jesus, the Son of God who became man, who as a man could understand our weakness, our ignorance, our immaturity, and could represent us before God. He is there as our intercessor. The fact that He is there as our representative priest gives us assurance that He will bring us into the presence of God.

The writer tells us He is there as our forerunner. In the Roman army, the word *fore-runner* signified the troops sent ahead to explore the terrain and the strength of the adversary before the army advanced. They prepared the way for the army to follow.

The fact that Jesus Christ has identified Himself with us as our High Priest and has gone into the presence of God signifies that all those He represents will be brought into God's presence as well. This is the settled assurance of the believer. Because of this assurance we can exercise patient endurance in spite of conflicts as we progress toward spiritual maturity.

4. Christ a priest in a superior order (7:1–28).

Having brought his readers back to the concept of Christ as a priest in the order of Melchizedek in Hebrews 6:20, the author now shows that Christ is a Priest in an order that is superior to Aaron's priestly order.

a. Melchizedek, the priest (7:1–3).

The individual, Melchizedek, around whom so much of the theme of Hebrews revolves, is referred to only twice in all previous Scripture: in Genesis 14:18–20 and in Psalm 110:4. In spite of his seeming insignificance, the author uses those references to demonstrate that Christ is a priest in an order that is superior to Aaron's.

The historical background to the first reference to Melchizedek is significant. After Lot had separated from Abraham and settled in Sodom, the Elamites formed a coalition under Chedorlaomer to subjugate the kingdom of Sodom and Gomorrah. Their invasion was successful, and Lot was taken captive. Abraham felt responsible to deliver his nephew, so he organized 318 of his shepherds into a fighting force. Since these men were shepherds, they may have been called on to fight wild beasts, but they

---

If a writer of the New Testament considered Old Testament episodes—even something so brief as this encounter with Melchizedek—so important, we would do well to become as familiar as possible with the wealth of information God has revealed in the Old Testament!

had never fought an organized army. Clearly, Abraham ventured into that conflict by faith. Land that had been given to Abraham by the blood covenant had been taken away from the rightful heirs. Abraham's faith in the promise/covenant was the basis upon which he moved to retake the land. Since Lot had been with Abraham when Abraham called on the name of the Lord (Gen. 13:1–5), Abraham believed that Lot also was a son of the promise. Therefore Abraham evidently believed that God would give him a victory over the conquerors so that Lot could inherit God's promised blessings. God responded to Abraham's faith and gave him a great victory.

As Abraham returned with the spoils of battle (Gen. 14:16), Melchizedek, who was identified as the priest of God Most High (Gen. 14:18), met him. Before the establishment of the Aaronic order some four hundred years later, God evidently appointed different individuals as mediators between Himself and people. Job, for example, seems to have held such a priestly appointment (Job 1:5). Melchizedek apparently was another of these divinely appointed priests. As he came out to meet Abraham, he pronounced a two-fold blessing. First, he pronounced a blessing upon Abraham (Gen. 14:19), evidently because he recognized that Abraham's victory was a victory by faith. He also pronounced a blessing upon God Most High (Gen. 14:20). Even though the conflict was waged in faith, the victory did not belong to Abraham. The victory was God's—through Abraham—so that the honor and the glory for the victory must be given to God Most High. Abraham's response was to give Melchizedek a tithe of all the spoils of the conquest (Gen. 14:20). In giving the tithes, Abraham was declaring that the victory was not his, but God's. Therefore all of the spoils did not belong to Abraham, but they rightly belonged to God. In giving a tithe he recognized God's right to all he had taken in battle. This is a very simple historical incident.

The writer of Hebrews, however, draws on this simple incident to present several important truths concerning the priesthood of Christ. In 7:1–3, many significant parallels between the order of Melchizedek and the priesthood of Christ are presented. For example, Melchizedek ministered in Salem, which without doubt is a reference to Jerusalem, the center of David's reign and eventually the center of the earthly reign of Christ following His second advent. Further, Melchizedek is identified as a priest of the Most High God. This emphasizes the universality of his priestly ministry as opposed to the limitations placed upon the Aaronic order, which ministered only to Israel. The two essential features of Melchizedek's priesthood are revealed in the names used in this passage. "Salem" means peace, so he was a king whose reign will be characterized by peace. "Melchizedek" means "king of righteousness," stressing the fact that righteousness as well as peace would characterize his reign. These are the two principle characteristics of the reign of Messiah as described by the Old Testament prophets (Isa. 9:6–7; 48:18).

Another significant feature is that Melchizedek united two offices in one person. He was both a king and a priest. No other individual in the Old Testament united these two offices within himself. Of course, the next one to exercise these two offices in one person will be Christ Jesus at His second advent, when as a King/Priest He will sit on David's throne to rule over David's kingdom.

When various religious groups propose their own views of what Jesus Christ would or would not do in today's world, reigning as "King of Righteousness" usually is not something they include. Be wary of those cultists, religious liberals, or radicals who say they "believe in Jesus." Always ask them to clarify which "Jesus" they believe in—the "Jesus" of their own philosophy or the Jesus of the Bible!

When the writer says that Melchizedek was "without father, without mother, without genealogy," he is emphasizing that as far as we know, he was individually appointed by God to this office and did not receive it by an inheritance from a father or grandfather who had been priest before him. Nor did he establish a king/priest line, since there is no record of any sons to whom the office might be passed on. We know nothing of his birth, nor do we know anything concerning his death, as we know about the death of Aaron (Num. 20:22-29). We know nothing of a time in his life before he became a priest, nor do we know anything of a retirement from the priesthood at the end of his life. In this respect—since he had neither beginning nor ending of days as far as is recorded—he stands as a timeless priest.

Notice that the writer is not comparing the person of Melchizedek with the person of Christ. Rather, he is comparing the biblical representation of Melchizedek in his role as a priest/king as given in Genesis 14 with the Priest/King office of Jesus Christ, the Son of God. Melchizedek did not approach Abraham as God's representative to pronounce judgment on Abraham, which characterized the ministry of the Aaronic priests. Instead, he pronounced blessing upon Abraham. And he not only pronounced blessing on Abraham, he also provided for Abraham's physical needs by offering bread and wine. Thus there were both spiritual and material benefits from Melchizedek's ministry to Abraham.

The lives of many people in the Old Testament are seen from beginning to end, like a video tape. We can view that tape in its entirety, or stop at any point and concentrate on one incident. The record of Melchizedek, however, is not like a tape at all, but a single snapshot. All that we know of him is what we can learn from that single snapshot. The similarity, then, is not between Melchizedek and Christ; it is between Melchizedek as he is presented in Genesis 14, and Christ.

The question is often raised about whether what is

recorded in Genesis 14 is a *theophany*; that is, a preincarnate appearance of the eternal Son of God. While many say it is, the context of Genesis 14 seems to argue against it. Every verifiable theophany in the Old Testament fulfills the purpose of bringing a message from God to men. But that is not the case here. Further, the details of the account—giving names and places—argue against it. Melchizedek could hardly be called the "king of Salem" unless he exercised legal authority there over an extended period of time. When the writer says he was "made like the Son of God," he seems to imply that only those things had been recorded that could be used later by the writer of the Hebrews to reveal truth concerning Christ's priestly office.

Thus, in the historical context, Melchizedek is an individual, universal, timeless, unique priest whose ministry resulted in spiritual and material benefits; and he is never known outside of that picture. In this, as the writer of the Hebrews will show, he represents a perpetual foreshadowing of the priestly order Christ will fill.

b. Melchizedek superior to Levi (7:4–10).

It is evident from the Genesis record that Abraham considered Melchizedek to be superior to himself. This is seen on two counts. First, Abraham gave tithes of his spoils to Melchizedek. He recognized that Melchizedek was God's priest and was a mediator between God and himself. In paying those tithes, he put himself in a position subservient to Melchizedek. Second, Abraham received blessing from Melchizedek. And as the writer will point out in verse 7, the lesser is blessed by the superior. Thus there can be no question that in that meeting Abraham was in the inferior position, and Melchizedek was in the superior position. God had ordained that the Aaronic priests would be the recipients of the tithes the people were obligated to offer to God. The priests then would offer those tithes to God on behalf of the people. Likewise, the acceptance of tithes by the Levitical priests put them in a position superior to those who offered tithes through them. Therefore no one living under the Law could escape the force of the apostle's argument here. If Abraham offered tithes to God through Melchizedek, it is obvious that Melchizedek was *superior* to Abraham.

Here the writer wants to make the point that the order of Melchizedek is superior to the Levitical order of priests. As he says in verses 9–10, "Levi, who receives tithes, paid tithes [that is, to Melchizedek] through Abraham, so to speak, for he was still in the loins of his father when Melchizedek met him." If Abraham was subordinate to Melchizedek, unborn Levi also was inferior to Melchize-dek. Therefore the priestly order subsequently established in the tribe of Levi would have been inferior to the order of Melchizedek. With careful logic, then, the writer has shown that the priestly order of Melchizedek is superior to the Levitical order.

c. The weakness of the Levitical priesthood (7:11–19).

1) transitory (7:11–14).

The Oriental view of superiority and subordination is a concept foreign to our modern Western culture. Therefore it is popular among unbelievers to stand in judgment of God and raise questions like, "How can a loving God allow suffering?" or "How could a God of love send people to hell?" Sometimes this attitude carries over into our Christian lives after we trust Christ as Savior, and we find ourselves questioning His wisdom, His love, or His understanding. Interestingly, the Bible seems to indicate that real understanding of God's work in our lives begins with our humble acknowledgement that He is superior to us, and based on that alone—whether we understand or not—we submit to His will in our lives. This was the lesson Job had to learn, and it was Abraham's attitude as well. Shouldn't it be ours?

The author points out that if they return to the Aaronic system, his readers are returning to an arrangement that can never bring them to maturity. That system was marked by certain weaknesses.

The first weakness the writer points out is that it did not bring to maturity those who were under its authority. As long as men were under the Law they were considered immature children (Gal. 4:1–3). But it was not God's intent to leave His own in a perpetual state of immaturity. So when at Christ's resurrection God appointed Him as priest in the order of Melchizedek (Ps. 110:4), it signified that God would not continue the system that consigned those under it to immaturity. Instead He instituted a new priestly order in which those under it could be brought to maturity.

But it was impossible for Christ to be appointed as high priest in the order of Melchizedek without first terminating the Levitical priestly system. The foundation on which that priesthood rested must be abolished. The Levitical system was a part of a covenant God made with Israel through Moses at Sinai. This was a *conditional* covenant that could be annulled without violating the character of the One who gave it. In Psalm 110:4 Messiah's appointment anticipated the termination of the Mosaic Law upon which the Levitical priesthood rested. This signified that the Aaronic priesthood was a changeable priesthood and that it eventually would be done away. A transitory system could not provide a basis for spiritual maturity.

2) temporary (7:15–19).

A second reason is given why the Levitical priesthood must be abolished. The Mosa-

Just as the Law could not bring to maturity those under its authority, so legalism (the teaching that our salvation depends on our ability to keep a set of rules or to obey the Bible's moral commands) in our churches can never bring anyone to spiritual maturity.

ic Law prescribed that priests must come from the family of Aaron in the tribe of Levi (cf. Num. 16–18). Since Jesus came from the family of David in the tribe of Judah, it would have been impossible for Him to have assumed the office of a Levitical priest. If Christ is to be inducted into a priestly order, it would have to be a different order. This is why he was appointed by His Father as a priest in the order of Melchizedek, not in the order of Aaron. That appointment again signifies that the existing Aaronic order was viewed by God as a temporary arrangement that would be done away.

In contrast to the Levitical priests, whose office would be done away, Christ was appointed "a priest forever" (7:17). The order to which Christ was appointed will never be terminated. And it follows logically that any order that is permanent is superior to that which is transitory and temporary.

The author summarizes his argument by pointing out the basic weaknesses of the Levitical system (7:18). It was temporary, for it was to be superseded by another priestly order. And it was unprofitable, because it did not bring to maturity those who were under it. In contrast, the new permanent order will introduce "a better hope"; that is, it will bring to maturity in Christ those who are under it. Therefore, today we do not attempt to draw near to God through the old temporary, unprofitable order, but through the new order instituted at Christ's appointment as a Melchizedekian priest.

d. Christ's priesthood is superior because it is based on a better covenant (7:20–22).

The Aaronic priesthood rested on the Mosaic covenant, which was temporary and conditional. Thus those serving in the Levitical order had no assurance of the continuation of their office. Jesus Christ, however, was inducted into the priesthood by an oath or covenant God the Father made with God the Son. Referring again to Psalm 110:4 the writer says, "The Lord has sworn and will not relent, 'You are a priest forever according to the order of Melchizedek.'" The statement appointing His Son as a priest is viewed as an unconditional, unchangeable covenant. No such foundation for the Levitical priesthood was ever given by God. Therefore Christ's Melchizedekian priesthood rests on a better foundation. And the "better covenant" (7:22) is the covenant the Father made with the Son confirming Him as an eternal priest in the Melchizedekian order. This means Christ is a unique priest, an individual priest, a timeless priest, a royal priest, a priest from whom spiritual and material blessings will come. And certainly any priesthood resting on such an eternal covenant is superior to the former priesthood which rested on a temporary and conditional covenant.

e. Christ's priesthood is based on resurrection life (7:23–25).

The Aaronic priesthood was made up of an endless number of priests who eventually died. No Aaronic priest was a permanent priest, because the function of each was terminated by death. Jesus Christ, however, was inducted into His priestly office following His resurrection; and as one who possesses endless resurrection life, His priesthood will never be terminated. Those who lived under the Levitical order would no sooner become accustomed to one priest than, because of his death, they would have to become accustomed to another. But because Christ's priesthood is

In relation to the Old Testament priesthood as well as in relation to all the world's religions, Jesus Christ is unique. He is the only religious founder who is not in the grave today. He is the only one who offers Himself, rather than a set of rules or a moral code, as the way to God. And He is the only one who proposes that He is God's ultimate and final word on the issue of sin, salvation, and eternal life.

founded on resurrection life, those who enjoy His ministry will never have to become accustomed to a successor, for He has "an unchangeable priesthood."

The author shows the consequences of having a priest who ministers out of endless resurrection life: "He is also able to save to the uttermost those who come to God through Him." Here the author is not referring to His saving work as the salvation of sinners from judgment and death, but rather using the words *to save* in the sense of "to bring to God's desired end"; that is, to bring them from immaturity to full maturity in Himself. That which the Law could not accomplish through an endless succession of priests whose temporary ministry rested on a conditional covenant, our High Priest will accomplish because His priesthood rests on the eternal covenant made by God His Father. This covenant established Him in an endless priesthood based on the fact that "He ever lives to make intercession for them."

f.   Christ's priesthood is superior because of the character of this Priest (7:26–28).

While those who lived under the old order received benefits from the Aaronic priesthood built on the Mosaic Law, in spite of its weakness and unprofitableness, yet they intuitively recognized that something more was needed. People intuitively knew that those who had to offer sacrifices for their own sins could not finally satisfy the demands of a just and holy God. That same intuition revealed what would be necessary. The writer now describes the kind of priest required to meet our need.

First, he must be *holy*. This word speaks of personal purity, of that which is intrinsically pure. In this sense the word can only be used of Jesus Christ. This shows His relationship to God. Next, he must be *harmless*. This brings out the fact that our priest must not practice evil. This would be His relationship toward people. "Undefiled" signifies freedom from any defilement or any impurity that would render the priest unclean and prevent him from fulfilling his priestly office. No priest could carry out his office until the required sacrifices were offered to remove his defilement. If our High Priest is to minister on our behalf without interruption, no defilement can interrupt His ministry. Only Christ is free from defilement to minister perpetually on our behalf.

The phrase "separate from sinners" seems to suggest the place in which the priest's ministry is to be carried on. The Aaronic priest ministered, surrounded by sinners who came to have him present their sacrifices for sin. Even though surrounded by sinners, the Aaronic priests withdrew into the recesses of the Holy of Holies on the Day of Atonement to present blood to cover the broken Law. But Christ, by His resurrection, has left this sphere in which sinful men dwell and has gone into the very presence of God to minister on our behalf. The final phrase, "has become higher than the heavens," shows the way by which our High Priest has become separate from sinners. The verb become emphasizes that He has entered into a permanent state of exaltation from which He will not withdraw, as the high priest on the Day of Atonement left the Holy of Holies to appear again in the midst of sinful people. Thus Christ in His personal character is far superior to any priest who ministered in the Aaronic tradition.

The author now states a second contrast, that is, the contrast in that which was being offered and in the frequency of what was offered. The Levitical priests offered

---

If Jesus Christ Himself is holy, harmless, and undefiled, what kind of life will characterize those who have drawn near to Him and are trusting Him to move them to spiritual maturity? Those who desire to live for Christ and who submit to His work in their lives will progressively become more like Him.

up animal sacrifices day after day. Because of the inadequacy of those sacrifices to make a final disposition of sin, they needed to be repeated. The sacrifices were offered for the priest himself as well as for the people.

In contrast, our High Priest made a single offering. He offered Himself. His sacrifice was a sacrifice that satisfied the demands of God's holiness and justice so that His sacrifice need never be repeated. That which He did, "He did once for all." His sacrifice of Himself was not for Himself, since He was without sin. Rather, it was a sufficient sacrifice for all sinners. It must be noted that while Christ was the sacrifice at His crucifixion, He was *not* functioning as a priest according to the order of Melchizedek. Instead, God the Father was the One who offered His Son as the sacrifice (Ps. 22:15; Isa.

53:10). Jesus Christ became the sacrifice by submitting Himself without reservation to the will of His Father, the same way Isaac became a sacrifice by submitting to the will of Abraham. He became a sacrifice "when He offered up Himself."

The Law appointed men who were sinful, weak, and dying to the office of priest; but when God confirmed a covenant to appoint a high priest in the order of Melchizedek, He appointed His own Son, who, because He "is holy, harmless, undefiled, separate from sinners, who has become higher than the heavens," is able to be the priestly mediator representing God to men and men before God.

To summarize what the apostle has been presenting in chapter 7 concerning the priesthood of Christ, he has pointed out that Christ is a universal priest representing

It is obvious that if Jesus Christ was God's perfect sacrifice, and He offered Himself "once for all," nothing whatsoever can be added to His sacrifice for our sins—not religious duty not moral restraint, not anything! Our salvation is based solely on His perfect sacrifice, "once for all."

God before all men, not like the Aaronic priest whose ministry was limited to the people of Israel. Christ combined in His Person the office of priest and the office of king. Such was not true in the Aaronic order, for no Aaronic priest ever occupied a throne. Christ's ministry as a King/Priest was characterized by righteousness and peace, whereas the Aaronic priesthood was concerned with sin and judgment. Christ was a unique priest for He did not inherit the priesthood from priestly forebearers nor did He transmit the office to sons who succeeded Him. Christ's ministry as King/Priest brought men to God's desired end; that is, to maturity, whereas those under the Aaronic order were kept in a state of perpetual infancy. Christ's ministry resulted in blessing, while the Aaronic order produced only that which was weak and unprofitable. Christ's priesthood rested on a covenant made by the Father with the Son that confirmed the Son as a Priest forever. Therefore Christ's ministry as priest was an unchangeable and permanent priesthood based on His resurrection life, whereas the Aaronic order was carried out

The more we study God's Word, the more we realize that the epicenter of His revelation is not our salvation, as wonderful as that is. Rather, the focus of Scripture is God's perfect plan for all creation, which will culminate in the reign and rule of His Son, Jesus Christ, over all things. It is only through the outworking of God's flawless plan that we were created, allowed to fall under Satan's dominion, only to be redeemed by His grace and thus escape the judgment that will fall on Satan and his rebellious host of angelic beings. Most incredibly, throughout His plan—including His covenant with Abraham, the giving of the Mosaic Law, and all those things which anticipated the ministry of Christ—there is not one mistake or contradiction!

by an endless succession of dying priests. And Christ's priesthood was based on the sinless character of the priest, whereas the Aaronic order was carried out through sinful men.

There can be no question, then, about the superiority of Christ's priesthood over the Levitical priesthood.

C. Christ has a superior priestly ministry based on a better covenant (8:1-13).

1 Now this is the main point of the things we are saying: We have such a High Priest, who is seated at the right hand of the throne of the Majesty in the heavens,

2 a Minister of the sanctuary and of the true tabernacle which the Lord erected, and not man.

3 For every high priest is appointed to offer both gifts and sacrifices. Therefore it is necessary that this One also have something to offer.

4 For if He were on earth, He would not be a priest, since there are priests who offer the gifts according to the law;

5 who serve the copy and shadow of the heavenly things, as Moses was divinely instructed when he was about to make the tabernacle.

For He said, "See that you make all things according to the pattern shown you on the mountain."

6 But now He has obtained a more excellent ministry, inasmuch as He is also Mediator of a better covenant, which was established on better promises.

7 For if that first covenant had been faultless, then no place would have been sought for a second.

8 Because finding fault with them, He says: "Behold, the days are coming, says the Lord, when I will make a new covenant with the house of Israel and with the house of Judah--

9 "not according to the covenant that I made with their fathers in the day when I took them by the hand to lead them out of the land of Egypt; because they did not continue in My covenant, and I disregarded them, says the Lord.

10 "For this is the covenant that I will make with the house of Israel after those days, says the Lord: I will put My laws in their mind and write them on their hearts; and I will be their God, and they shall be My people.

11 "None of them shall teach his neighbor, and none his brother, saying, 'Know the Lord,' for all shall know Me, from the least of them to the greatest of them.

12 "For I will be merciful to their unrighteousness, and their sins and their lawless deeds I will remember no more."

13 In that He says, "A new covenant," He has made the first obsolete. Now what is becoming obsolete and growing old is ready to vanish away.

1. A superior place of ministry (8:1– 5).

We have seen in the previous references to Psalm 110:4 that Christ did not enter His priestly ministry until after His resurrection and ascension. With the words, "Sit at My right hand, till I make Your enemies Your footstool" (Ps. 110:1), God the Father welcomed God the Son into the glory which He had with the Father before the world existed. At the time of His ascension, Christ was "seated at the right hand of the throne of the Majesty in the heavens" (Heb. 8:1). To be seated at the Father's right hand signified Christ's appointment to the position of honor and authority. The throne He occupies and from which He ministers is not David's throne, which He will one day occupy here on earth as the promised Messiah (Matt. 25:31). Rather, He was identified with the throne of "the Majesty in the heavens." The authority

It has been said that there is no more concise overview of God's plan for the ages than Psalm 110:1. "The Lord said to my Lord" shows the eternality of God the Son and the Father's perfect plan. The phrase ". . . sit at my right hand until . . ." shows the position the Son assumes between the time God first sent Him to His people Israel and was rejected by them, and the time He would return to establish His kingdom. It also accounts for the current time period, when Christ is seated at the Father's right hand. And ". . . I make your enemies a footstool for your feet" foretells what will happen when He returns to establish His kingdom, as is revealed more fully in other prophetic portions of Scripture.

assigned to the One so enthroned was to be "a Minister of the sanctuary and of the true tabernacle" (Heb. 8:2). Thus He was not appointed to be a king in an earthly domain, but rather He was appointed to function as a High priest in a new sanctuary. And the appointment as High Priest, according to Psalm 110:4, follows the enthronement of Christ at His Father's right hand.

The writer very logically shows us the necessity of installing Christ in a new sanctuary. It was the function of priests to offer gifts to God from the people and sacrifices on behalf of them. By divine appointment the tabernacle was the place where gifts were presented and sacrifices were offered. As a priest, Christ must present to the Father the gifts of those whom He represents, and present the benefits of His sacrifice on their behalf in any time of need. It was impossible for Christ to fulfill His priestly function in the tabernacle here on earth, for only the sons of Aaron from the tribe of Levi were permitted to function in that earthly tabernacle. Had Christ attempted to operate in that tabernacle, He would have been an intruder and the gifts He presented as well as the sacrifices He offered would have been unacceptable. He would not have been considered a priest and therefore could not have had a ministry in that tabernacle.

Therefore, in order for Him to function as High Priest, it was necessary that He be provided with a better sanctuary. And since His ministry is on the basis of resurrection life, that new tabernacle cannot be an earthly tabernacle. It must be a heavenly tabernacle in which a resurrected High Priest can function.

The author points out (8:5) that the entire Levitical system, of which the tabernacle was a part was viewed as temporary from the very time of its inception. The tabernacle and all that was conducted by the priests in it was only "the copy and shadow of the heavenly things" (8:5). And while men could learn from that which was a copy and shadow, those were not the realities they were designed to anticipate. The covenant given to Israel through Moses—upon which the Levitical system was built—was viewed as a temporary arrangement that ultimately would give way to the reality it foreshadowed. The earthly tabernacle must give way to the heavenly. The temporary tabernacle must give way to the eternal. An earthly priesthood must give way to a heavenly one. The system that rested on a temporary arrangement must give way to a ministry whose foundation is an eternal covenant the Father made with the Son when He appointed Him as High Priest according to the order of Melchizedek.

2. A superior covenant (8:6–13).

Beginning in verse 6, the apostle draws the conclusion that Christ, although disqualified from serving as a priest here on earth, serves in heaven in a more excellent ministry. This ministry is based on a covenant better than the Mosaic covenant upon which the Levitical priesthood was based. He possesses a superior priesthood because of the superior basis on which it rests. The apostle shows conclusively that the foundation for the Levitical priesthood was a temporary covenant, and he affirms that Christ's priesthood rests on "a better covenant" (8:6), that is, a covenant that was superior to the Mosaic covenant. This better covenant is the covenant the Father made with the Son in Psalm 110:4, which appointed the Son an eternal priest.

To show that God viewed the Mosaic covenant as temporary, the writer of Hebrews quotes from Jeremiah 31:31–34. Because Israel had failed in their obligations under the Mosaic arrangement, Jeremiah had announced the deportation of the people from the Promised Land and the removal of a Davidic descendant from the throne. The penalty for disobedience, as forewarned in Leviticus 26 and Deuteronomy 28, had fallen upon them. Since the nation's enjoyment of covenant blessings depended on their obedience, and since Israel had demonstrated conclusively that the people could not produce the required obedience, God announced that He would terminate the Mosaic covenant and would introduce a new covenant. In the new covenant God said, "I will put My laws in their mind and write them on their hearts; and I will be their God, and they shall be My people" (Heb. 8:10). God Himself would do a work that would so change the minds and heart of the people that they would walk in obedience to God. This obedience would become possible because God, under the terms of this new covenant, would put His Spirit within them (Ezek. 36:25–27; Joel 2:28–29). Under the terms of this new covenant, there would be universal knowledge of God in recognition of what God expected of those who walk in fellowship with Him to receive the promised blessings (Heb. 8:11). Further, this covenant would make provision for the forgiveness of

Because the Mosaic Law is now obsolete, some people mistakenly think it has nothing to offer Christians and thus does not deserve study. According to the Bible, however, the Law served two purposes in relation to the people of God. The first purpose was regulatory, in that it minutely regulated life for the redeemed Jew. That purpose has indeed been supplanted by the superiority of Christ. The second purpose, however, was revelatory, in that it provided revelation concerning the nature of God, man, and the relationship between the two. That purpose of the Law has never ceased, as we can see from the way the author of Hebrews used the Law to teach truth concerning Jesus Christ and the Christian life. Thus the eternal Word of God—even the Law—always has something to offer the child of God who will carefully study it.

their sins (8:12). None of the things guaranteed in this new covenant which God would make with the house of Israel and the house of Judah (8:8) were received through the Mosaic covenant.

The logical conclusion the author draws, then, is found in verse 13: "In that He says, 'A new covenant,' He has made the first obsolete." At the moment Jeremiah announced that God would make a new covenant, he served notice that the old covenant was to be viewed as temporary, not permanent, and that it eventually would be terminated. While the tearing of the veil of the temple at the time of Christ's death (Matt. 27:51) signified that the Law had been done away, its practices were carried on until the destruction of Jerusalem by Titus in A.D. 70. The writer evidently anticipates that event when he says, "Now what is becoming obsolete and growing old is ready to vanish away." Because the temple was still standing, some Hebrews might not understand that the old order had been terminated. But the apostle recognized the imminence of the coming destruction of the temple after which the Levitical system could no longer be carried on. Remember, Christ Himself had predicted that the generation of Israel that rejected Him would come under physical, temporal judgment (Matt. 12:31–32; 23:37–24:2; Luke 21:24).

Thus Jeremiah's announcement of a forthcoming new covenant served notice that the existing covenant must be viewed as a temporary covenant. Even though generations would pass before that old covenant would be terminated at Christ's death, the old covenant nevertheless was temporary. When in the upper room on the eve of His crucifixion our Lord instituted a memorial of His body that was broken and His blood that was shed, He revealed that His death would institute that promised new covenant (Matt. 26:28; Mark 14:24; Luke 22:20; 1 Cor. 11:25). And while some of those to whom the author was writing could flee to the temple for refuge because it was still standing, they would be returning to that which was temporary and which would soon pass away. From its inception, the Levitical system was a temporary arrangement, whereas Christ's priesthood is based on an eternal covenant made by the Father with the Son, which confirmed Him as a high priest forever after the order of Melchizedek.

D. Christ ministers in a superior sanctuary on the basis of a better sacrifice (9:1–10:18).

1 Then indeed, even the first covenant had ordinances of divine service and the earthly sanctuary.

2 For a tabernacle was prepared: the first part, in which was the lampstand, the table, and the showbread, which is called the sanctuary;

3 and behind the second veil, the part of the tabernacle which is called the Holiest of All,

4 which had the golden censer and the ark of the covenant overlaid on all sides with gold, in which were the golden pot that had the manna, Aaron's rod that budded, and the tablets of the covenant;

5 and above it were the cherubim of glory overshadowing the mercy seat. Of these things we cannot now speak in detail.

6 Now when these things had been thus prepared, the priests always went into the first part of the tabernacle, performing the services.

7 But into the second part the high priest went alone once a year, not without blood, which he offered for himself and for the people's sins committed in ignorance;

8 the Holy Spirit indicating this, that the way into the Holiest of All was not yet made manifest while the first tabernacle was still standing.

9 It was symbolic for the present time in which both gifts and sacrifices are offered which cannot make him who performed the service perfect in regard to the conscience--

10 concerned only with foods and drinks, various washings, and fleshly ordinances imposed until the time of reformation.

11 But Christ came as High Priest of the good things to come, with the greater and more perfect tabernacle not made with hands, that is, not of this creation.

12 Not with the blood of goats and calves, but with His own blood He entered the Most Holy Place once

for all, having obtained eternal redemption.

13 For if the blood of bulls and goats and the ashes of a heifer, sprinkling the unclean, sanctifies for the purifying of the flesh,

14 how much more shall the blood of Christ, who through the eternal Spirit offered Himself without spot to God, cleanse your conscience from dead works to serve the living God?

15 And for this reason He is the Mediator of the new covenant, by means of death, for the redemption of the transgressions under the first covenant, that those who are called may receive the promise of the eternal inheritance.

16 For where there is a testament, there must also of necessity be the death of the testator.

17 For a testament is in force after men are dead, since it has no power at all while the testator lives.

18 Therefore not even the first covenant was dedicated without blood.

19 For when Moses had spoken every precept to all the people according to the law, he took the blood of calves and goats, with water, scarlet wool, and hyssop, and sprinkled both the book itself and all the people,

20 saying, "This is the blood of the covenant which God has commanded you."

21 Then likewise he sprinkled with blood both the tabernacle and all the vessels of the ministry.

22 And according to the law almost all things are purified with blood, and without shedding of blood there is no remission.

23 Therefore it was necessary that the copies of the things in the heavens should be purified with these, but the heavenly things themselves with better sacrifices than these.

24 For Christ has not entered the holy places made with hands, which are copies of the true, but into heaven itself, now to appear in the presence of God for us;

25 not that He should offer Himself often, as the high priest enters the Most Holy Place every year with blood of another--

26 He then would have had to suffer often since the foundation of the world; but now, once at the end of the ages, He has appeared to put away sin by the sacrifice of Himself.

27 And as it is appointed for men to die once, but after this the judgment,

28 so Christ was offered once to bear the sins of many. To those who eagerly wait for Him He will appear a second time, apart from sin, for salvation.

10:1 For the law, having a shadow of the good things to come, and not the very image of the things, can never with these same sacrifices, which they offer continually year by year, make those who approach perfect.

2 For then would they not have ceased to be offered? For the worshipers, once purified, would have had no more consciousness of sins.

3 But in those sacrifices there is a reminder of sins every year.

4 For it is not possible that the blood of bulls and goats could take away sins.

5 Therefore, when He came into the world, He said: "Sacrifice and offering You did not desire, But a body You have prepared for Me.

6 In burnt offerings and sacrifices for sin You had no pleasure.

7 Then I said, 'Behold, I have come--In the volume of the book it is written of Me--To do Your will, O God.'"

8 Previously saying, "Sacrifice and offering, burnt offerings, and offerings for sin You did not desire, nor had pleasure in them" (which are offered according to the law),

9 then He said, "Behold, I have come to do Your will, O God." He takes away the first that He may establish the second.

10 By that will we have been sanc-tified through the offering of the body of Jesus Christ once for all.

11 And every priest stands ministering daily and offering repeatedly the same sacrifices, which can never take away sins.

12 But this Man, after He had offered one sacrifice for sins forever, sat down at the right hand of God,

13 from that time waiting till His enemies are made His footstool.

14 For by one offering He has perfected forever those who are being sanctified.

15 But the Holy Spirit also witnesses to us; for after He had said before,

16 "This is the covenant that I will make with them after those days, says the LORD: I will put My laws into their hearts, and in their minds I will write them,"

17 then He adds, "Their sins and their lawless deeds I will remember no more."

18 Now where there is remission of these, there is no longer an offering for sin.

1. The earthly tabernacle (9:1–5).

The writer assumes his readers are familiar with the details of the tabernacle as God had revealed them to

Moses at Mount Sinai. There are many allusions and references to Leviticus 16 in Hebrews 9:1–10:18. The author makes no reference to the structure itself; nor to the outer curtains that set it apart from the camp; nor to the altar and laver that were set up outside of the tabernacle, though he does briefly mention four articles of furniture that were put in the tabernacle.

The tabernacle was divided into two parts, referred to here as the "first part" and "the Holiest of All." In the first part were two articles of furniture. The first was the lampstand (Ex. 25:31–40), which was designed to be a perpetual reminder that the redeemed nation was to be light to the world, a kingdom of priests who would receive revelation from God and communicate that revelation to people (Ex. 19:6). While the nation never fulfilled this ministry, it will eventually be fulfilled through Israel's Messiah, Jesus Christ, who came as light into the world that was in darkness (John 1:4, 9; 8:12). The second article of furniture was the table on which the showbread was placed (Ex. 25:23–30). This was a reminder to Israel that the God who had redeemed them and had made them to be light to the world would provide that which would support and sustain them in their daily walk before Him. This bread also foreshadowed the One who would come as the Bread of Life (John 6:32–35).

The writer then moves behind the veil that divided the outer portion of the tabernacle from the Holiest of All, and he mentions two articles of furniture that were found there. The first was the golden altar of incense (Ex. 30:1–10). This altar represented the congregation's worship

Although the superiority of Jesus Christ supplanted the practice of tabernacle worship by (regulatory), it has much to offer us in understanding Christ's position and ministry (revelatory).

and prayers directed toward the God who had redeemed them. This altar was attended daily by the priests. Each morning and each evening the priests placed especially prepared incense upon that altar that was kept burning continuously in the presence of God, whose presence dwelt between the cherubim above the mercy seat.

Because Hebrews 9:7 says that "the high priest went alone once a year" behind the veil, it has generally been assumed that the altar of incense must have been located in the first part of the tabernacle so that the only article of furniture in the Holiest of All was the ark of the covenant with its mercy seat. However, the writer of Hebrews specifically states that the golden altar of incense was located within the Holiest of All. To better understand this, it helps to look at the instructions given to Moses concerning where he was to locate the altar of incense. In Exodus 30:6, we read, "You shall put it [the altar of incense] before the veil that is before the ark of the Testimony before the mercy seat that is over the Testimony, where I will meet with you." We can see that the altar of incense was "before" the veil—but the point of reference is the ark of the testimony. This means that the altar of incense was not put *outside* the veil, separated from the ark of the testimony, but was put *behind* the veil, in the Holiest of All, in front of the ark of the testimony. Since the function of the altar of incense was to offer worship and prayer to God, it was entirely fitting that it should be located within the Holiest of All in the presence of the Shekinah, the glory of God. In discussing the Day of Atonement, as the writer is doing in Hebrews 9, he stresses that only the high priest could enter the Holiest of All on that day—but that did not preclude other priests from entering daily to tend the altar of incense.

The second article of furniture within the Holiest of All was the ark of the covenant. This was the repository of the golden pot that had manna within it as a perpetual reminder of God's faithfulness to provide for His people in their wilderness experience (Ex. 16:33). It also contained Aaron's rod that budded, a perpetual reminder that God had singled out the tribe of Levi and the house of Aaron as those who would occupy the priestly office (Num. 17:10). And it contained the tablets on which the Law delivered to Israel had been written, a reminder that God was judging His redeemed people by that Law, holding them responsible for its observance (Ex. 25:16).

Above the ark of the covenant was the mercy seat (Ex. 25:10–22). The mercy seat was overshadowed by the cherubim, a representation of the highest rank of angelic beings, signifying that all the heavenly hosts observe the graciousness and mercy of God that provides a covering for sin so that God may accept sinners to Himself and dwell among them. The broken law, which carried a death penalty for violation, was quite literally being covered by blood—the blood of an innocent substitute rather than the blood of the guilty. The mercy seat was the place where a propitiatory sacrifice was placed before God as a covering for the sins of the nation so that God could continue to dwell in the midst of a sinful people and could have a basis on which to postpone the collection of the debt incurred by their sins.

2. The temporary value of the Levitical sacrifices (9:6–10).

Through Moses, God had given the priests specific instructions concerning the service that was to be conducted within the tabernacle. The lampstand had to be tended daily, "from evening until morning" (Ex. 27:-20–21), and was never permitted to be extinguished. Incense was to be placed on the altar of incense every morning and every evening (Ex. 30:7–8) so that the fragrance of the incense was continually ascending to God, symbolizing the redeemed people's worship and prayers to God. Each week the priests were to bake the twelve cakes to be placed on the table on the Sabbath, after which the priests were permitted to eat the showbread that had been replaced.

What the writer is saying, then, is that "priests always went into the first part of the tabernacle, performing the services" (Heb. 9:6). Some of the work was done daily and some weekly. But the point is that the work needed to be done again and again. This emphasizes that all that was carried on in the tabernacle had only temporary value. It brought nothing to completion.

The writer now turns from the daily or weekly ministries of the priests to the ritual that was observed by the high priest himself. The highest function that one other than the high priest could perform in the tabernacle ritual was to preside at the golden altar of incense. This privilege was determined by lot and could be performed only once during the course of a priest's life. Such was the privilege afforded Zacharias (Luke 1:8–9). If, as the writer of Hebrews indicates, Zacharias was privileged to enter behind the veil and go into the Holiest of All to place incense on the golden altar, it is no wonder he was overcome with fear when an angel of the Lord stood at the right side of the altar.

To the high priest alone was given the privilege of presiding over the most significant ritual in all Israel's calendar year, the Day of Atonement. But even as significant as was the offering of the blood of the goats on the Day of Atonement, it too had only temporary value and needed to be repeated year after year.

Is this our personal perspective on God's holiness? Do we stand in awe of His perfection, of our imperfection and impurity before Him? Church historians have noted that the church has never risen above its collective concept of God. It could well be that the many moral crises we face in our culture today are directly related to the church's lost concept of God's holiness.

What the writer is stressing in verses 6–8 is that all that was carried on by the priests in the earthly tabernacle had temporary, not permanent, value.

The author himself interprets the significance of all this when he says, "The Holy Spirit indicating this, that the way into the Holiest of All was not yet made manifest while the first tabernacle was still standing" (9:8). Every detail of the service in the tabernacle was symbolic (9:9), foreshadowing through a temporary arrangement that which would be accomplished permanently by Jesus Christ through His death. It is stressed again that as detailed as were the services and observances in the tabernacle, they "cannot make him who performed the service perfect" (9:9). That which was temporary could not bring the observers to maturity nor could it provide a permanent cleansing of the conscience from the guilt of sin. The Mosaic system was concerned with cleansing from external defilement (9:10), but it could not cleanse the conscience.

Again the whole Levitical system was viewed as a temporary arrangement, for it was to continue "until the time of reformation" (9:10), a new age in which a new and better program would be inaugurated that would accomplish that which the Law could not do.

3. The superiority of Christ's sacrifice (9:11–12).

To understand the truth the writer presents here, it is necessary to review what took place on the Day of Atonement, one of the annual feasts ordained by God to be observed by all Israel.

While the other six feasts outlined in Leviticus 23 were joyful celebrations, the Day of Atonement observed on the tenth day of the seven month was "a holy convocation for you; you shall afflict your souls, and offer an offering made by fire to the Lord. . . . It shall be to you a sabbath of solemn rest, and you shall afflict your souls; on the ninth day of the month at evening, from evening to evening, you shall celebrate your sabbath" (Lev. 23:27, 32).

Instructions concerning observance of the Day of Atonement are recorded in Leviticus 16. This was the day on which the nation as a nation acknowledged its sinfulness before the Lord, and on which an atoning offering for national sin was made.

From the inception of the Day of Atonement, Aaron represented the people before God as blood was offered to cover their sin. But since Aaron was a sinner, it was necessary that elaborate preparation be made so he could stand in the presence of a holy God as the representative of a people who acknowledged their sinfulness. The day began with a selection of animals that were set apart to be sacrificed. First, a bull was selected for sacrifice by Aaron and his sons who served with him in the priesthood, then two goats were chosen as a sin offering for the people (Lev. 16:5–6). The sin offering (Lev. 4) was an offering that dealt with the guilt of sin. Aaron sacrificed the bull to "make atonement for himself and for his house" (Lev. 16:11). Aaron, who by this offering had acknowledged his guilt before God, still could not go unveiled into the presence of God to offer the blood of the sacrifice as a covering for his sin. So he was instructed to "take a censer full of burning coals of fire from the altar before the Lord, with his hands full of sweet incense beaten fine, and bring it inside the veil. And he shall put the incense on the fire before the Lord, that the cloud of incense may cover the mercy seat that is on the Testimony, lest he die" (Lev. 16:12–13). The smoke from this incense became Aaron's protective veil so that he could place the blood of the bull on the mercy seat. This he was to do seven times (Lev. 16:14).

Having satisfied the penalty the Law placed upon him, Aaron could now emerge from the Most Holy Place to offer a sin offering on behalf of the nation. Having cast lots to determine which goat would be sacrificed and which would live (Lev. 16:8), Aaron now proceeded to kill the goat of the sin offering and to "bring its blood inside the veil, do with that blood as he did with the blood of the bull, and sprinkle it on the mercy seat and before the mercy seat. So shall he make atonement for the Holy Place, because of the uncleanness of the children of Israel, and because of their transgressions, for all their sins" (Lev. 16:15–16). While the sin of the nation could not defile the Most Holy Place where God manifested His presence, all the area outside that place was viewed as having been defiled by Israel's sin. Therefore the blood of the goat had to be applied to all that was in the Holy Place and to the altar that was in the courtyard. Then that which had been defiled was seen as having been sanctified or set apart to the Lord (Lev. 16:18–19).

Aaron now proceeded to take the second goat, called the scapegoat, and did as he had been instructed: "Aaron shall lay both his hands on the head of the live goat, confess over it all the iniquities of the children of Israel, and all their transgressions, concerning all their sins, putting them on the head of the goat" (Lev. 16:21).

Laying on hands was a sign of identification, so that the scapegoat is identified with the nation acknowledging its sin. That physical act also signified a transfer of guilt from the guilty to the goat, which then stood as a substitute for the nation. The scapegoat then was led so far off into the wilderness that it was impossible for it to find its way back, so it could not bring back to the nation the

When we see how serious about sin God has always been, we see that the blood of Jesus Christ has indeed saved us from God's inevitable response to sin—which the Bible calls His "wrath." God's wrath is not exclusive to the Old Testament. It always has been and always will be His response to sin. But as we will see, the method of satisfying God's wrath has gone from that which was temporary to that which is permanent.

sins that had been removed. Because Aaron had been involved as a mediator between God and the guilty people, another sacrifice for sin also was necessary. Aaron was instructed to offer a burnt offering for the people and for himself (Lev. 16:24). The burnt offering is an offering to God in worship for the benefits that come to those for whom blood has been offered to God. The guilt of sin was taken care of by the sin offering; and as the people received the benefits of the sin offering, they offered a burnt offering in worship for those benefits. The people then concluded the observance of the Day of Atonement in thanksgiving for the benefits that came to them through the blood that had been presented to God.

To understand the significance of this in relation to Hebrews, we must visualize what took place behind the veil in the Most Holy Place. As we have already seen, the most significant article of furniture in the Holy of Holies was the ark of the covenant. The mercy seat was the cover of the ark, and on that cover were two cherubim with their wings extended and their faces looking down toward the mercy seat itself. Because God revealed His presence by the shining of the Shekinah between the cherubim above the mercy seat, God was viewed as dwelling in the midst of His people, measuring them by the Law stored in the ark of the testimony. When so judged, the nation was deemed guilty; and the penalty for that violation was death. The people of Israel stood outside the tabernacle, acknowledging their guilt and the justice of God's judgment upon them. But in keeping with the divine arrangement within the Levitical system—which was the manifestation of God's grace—the nation's guilt could be covered by blood and a penalty carried out on a substitute, a sin offering on behalf of the people. Thus the Day of Atonement was the day on which God's just judgment was paid by a substitute. That blood offered *satisfaction* to God, because God did not overlook their sin; He did not condone their sin; He did not ignore their sin. He still demanded that the penalty for sin be paid. Blood was offered as a payment for that indebtedness. So this was the day in which God was satisfied, or *propitiated.* The righteous demands of a holy God were met. By grace, they were met by a substitute in death rather than by the death of the guilty.

Here we should notice several important things. On the Day of Atonement, God was the One being propitiated or satisfied. The blood satisfied God. The mercy seat was the place of propitiation. And the guilty people were those for whom propitiation was being offered. As a result, the penalty of the Law was carried out, although by a substitute rather than by the guilty. By this it became possible for a holy God to dwell in the midst of a sinful people, and to deal with them on the basis of a propitiatory sacrifice. As by faith the people visualized the blood being put on the mercy seat, they felt that their sins had been covered by blood. And as they watched those sins transferred from themselves to the scapegoat that was led away, they sensed that those sins—having been covered by blood—were removed from the guilty. Therefore by faith they experienced peace with God.

We must understand the significance of the Day of

Notice that God's cure for guilt always has been satisfaction of His wrath and forgiveness of the sinner. The same is true today. Psychologists tell us that over half of all mental and emotional illness is guilt-related; yet even the Christian church has begun to abandon God's cure—forgiveness—for the convoluted "logic" of blaming one's upbringing, environment, or something other than one's own sin and guilt before God. God has not changed, and His grace—offering forgiveness and peace with Him—is still the only cure for guilt.

Atonement in the old order before we can adequately understand what the writer of Hebrews wanted to teach concerning the work of Christ. Specifically, Christ's sacrifice is the ultimate fulfillment of the Day of Atonement. At the Cross, God was the one being propitiated (satisfied); the blood of Christ was that which propitiated a holy God; the body of Christ was the place of propitiation (the mercy seat); and all guilty sinners were those for whom propitiating blood was being offered to God.

The word *but* in verse 11 is designed to draw a contrast between that which was the most important event in the calendar year within the Levitical system, and that which Christ accomplished through His death on the cross, which became the basis for the ministry of our great High Priest. The writer does not contrast the offering of Christ with the Levitical offerings described in Leviticus 1–6. The first three offerings—the burning offering, the meal offering, and the peace offering—were offerings by which a worshiper expressed thanksgiving to God in response to the blessings he had received. These three were a sweet fragrance to God. The sin offering and the trespass offering were offerings by which the offerer acknowledged his sin and through which he was restored to fellowship with God. These two offerings dealt with sin and were a stench to God. But all of these offerings were acceptable to God because they were based on the blood offered on the Day of Atonement. Apart from that observance, none of these offerings would have

How interesting that three of the most significant practices in the life of the Jew were expressions of thanksgiving to God for His blessings. Are we this careful to acknowledge our thanks to Him? The giving of thanks for specific blessings should always be a part of our personal and family devotions.

been acceptable nor would they have had any value.

What the writer does throughout this portion of the letter, then, is focus our attention on the contrast between the work of Aaron on the Day of Atonement and the work of Christ, to show the superiority of Christ's work. Christ's work is viewed as a superior work first of all because of the location where His high priestly work is carried on. He does not minister in the tabernacle that was erected by Moses here on earth (Heb. 9:1–5); rather, He ministers in heaven. The tabernacle in which Christ ministers as a priest is the divine ideal, the very presence of God of which the earthly tabernacle was only a shadowed copy. He ministers in a perfect tabernacle, and through His ministry there, He brings those whom He represents to the perfection or maturity that God had designed.

The second point of contrast concerns the sacrifice that is the basis of Christ's priesthood. In the old order, two different offerings were required. The blood of the bull was offered for Aaron and his sons, and the blood of the goat was offered for the sins of the people. The high priest could not enter into the Most Holy Place without blood, both for himself and for the people. But Christ entered into His priestly ministry not with blood, as our translation suggests (9:12), but as a preferable reading would indicate, He entered "by or through His own blood." It was not necessary for Christ to physically transport His physical blood into heaven to provide a basis for His priestly ministry; but because of His shed blood on the cross, He was able to enter into His priestly ministry. The high priest on the Day of Atonement had to enter the Most Holy Place twice, once to make an offering for himself and a second time to make an offering for the sin of the people. But it was not necessary for Christ to repeat His entrance, for "He entered the Most Holy Place once for all" (9:12).

The third superiority of the work of Christ is the salvation that was provided.

blood of the Day of Atonement was effective for twelve months. During that time one who sinned willfully could flee and put himself under the blood on the mercy seat placed there on the Day of Atonement. This is what David did in Psalm 51 when he cried, "Purge me with hyssop, and I shall be clean; wash me, and I shall be whiter than snow" (Ps. 51:7). This also is what the tax collector did when he prayed, "God be merciful to me a sinner" (Luke 18:13); or as his plea could be understood, "God be *propitiated* to me a sinner," or, "God see me under the mercy-seat blood."

However, because that blood lost its effectiveness with the expiration of the year, the ritual had to be repeated again. Not so with the offering of Christ. He "obtained eternal redemption" by the one sacrifice of Himself. As gracious and merciful as was God's provision for remedy for sin through the Day of Atonement, far greater was the mercy, grace, and love that provided eternal salvation through the one sacrifice of Him who became our great High Priest.

4. *The results of Christ's sacrifice (9:13–22).*

a. Purification (9:13–14).

David's prayer of repentance and plea for cleansing by Day of Atonement blood was the basis of his forgiveness before God. And though we know from the biblical account that the consequences of his sin continued, he did not suffer the death penalty as prescribed by the Law. In our own dealing with sin, we should keep in mind both of these aspects of God's provision: (1) It is only by the blood of Jesus Christ that we are forgiven, not by our own merit or our promises that we are going to "straighten up"; (2) The consequences of our sin may well continue, even though we are forgiven. This alone should be enough to motivate us to live holy lives and do all we can to avoid sin in the future.

In verse 13, the author refers to two Levitical rituals that provided for external cleansing. The first was the propitiatory sacrifice on the Day of Atonement (Lev. 16). The second was the cleansing through the ordinance of a red heifer (Num. 19). The first had to do with national uncleanness; the second dealt with individual uncleanness. Both of these provided for purification, but it was a purification "of the flesh," that is, they dealt with external purification. They removed outward defilement and gave outward cleansing.

But the need of the sinner went far deeper than the external. There was a need in the sphere of the conscience, which was internal. This need was spiritual rather than physical. And to meet this need, an offering of greater value than the offering of bulls or goats or heifers was required. Remember, animals were under the curse of Genesis 3:14, and that which remained under a curse could not render complete satisfaction to a holy God. But since Jesus Christ was "without spot," His blood was offered to provide a propitiatory sacrifice wholly acceptable to God. While the blood of animals provided for external cleansing, the blood of Christ could "purge your conscience." It alone could satisfy the sinner's deep spiritual need.

Here the author draws several contrasts. The first in the kind of blood that was being offered. There is a difference between the blood of animals under a curse and the blood of Christ who was without the taint of sin. The second con-

Never forget that it is the human conscience that needs cleansing—not just our behavior. If you are living a life that is externally acceptable, but you are not living with a clean conscience before God, your relationship with Christ is lacking. Always let the Word of God search not only your actions, but also the "thoughts and intentions of the heart."

trast is in the kind of cleansing—the difference between external cleansing through the blood of animal sacrifices, and internal cleansing through the offering of Christ's blood.

Then there is a contrast in that the animal sacrifices were involuntary, while the sacrifice of Christ was voluntary. He "offered Himself," and that which was voluntarily offered to God had greater value than that which was involuntary. In this regard, it is stated that He offered Himself "through the eternal Spirit." The Spirit may be a reference to the Holy Spirit, which would seem to be supported by the use of the word *eternal.* However it may refer to Christ's human spirit, which is said to be eternal because of the perfect union between His humanity and His deity. While the first interpretation may refer to Christ's enablement by the Holy Spirit to offer Himself as a sacrifice, the second interpretation seems preferable. The apostle's argument seems to be that animals were an invol-

untary sacrifice, while Christ's offering was voluntary. By a decision of His will He offered Himself to death as the sinner's substitute. His offering was therefore a spiritual act, not an outward fleshly act. As a result of the kind of offering that was made, Christ's death not only removed the defilement, but also the *source* of the defilement. The conscience was cleansed so it did not continue to do its condemning work. The result was that men felt free to serve God. One under the condemnation of conscience has no liberty to serve God; but the individual who is freed from the nagging guilt of sin can serve God joyfully.

b. The ratification of a new covenant (9:15–22).

Because of the kind of offering Christ offered, and because of the nature of the blood that was offered (9:14), a conclusion is drawn in verse 15. By His death Christ has enacted "the New Covenant," and this new covenant is the basis of "eternal redemption" (9:12). This new covenant was enacted "by means of death." And this new covenant provided first "for the redemption of the transgressions under the first covenant."

The "first covenant" here refers to the Mosaic covenant. On the Day of Atonement, the nation's sins were covered by blood until the next Day of Atonement, when those accumulated sins had to be covered once again. To better understand this process, we might compare the Day of Atonement to a note of indebtedness. That note fell due each year, and because the debtors were unable to pay, they asked for an extension of their indebtedness for another twelve months. In the same way, the sins of the nation accumulated year after year. The Day of Atonement did not retire the debt; it only forestalled collection for another year. But then Jesus Christ came, so that by His death He might make payment in full for those accumulated transgressions. This is what Paul affirmed in Romans 3:25 where, speaking of Christ, he wrote, "whom God set forth to be a propitiation by His blood, through faith, to demonstrate His righteousness, because in His forbearance God had passed over the sins that were previously committed."

The second result is that those who live after the new covenant was inaugurated "may receive the promise of the eternal inheritance" (9:15). Having stated that the new covenant was inaugurated "by means of death," the writer goes on in verses 16 to show that death was neces-

A desire to serve God will be a natural consequence of the cleansing of the conscience. That's why the New Testament teaches that those who profess to know Christ but do not show any evidence of a desire to serve God actually do not know Him at all. More positively, those who come to Christ for His perfect cleansing are free to serve God joyfully from a clear conscience!

sary to inaugurate the new covenant—that which can provide redemption for past sins and provide a future eternal inheritance.

The word translated *testament* in verse 16 would be better translated *covenant,* as it has been previously translated (Heb. 7:22; 8:7–13). The reason is that the writer is not referring to a will by which an inheritance is transferred to an heir after the death of the one making the will. Rather, he is referring to the formalization or ratification of a covenant. In biblical times, covenants could be made by shaking or striking the hands together (Ezra 10:19), by exchanging sandals (Ruth 4:7), or by exchanging salt (2 Chron. 13:5). By the form of their enactment, these covenants were considered temporary covenants. To enact a permanent covenant, on the other hand, the blood of a sacrifice was required (see Gen. 15:9–21). As discussed earlier, when entering into a blood covenant, the terms of the covenant would be agreed upon by the two making the covenant. An animal then would be sacrificed, the carcass divided into two pieces, and laid on the ground. That animal was viewed as a substitute in death for the two making the covenant. The two then walked together between the pieces of the animal and thus were bound by blood. Since the animal was viewed as a substitute for the two making the covenant, it signified that since the two had died, it was impossible for them to change the terms of the covenant.

Here it must be emphasized that in a blood covenant, the sacrifice was a substitute in death for those making the covenant. The new covenant that guarantees

If personal salvation today is based on the same certainty as God's covenant with Abraham and is dependent on God's ability to keep that which He has promised, there is no way believers can "lose" or forfeit their salvation once God has bestowed it on them.

eternal redemption was a blood covenant. Therefore, since Christ is the one inaugurating that covenant, His death was essential (9:16). While two entering into a blood covenant might agree on the terms, they were not bound by the covenant until after the animal had been sacrificed. Logically, then, while the Old Testament promised eternal redemption, the benefits of that promise were not available until after the one making that new covenant had offered Himself as a sacrifice for the sins of the world. Now that Christ has shed His blood and offered that blood to God as a sacrifice, the benefits of the new covenant are readily available.

Anticipating the enactment of this new covenant through the death of Christ, Jeremiah 31:34 promised, "I will forgive their iniquity, and their sin I will remember no more." What was foreshadowed concerning the removal of sin from the guilty (by sending the scapegoat off into the wilderness on the Day of Atonement) has now been realized through the enact-

ment of the new covenant. The necessity of blood to enact a covenant is seen in that "not even the first covenant [the Mosaic covenant] was dedicated without blood." By referring back to Exodus 24:1–8, the readers are reminded that the Mosaic covenant was dedicated by blood. While the entire Levitical system was commanded by God, it was useless without the blood on which it all was based, for "without shedding of blood there is no remission" (9:22).

Thus the writer shows that removal of sin and the eternal salvation God has provided through the new covenant is based on Christ's voluntary, rational, spontaneous offering of uncorrupted blood. Christ did not ratify His covenant with the blood of an animal, but with His own blood. Since the new covenant was ratified by the blood of an eternal person, that covenant is therefore eternal and unchangeable, and provides an eternal inheritance. Just as ratifying the old covenant with blood showed that covenant was unchangeable, so ratifying the new covenant with Christ's superior kind of blood shows that the new covenant is eternal and immutable.

5. *Christ's ministry in the new tabernacle (9:23–28).*

   a. The ministry in heaven (9:23–24).

In contrasting the work of our great High Priest with the work of Aaron on the Day of Atonement, the writer first contrasts the place of ministry. Christ did not enter into an earthly tabernacle, "but into heaven itself, now to appear in the presence of God for us" (9:24). When the author refers to "the copies," he is referring to the earthly tabernacle with all its articles of furniture, its priesthood, and its rituals. The earthly is not the reality, but only a shadowy representation of the divine ideal. On the Day of Atonement, all outside the Holiest of All had to be cleansed by blood, for all outside the place where God dwelt were viewed as having been defiled by sin. The writer states that "the heavenly things themselves [should be purified] with better sacrifices" (9:23).

The writer may have said that the heavens need to be cleansed for several reasons. Since the earthly things needed cleansing, and these are copies of heavenly things, it corresponds that the heavenly things need cleansing. Fur-

---

In our day of religious plurality, we need to separate the idea of tolerance—graciously tolerating the presence of many ideas—from the idea of latitude, which is the acceptance of many opposing views as being equally valid. The Bible makes it clear that the salvation God has provided through Jesus Christ cannot be improved upon and will never be changed. And while we graciously allow other religions' adherents to express their views, nowhere does the Bible teach that we should accept those views on a plane co-equal with what God has revealed through the Scriptures.

ther, it is clear from various passages that the heavens are not clean (Job 4:18; 15:15; 25:5). It is also clear that people are identified with creation (Rom. 8:19ff), so that when people sinned, that defilement extended beyond the earth to the heavens themselves, so that the heavens need cleansing (cf. Col. 1:20). This is why all creation is awaiting its redemption (Rom. 8:19–22). Thus Christ as High Priest not only appeared in the presence of God for us, but He also appeared to provide cleansing for "the heavenly things."

b. Christ's ministry is based on the sacrifice of Himself (9:25–26a).

Christ did not come to offer Himself "often," like the Levitical offerings, but He offered Himself once and for all. So perfectly acceptable to God was the sacrifice of His Son that no more sacrifices were required.

c. By His sacrifice, Christ made a permanent disposition of sin (9:26b–28a).

When the author states that Christ has "put away

sin," he is drawing a vivid contrast between the work of Aaron and the work of Christ. The blood of the Day of Atonement provided a temporary covering for sin. But Christ has put away sin permanently. Repeated atonement was necessary because of the kind of blood Aaron offered; but the kind of blood Christ offered made His sacrifice an acceptable sacrifice, a sufficient sacrifice that never needed to be repeated. His sacrifice consequently is effective eternally. We must distinguish between "to put away sins" and "to put away sin."

The first has to do with individual transgressions. Christ certainly dealt with these by His sacrificial death. However, "to put away sin" has to do with settling the sin question itself. Sin was brought under judgment so that a disposition might be made of all that was contrary to the holiness of God, so that all that was contrary to Him might be permanently removed. The sin question was settled at the cross. The penalty for Adam's sin was death, and death came upon all human beings because of his disobedience. But after death, all who are under the condemnation of sin face judgment. Therefore "Christ was offered to bear the sins of many." The "many" refers back to all people who die (9:27). While the benefits of Christ's death come only to those who believe, yet Christ's death nevertheless was on behalf of all sinners. Because of the nature of the sacrifice that was made and the blood that was offered, the one death was sufficient for all to put away sin.

d. Christ's ministry brings promised blessings (9:28b).

After completing the sprinkling of the mercy seat with the blood of the animal sacrifice on the Day of Atonement, Aaron emerged from behind the veil to pronounce a blessing on the assembled congregation. The simple fact that Aaron *emerged* signified that the broken Law had been covered by blood and God was satisfied with that sacrifice. Therefore Aaron could dismiss the assembled congregation with a conscience that had been quieted by the

blood that had been offered. Based on that scene, the writer of Hebrews states that the one who has entered into the presence of God to minister as our great High Priest "will appear the second time." He will leave the scene of His heavenly priesthood to appear to those awaiting His return. When He returns the second time, He will not deal further with the sin question, because He has already put away sin by the sacrifice of Himself. But He will appear the second time "for salvation"; that is, to bring those who have received His salvation to the realization of "the promise of the eternal inheritance" (9:15).

This inheritance was graphically described by the Lord to those with Him in the upper room on the eve of His crucifixion when He said, "In My Father's house are many mansions; if it were not so, I would have told you. I go to prepare a place for you. And if I go and prepare a place for you, I will come again and receive you to Myself; that where I am, there you may be also" (John 14:2–3).

6. The sufficiency of Christ's sacrifice (10:1–18).

The author now draws a vivid contrast between the Old Testament sacrifices offered under the Levitical system and the sacrifice of Christ.

a. The inadequacy of Old Testament sacrifices (10:1–4).

Again it is stressed that the Law was only a foreshadowing of the benefits that were to come through the one acceptable sacrifice Christ offered to God. The Law was the shadow from which those who were under it could grasp all the benefits God would one day provide. While the Law made temporary provisions, it was incapable of making a final disposition of the sin question. The Law held those over whom it ruled in a perpetual state of infancy and could not liberate them from its oversight so that they could come to maturity. While those living under the Law by faith could be accepted by God, their acceptance was provisional and depended on the future sacrifice of Christ to bring them to a state of perfection before God.

Had that perfection been obtainable through animal sacrifices, those sacrifices would not have been repeated again and again. But their very repetition proved the inadequacy of those sacrifices. If the conscience was fully cleansed from the guilt of sin, the sacrifices would have ceased. If those sacrifices were efficacious, "the worshipers, once purged, would have had no more conscious-

---

How often do we take the time each day to look beyond the earthly, the material, the immediate and catch sight of the heavenly, the spiritual, the eternal aspects of all Christ has done for us and will do for us? In light of eternity, our time in this world truly is a mere moment in time. Daily we can ask ourselves: "Is my behavior here on earth worthy of the work Christ has done for me and the mansion where I will spend eternity?"

ness of sins" (10:2). But rather than purging the conscience, the sacrifices on the Day of Atonement were "a reminder of sins every year." The closer the Day of Atonement came, the more conscious the people became of their sins. That is why the Day of Atonement was not like the other festive day but rather a day of deep mourning. The people stood acutely conscious of their condemnation by a holy and just God. Their only hope was that God might be gracious and accept the blood of bulls and goats as a temporary covering for their sins so that they would not come under immediate divine judgment. It was a recognition that it was "not possible that the blood of bulls and goats could take away sins" (10:4). The blood of bulls and goats could only provide a temporary covering for sin. The removal of sin awaited the coming of the One anticipated in Isaiah 53, who would take the sin of the nation upon Himself, offer a payment to God in behalf of that sin, make a full settlement of the sin question, and consequently remove the guilt of sin forever from the guilty by cleansing the conscience.

b. The adequacy of Christ's sacrifice (10:5–10).

In a vivid contrast the writer shows that what the blood of animals could not do, Jesus Christ by His sacrifice has accomplished, for "we have been sanctified through the offering of the body of Jesus Christ once for all" (10:10). The author had previously shown that the sacrifice of Christ has value because of the nature of the blood that was offered in sacrifice (9:12–14). Now he shows the sacrifice of Christ is superior to that of animals because of the nature of the sacrifice itself. It was a voluntary sacrifice offered in obedience to the will of God.

In Psalm 40, David cried to God in desperate circumstances (10:1). The One to whom David had appealed is to be trusted (10:4) because of all that He has demonstrated to people through His works (10:5). But what God demands of people is obedience (10:6). And such obedience is more acceptable to God than burnt offerings and sin offerings. The psalmist responds by declaring that He delights to do God's will (10:7–8). And because of that obedience he can claim God's tender mercies to meet his need (10:11).

The writer of Hebrews uses David's testimony to stress Christ's obedience to the will of His Father. That obedience gave special merit to His sacrificial death. The coming of Christ into the world was an act of obedience to the will of His Father, for it was the Father who gave His Son to become incarnate (John 3:16; Phil. 2:5–8). This obedience characterized Christ not only in His Incarnation, but throughout the course of His entire life. And that obedience reached its climax when He offered Himself as a sacrifice in obedience to the will of God.

The statement "sacrifice and offering You did not desire" means that God found no lasting pleasure in the Levitical system. *Sacrifice* is a reference to the burnt offering, one of the three sweet-smelling offerings that repre-

Though the whole concept of "animal rights" sounds ridiculous, some well-meaning Christians struggle to understand the value God places on animals in contrast to people.

From the Levitical system of sacrifice, we can draw at least three conclusions. First, man is inherently superior and thus of greater worth than animals, since animal sacrifice could not effectively pay the price for people's sins before the Creator, but only forestall that payment. Second, killing animals for biblically sanctioned purposes (food, protection, and sacrifice) could not be inherently immoral, for God could not use an immoral practice to atone for sin. And third, God's purpose for animals on the earth is subordinate to His purpose for individual people, for any individual—in his or her quest for fellowship with God—could sacrifice many, many animals over the course of a lifetime.

sented the worship of God's people in recognition of the benefits He provided. *Offering* is a reference to the sin offering, one of the two non-fragrant offerings the guilty presented to be restored to fellowship with the God whose Law they had broken. To render satisfaction to God, Jesus Christ came "to do Your will, O God." Christ's purpose in coming was to obey His Father. This obedience culminated at the cross. Christ came to do what people under the Law found they could not do—obey to attain perfection.

There are several reasons that the Old Testament sacrifices were unacceptable to God. As we have already noted, animals came under the curse that was passed upon all creation because of Adam's sin (Gen. 3:14), and what was accursed could not satisfy the demands of a holy God. But the main point the author makes here is that no animal ever went voluntarily to its death. That is why instruction was given to "bind the sacrifice with cords to the horns of the altar" (Ps. 118:27). Any animal brought

to sacrifice would be overcome with fear at the scent of death and would seek to return to the safety of its flock or herd. That which had been dedicated to God could not be returned to secular uses and therefore was to be secured to the horns of the altar. But God could find no lasting pleasure in that which was sacrificed contrary to its own will.

In contrast to this, Jesus Christ could say to His Father, "Behold, I have come to do Your will, O God" (Heb. 10:9). Christ's submission to His Father's will was clearly displayed in Gethsemane when Jesus faced death on the cross, being made sin on the sinner's behalf, entrance into spiritual death, and separation from His Father. There He said three times, "Not as I will, but as You will" (Matt. 26:36–44). By His voluntary sacrifice, Christ terminated involuntary sacrifices, and by His obedient sacrifice "we have been sanctified." Christ, by His obedience to the will of His Father, has accomplished once and for all time that which the involuntary sacrifices of the Old Testament could never accomplish.

c. The effectiveness of Christ's sacrifice (10:11–14).

Previously the writer pointed out that the Law "can never with these same sacrifices, which they offer continually year by year, make those who approach perfect" (10:1). By contrast, the author now points out that "by one offering He has perfected forever those who are being sanctified" (10:14). This sacrifice has obtained eternal redemption (9:12) and has made an eternal inheritance available (9:15). God's purpose for His own is being accomplished. That which Aaron was not able to accomplish even by offering repeated sacrifices (10:11), Jesus Christ has accomplished through His one sacrifice (10:12).

The evidence that His sacrificial work is forever completed is that He "sat down at the right hand of God." The contrast is made between the Old Testament priest—who continuously stood to minister—and Christ, who, having finished His work, could be enthroned in honor and glory at the right hand of God. At the time of His enthronement, Jesus Christ did not institute or begin to execute the authority of a king promised to Him by the decree made with Him by His Father (Ps. 2:6–9). That kingdom will be established here on the earth in fulfillment of the Davidic covenant (2 Sam. 7:16), with Jerusalem as the center of His reign. But having completed the work that provided eternal redemption, the Lord could be restored to the glory that He had with the Father before the world began (John 17:5). And He awaits the Father's appointed time for His return to establish the earthly Davidic kingdom, at which time "His enemies are made His footstool" (10:13). Seated at the Father's right hand until that time (Ps. 110:1b), the Son can look back to His accomplished work and also look in anticipation to His work as King/Priest that remains to be completed.

d. The enactment of a new covenant (10:15–18).

Referring to the great promise God made with the

house of Israel and the house of Judah through Jeremiah (Jer. 31:31–34), the author points out that it is God's revealed purpose to terminate the Mosaic Law by the introduction of a new covenant. And as a result of that new covenant God can affirm that "their sins and their lawless deeds I will remember no more" (10:17). Because of the new covenant, it will no longer be necessary to make an offering for sin, for there will no longer be a remembrance of sin by God. And there will be no more conscience concerning sin on the part of the believer. An important feature of Christ's sacrifice was to provide forgiveness of sin; and this work was accomplished so completely that God does not even remember the sins covered by the blood of Christ.

Sin incurs a debt, which requires forgiveness. It enslaves in a bondage, which requires redemption. And it causes an alienation, which requires reconciliation. All three results of sin must be dealt with to "put away sin" (9:26). Therefore the author deals here with the first of these consequences—namely, forgiveness. The root concept in forgiveness is to separate or to remove. Sin transferred from the guilty to the guiltless (so that He by death could render payment for indebtedness) has made it possible for the sinner to be forgiven. While we have no control over our memory so that we can dismiss sin from our minds, God by a sovereign act of His will can and does dismiss from His memory every sin that has been covered by the blood of Christ.

In Scripture there is a difference between that which is true of believers positionally, and that which takes place experientially. One of the great benefits of spiritual maturity, however, is that as we grow spiritually, what we experience from day to day becomes more consistent with what is true of our position in Christ.

That which has been dismissed from God's memory need not be a weight on the conscience of the one who has been forgiven. By the offering of Christ through the new covenant, sin's debt has been canceled by a full payment, and the conscience of the one who has been forgiven is cleansed. Because of the accomplished work of Christ, what need can there possibly be to continue Levitical sacrifices? The application of this truth to the readers, then, is this: What excuse can be found for those who take refuge in animal sacrifices to escape persecution?

In this extended section, the author has shown us that we have a High Priest who is superior to the Aaronic priests who ministers in a superior tabernacle to that tabernacle in which Levitical priests served God. He serves in a superior place—that is, in heaven not on earth. His priesthood is built on a better foundation—namely, the covenant God made with His Son in appointing Him a priest (rather than in the covenant God made with Israel through Moses). He ministers on the basis of a better sacrifice—the blood of Christ rather than the blood of animals. And His ministry is based on a better covenant —one that does not remind the guilty of their indebtedness year after year but guarantees them the forgiveness of sins.

Those who struggle with the nagging memory of past sins can take great encouragement from the fact that God Himself does not remember sins covered by the blood of Christ. If God does not remember them, surely He does not intend for us to hang onto those obsolete memories!

IV. The Application of Christ's Superiority to the Life of the Believer (10:19–13:25).

The author introduces this new section with the word *therefore*. As suggested earlier, this epistle was not designed so much as a theological treatise to acquaint the readers with Christ's superiority over the old Levitical system as it was to exhort believers to faith and patient endurance based on the theological truth it presents. The author is not so much attempting to enlighten their minds in important doctrinal issues as he is attempting to use those doctrines to move their wills to obedience to the truth. To apply the truth, then, the writer begins with an exhortation.

A. The exhortation (10:19–25).

19 Therefore, brethren, having boldness to enter the Holiest by the blood of Jesus,

20 by a new and living way which He consecrated for us, through the veil, that is, His flesh,

21 and having a High Priest over the house of God,

22 let us draw near with a true heart in full assurance of faith, having our hearts sprinkled from an evil conscience and our bodies washed with pure water.

23 Let us hold fast the confession of our hope without wavering, for He who promised is faithful.

24 And let us consider one another in order to stir up love and good works,

25 not forsaking the assembling of ourselves together, as is the manner of some, but exhorting one another, and so much the more as you see the Day approaching.

In this exhortation the readers are viewed as priests. This is the same truth Peter affirmed when, addressing believers, he said, "You also, as living stones, are being built up a spiritual house, a holy priesthood, to offer up spiritual sacrifices acceptable to God through Jesus Christ" (1 Pet. 2:5). John reiterates that same truth when he states that Christ "has made us kings and priest to His God and Father" (Rev. 1:6). The imagery of this exhortation is based on the concept that all believers have been constituted as priests before God. In setting Aaron and his sons aside to the office of priests, God said you shall "consecrate them, and sanctify them, that they may minister to Me as priests" (Ex. 28:41). Again God said, "I will also sanctify Aaron and his sons to minister to Me as priests" (Ex. 29:44).

Careful instruction was given concerning the garments the priest wore as he ministered in the tabernacle. Before those garments were placed on Aaron or his sons, they were washed with water (Ex. 29:4). Aaron then was robed, and following that was anointed with a special anointing oil God had commanded be made (Ex. 30:22–29). God said, "You shall anoint Aaron and his sons, and sanctify them, that they may minister to Me as priests" (Ex. 30:30). Only after the washing, the robing, and the anointing was Aaron able to assume his ministry in the tabernacle. Aaron was confident that he was able to minister in the presence of God, for in connection with the institution of the continual burnt offering God had said, "I

will meet you to speak with you. And there I will meet with the children of Israel . . . . I will dwell among the children of Israel and will be their God. . . . I am the Lord their God" (Ex. 29:42–46).

The same privilege Aaron received—to minister in the very presence of God—is viewed as the privilege of the believers to whom the apostle is writing. Therefore he exhorts them, "Let us draw near with a true heart in full assurance of faith." When he states that our hearts have been "sprinkled from an evil conscience" (10:22), he no doubt is referring to the anointing of Aaron with the specially prepared anointing oil. And in his reference to "our bodies washed with pure water" (10:22), he must have had in mind the washing that prepared Aaron to enter into his priestly ministry. Since we have been cleansed and anointed or set apart to a priestly ministry, it is our privilege to draw near to the presence of God in order that we might minister before Him. There would be natural trepidation about entering into the presence of God; but the author asserts that we have boldness to enter the Holiest, for the veil that once separated the priest from the presence of God has been removed. Moreover, we enter with boldness because we enter "by the blood of Jesus" (10:19). The blood of Christ so cleanses us that there is no obstacle to our entering into the very presence of God as believer/priests.

While this entrance into God's presence under the old order was reserved for the priests, this privilege is now granted to all believers who are identified here as "brethren." Our entrance is not only "by blood," but it is also "through the veil." This may possibly be understood to mean that whereas the veil in the tabernacle barred entrance into the presence of God, now that the veil has been rent asunder (Matt. 27:51), we can come in the presence of God with no veil between. But an even better understanding, which seems to be the intent of the writer here, is that Christ's human body—united to eternal deity by incarnation—is the veil; with the sacrifice of Christ on the cross—viewed as the rending of the veil—we have

---

Perhaps you have had the experience of spending time with "name droppers"—people who love to recount the many famous people they have met. Something inside us tells us that the privilege of drawing near to a person of means and influence says something significant about us as well. Whether or not that is true, the Bible tells us that knowing Christ enables us now to draw near to the very presence of God. That does say something significant about us! That says that we now have direct access to the Creator of the universe, for whom nothing is impossible. We have a direct line of communication for every need or trouble. And because our sins have been washed away by the blood of Christ, we are as beloved by God as is His Son.

direct access to God. When Christ became flesh it was necessary that His glory be veiled lest He consume men by the brightness of that glory. Just as the people of Israel who assembled at the tabernacle could not see the Shekinah that dwelt above the mercy seat in the Holy of Holies, so those who looked upon Jesus Christ during the years of His ministry could not see His essential glory. His flesh was that which veiled His glory. But at his crucifixion that flesh was rent so that through that rending of the veil we might approach the unveiled presence of God.

While believers are priests and have the right of direct access to God, they are under the authority of a High Priest who rules over the house of God. This High Priest not only invites us to come into God's presence, but so works in us that we draw near with a "true heart" and in "full assurance of faith." A "true heart" is one that by faith has confidence that he is acceptable to God and has direct access to God. The only alternative to this is a heart that doubts and enters with fear.

The second exhortation, based on our privileged position, is, "Let us hold the confession of our hope without wavering" (10:23). The word

Businesses have found that one of the most effective ways to get new customers to call is to let them know about a toll-free "800" number—one they can call without charge to place orders or obtain information. In the world of marketing, people are eager to use free access. Sometimes, however, this is not true in the spiritual realm. We have free access to the throne of Almighty God, and yet often we do not avail ourselves of that marvelous privilege. If a daily time of prayer is not on your priority list right now, perhaps you will re-evaluate your privilege of access to God and begin to avail yourself of the most marvelous privilege known to humankind.

confession as the author used it previously (Heb. 4:14), referred to his readers' public acknowledgment of faith in Jesus Christ and of their identification with Him by baptism. He is not asking them to make another such confession, but to cleave without hesitancy, without doubt, without wavering in regard to that which they had already made confession. The basis of his appeal is the faithfulness of God, for "He who has begun a good work in you will complete it until the day of Jesus Christ" (Phil. 1:6). What the writer is asking is quite in contrast to Israel's experience at Kadesh Barnea, when after receiving the promise of possession of the land and the enjoyment of covenant blessings in it, they doubted, wavered in their commitment, and turned in unbelief from the conflict that lay before them.

A third exhortation follows: "Let us consider one another." This is in keeping with Paul's injunction, "For I say, through the grace given to me, to everyone who is among you, not to think of himself more highly than he ought to think, but to think soberly, as God has dealt to each one a measure of faith. For as we have many members in one body, but all the members do not have the same function, so we, being many, are one body in Christ, and individually members of one another" (Rom. 12:3–5). The object of this exhortation is to "stir up love and good works." Love will be the atti-

This attitude of humility and self-effacement is literally un-American! Yet it is the model for biblical Christianity lived out in our everyday lives. Regardless of what the success merchants and motivational speakers may say, there is no place in the Christian church for the world's idea of "movers and shakers" or for anyone who insists on placing himself and his own ideas above the needs of other Christians.

tude toward other believers, while good works will be the actions directed toward the needs of fellow believers as a demonstration of that love.

Next, a negative and a positive aspect are considered. The negative exhortation is found in the statement, "not forsaking the assembling of ourselves together" (10:25). It seems evident that some readers, having grown weary in the conflicts that came through persecution from the religious community, wanted to hide the fact that by baptism they had left the old order. Therefore they sought to again identify externally with the old system to relieve their trials. Some seem to have already lapsed back into the externalisms of Judaism. This is not an evidence of love and good works.

But on the positive side, they are to exhort one another. This exhortation provides encouragement and help for suffering believers, which is evidence of their love for the brethren. Encouragement to show love and good works is found in the fact that they "see the Day approaching."

Christ had warned the religious leaders who concluded that His miracles were performed by the power of Satan that if they persisted in their rejection, that generation of Israel would be guilty of a sin for which there could be no forgiveness (Matt. 12:31–32). Because the nation persisted in its rejection, Christ announced a coming judgment on that generation (Matt. 23:37–24:2). He said, "There will be great distress in the land and wrath upon this people. And they will fall by the edge of the sword, and be led away captive into all nations. And Jerusalem will be trampled by Gentiles until the times of the Gentiles are fulfilled" (Luke 21:23–24).

When Pilate consented to the leaders' demand that Christ be crucified (John 19:15), that generation of Israel came under a physical, temporal judgment. Peter recognized that state of the nation when, on the day of Pentecost, he pled with the nation to "be saved from this perverse generation" (Acts 2:40). As long as people remained citizens of that nation, they were under the judgment God had decreed upon that generation. Only those who identified themselves with Christ by baptism and thus terminated their citizenship in the nation would escape that coming judgment. As he pens the words "you see the Day approaching" (Heb. 10:25), the writer recognizes that the generation which demanded the crucifixion of Christ and consequently came under judgment is coming to a close. The beginning of Rome's war against the Jews was already being anticipated, and in a short time Titus would lead the Tenth Roman Legion into the land of Israel. He would subjugate the land to himself, and in that conquest would destroy the city of Jerusalem along with its temple. "The Day," then, refers to God's judgment accomplished through Titus in which the land and the people would be forcibly subjected to the authority of Rome. Thus the writer is encouraging believers to exercise patient endurance, for shortly God would judge the generation of Israel

Historically, those believers who did not forsake their assembling together, even more as the fall of Jerusalem approached, suffered persecution together. But that persecution, in fact, drove them from Jerusalem so that they did not suffer the atrocities God allowed that city to suffer at the hands of the Roman general, Titus. God's answer to today's persecution of the conservative, evangelical church is not disassociation and distance, but unity, communion, and an ever-growing witness to unbelievers. Rather than trying to figure out how to make the church more like the world so the world will go to church, we should be trying to figure out how to make the church more like Christ so the church will go to the world. And the more the opposition increases, the more we should assemble together for that purpose.

that crucified Christ and had been showing their hatred of Christ by persecuting believers. And that judgment would terminate the persecutions by that nation.

B. The warning (10:26–31).

26 For if we sin willfully after we have received the knowledge of the truth, there no longer remains a sacrifice for sins,

27 but a certain fearful expectation of judgment, and fiery indignation which will devour the adversaries.

28 Anyone who has rejected Moses' law dies without mercy on the testimony of two or three witnesses.

29 Of how much worse punishment, do you suppose, will he be thought worthy who has trampled the Son of God underfoot, counted the blood of the covenant by which he was sanctified a common thing, and insulted the Spirit of grace?

30 For we know Him who said, "Vengeance is Mine, I will repay," says the Lord. And again, "The Lord will judge His people."

31 It is a fearful thing to fall into the hands of the living God.

The word *for* in verse 26 introduces the reason believers should heed the exhortations just given. The consequences of walking not by faith but by the flesh in unbelief are indeed serious. Forsaking the assembling of themselves together in light of all the writer has explained to them and returning to the external forms of Judaism would be a willful sin. The writer assumes that through this epistle they "have received of the truth." Since the law has been terminated and has been superseded by the ministry of a great High Priest in the heavenlies, they would be returning to a system in which "there no longer remains a sacrifice for sin" (10:26). While the Levitical system from the time of its inception at Sinai until the death of Christ was the system that provided a sacrifice for sins, now that it has been done away there is no longer any value in offering those antiquated sacrifices. Therefore there could be no benefit to those who left their fellowship with other believers to return to a dead system. Rather than finding benefit, there would be "a certain fearful expectation of judgment, and fiery indignation" (10:27). This judgment is the judgment Christ had predicted would fall on that generation if they rejected Him as Savior and Sovereign. The adjectives *fearful* and *fiery* describe the severity of that physical temporal judgment that will soon be coming.

Jesus had promised such a judgment. In response to the question regarding what would be done to those who rejected the Son it was stated: "He will destroy those wicked men miserably" (Matt 21:41); and again, "He will come and destroy those vinedressers and give the vineyard to others" (Luke 20:16). The nation that for several generations had enjoyed a certain amount of freedom under Roman rule would be desolated by a ruthless invader. That judgment was inevitable.

Under the old order, if someone sinned unintentionally, a sin offering could be offered (Num. 15:22–29). But if a person sinned presumptuously or intentionally, no sacrifice was provided, and the willful sinner "shall be cut off

from among his people" (Num. 15:30). Judgment followed deliberate sin. The sinner's only hope was to plead for mercy on the basis of the Day of Atonement blood applied to the mercy seat. As revealed in Psalm 51, this was David's refuge after his presumptuous sin.

On the basis of this principle, a severe warning is given to those who have understood that the Law has been terminated by the death of Christ, but who are considering a return to the externals of Judaism. Not to walk by faith is sin (Rom. 14:23). If they do return, they are returning to a system in which there are no longer any effective sacrifices that can be offered, and because of their willful sin, they can anticipate the judgment of God. Because they had identified themselves with Christ through baptism, they were no longer under the judgment pending against that generation. But if they forsook the assembling of themselves together with other believers and returned to fellowship in the temple, they would be re-identifying themselves with a nation under judgment and there would be no escape when that judgment fell.

The apostle certainly is not threatening them with loss of salvation, but rather warning them that the physical, temporal judgment that was to come on those who were the adversaries of Christ and His followers would fall upon them as well.

The Law demanded that those who sinned willfully against the Law should be put to death by stoning. Such was the penalty for the sin of blasphemy (Lev. 24:15–16, 23); for adultery (Deut. 22:21–24); for idolatry (Deut. 17:2–5; Lev. 20:2); for violation of the Sabbath (Num. 15:32–36). The same penalty was pronounced upon false prophets (Deut. 13:10); upon the spirit medium (Lev. 20:27); and upon a rebellious son (Num. 21:21–23). Lest there be miscarriage of justice, a minimum of two witnesses was required before the penalty could be carried out (Deut. 17:4–7). The author sounds a severe warning that those who might commit the willful sin contemplated here would deserve "much worse punishment" (10:29). It is difficult to conceive of a punishment worse than death by stoning; nevertheless, those who would forsake the assembling of themselves together to identify with outmoded ritual would deserve such punishment. The reason that those who identify with the generation of Israel that willfully rejected Jesus Christ as Savior and Sovereign would in effect be condoning that sin. "Trampled under foot" signifies a flagrant con-

---

As much as we should respond in a sensitive and loving way to those among us who struggle with sin, we also should be ready and willing to speak truthfully and plainly to those who willfully choose a life of habitual sin. Sin always has its consequences, consequences that can be extremely unpleasant and painful for the rebellious child of God.

tempt for the Son of God. Further, in the light of the knowledge that had been brought to him through this epistle, he would deem the blood by which he had been sanctified as of no more value than the common blood of Old Testament sacrifices. By his action he would be revealing an attitude that suggested that the blood of Christ was in no way superior to the blood of animals.

Finally, such an act would indicate hostility toward the Holy Spirit through whose gracious ministry he had been brought to faith in Jesus Christ. The word *for* in verse 30 gives the reason that judgment must follow willful sin, and the reason stems from the character of God. In quoting Deuteronomy 32:35–36, the author reiterates what was a well-established principle. God is a righteous God, and when the holiness of God is violated, the character of God demands that the wicked be punished. God cannot and will not overlook such willful sin. And the author reminds those contemplating such action that "it is a fearful

thing to fall into the hands of the living God" (10:31). Those who identified with the nation under judgment would not themselves be counted the objects of that judgment; but because of their identification with the nation, they would not escape the consequences of that judgment.

C. A word of encouragement (10:32–39).

32 But recall the former days in which, after you were illuminated, you endured a great struggle with sufferings:

33 partly while you were made a spectacle both by reproaches and tribulations, and partly while you became companions of those who were so treated;

34 for you had compassion on me in my chains, and joyfully accepted the plundering of your goods, knowing that you have a better and an enduring possession for yourselves in heaven.

35 Therefore do not cast away your confidence, which has great reward.

36 For you have need of endurance, so that after you have done the will of God, you may receive the promise:

37 "For yet a little while, And He who is coming will come and will not tarry.

38 Now the just shall live by faith; But if anyone draws back, My soul has no pleasure in him."

39 But we are not of those who draw back to perdition, but of those who believe to the saving of the soul.

By way of encouragement, the writer reflects on those things they already have suffered because of their identification with Christ. No sooner had they by baptism severed their ties with the old order than they were subjected to suffering. They were reproached, and they were persecuted. Some of this came to them directly, while some suffered indirectly because they identified with those who were being so treated. The author himself was one of those to whom, after coming to Christ, they had shown compassion while he was in prison. They had endured personal testings; and when tested in material things, they had responded in joy. Such material possessions as they had were counted as nothing in comparison to the "enduring possession" that was theirs in heaven. All that they had endured joyfully and sacrificially was an evidence of their "love and good works" (10:24). All these were evidence of the genuineness of their faith in Jesus Christ and a manifestation of faith's outworking in their lives.

Now the writer gives an exhortation based on their previous experience of walking by faith. As faith had sustained them in their past deprivations, so faith could and would sustain them in their present experiences. The phrase cast away is very strong. It means "to fling away." This could be ren-

God's Word always speaks highly of those who have suffered for their faith. Though it is not a path we might normally choose for ourselves, if we are called upon to suffer ridicule, isolation, or persecution for our faith in Christ, we should always count it a privilege and an honor.

dered, then, "Do not fling, as though it was of no value, the boldness which you once had made your very own." The trials they were undergoing were a part of the life of faith. Thus they did not need more faith, for faith had demonstrated its sufficiency in days past. But they did need patience, so that through the patient endurance produced by their faith they might eventually obtain that which had been promised to them.

To illustrate this point, the author quotes Habakkuk 2:3-4. There the prophet had expressed his concern over the sin so evident in his nation. It appeared that God took no notice of it, for it seemed to go unjudged. But God responded by promising He would judge that nation by bringing the Chaldeans against them. They would be God's instruments through which judgment would come. Even though the judgment was delayed to give the people an opportunity to repent, the judgment was certain. However, while the righteous wait for that judgment to fall upon the guilty, they must live by faith (Hab. 2:4). The application is that the just must live by faith *in the faithfulness of God*. Even though judgment on the unbelieving nation is delayed and believers are undergoing persecution, they must live by faith. The prophet anticipated that some might not

---

While Israel certainly had a greater responsibility to obey God because of the Word of God entrusted to it, God never treats national sin lightly. More than a call to political activism, this should be to us a mandate to call the people in our nation to repentance and faith in Christ, and also to be bold in proclaiming the possible consequences we might face if we continue to flaunt our national disregard for the things of God. And if this is a responsibility you take seriously, be prepared for the privilege of being ridiculed for His sake!

live by faith, but might instead draw back. The phrase "draw back" has in it the idea of shrinking because of fear or cowardice. One who did this was certainly not walking by faith. His drawing back would be considered an act of disobedience that stemmed from his unbelief.

The writer of Hebrews still has in mind the sin of Israel at Kadesh Barnea. Before them lay the land and a life of peace and rest that, in obedience to the command of God, they were to possess by faith. But that redeemed generation did not respond to the promises of God by faith but rebelled because of unbelief. God's displeasure toward those who refused to live by faith resulted in the judgment passed upon them. While they did not forfeit their status as a redeemed people, they did lose the blessings they could obtain only by faith.

In verse 39 the writer states his confidence that his readers will not repeat the sin of their forefathers at Kadesh Barnea by refusing to live by faith and thus forfeit the blessings God has provided

for those who live by faith. He identifies himself with these, and while some view those addressed in verse 39 as unbelievers, the writer's identification with his readers seems to make it mandatory they be regarded as believers. "Those who draw back" would be those who are "forsaking the assembling of ourselves together" (10:25). Leaving the assembly of believers to identify with temple services to escape persecution would not be an act of faith. It would be a public declaration that they did not believe God could or would sustain them through their trials and that they needed another solution to their difficulties.

Many believe this exhortation is addressed to unbelievers because the author says they would be drawing back to *perdition*, which usually refers to the eternal punishment of the unsaved. However, in this instance the author is using that same word to describe the awesome judgment that soon will fall upon Jerusalem (Luke 21:24). Here *perdition* is used of that "fearful expectation of judgment, and fiery indignation which will devour the adversaries" (10:27).

The alternative to drawing back is faith. The author is confident that those to whom he is speaking are "those who believe." Evidence of their faith has already been given in verses 32–34. Those who draw back, then, would be those who—while they had once walked by faith—were not continuing to walk in faith. The evidence of their departure from a walk by faith is that they would forsake the assembling of themselves together, and thus would re-identify themselves with a nation under impending judgment. But the writer is confident that in spite of whatever temptation they may have experienced to abandon the life of faith, they will walk by faith and will experience "the saving of the soul." Since this is addressed to believers whose faith had been validated by their works, the salvation the writer refers to here cannot be the initial act of salvation, but must refer to deliverance from the consequences of unbelief.

The apostle's thinking here is very similar to that which he had previously presented in chapter 6. All the spiritual blessings they had experienced validated the genuineness of their faith. But if their walk by faith should be interrupted, and they should not go on to maturity, they would suffer the consequences that would come from abandoning the life of faith. Thus their

Sometimes we may think that the obstacles we are facing, those things that are preventing us from going on to maturity, are far greater than anything we can overcome. We are not alone in that regard! Many saints of God have faced seemingly insurmountable obstacles in their walk of faith. That is why the author will go on to recount an impressive list of believers who faced such obstacles and, by faith in God's ability to fulfill what He promised, overcame them.

need is not to come to faith, but rather to continue to walk by faith and to let faith produce its fruit, which is patient endurance.

D. Examples of a life of faith (11:1–40).

1 Now faith is the substance of things hoped for, the evidence of things not seen.

2 For by it the elders obtained a good testimony.

3 By faith we understand that the worlds were framed by the word of God, so that the things which are seen were not made of things which are visible.

4 By faith Abel offered to God a more excellent sacrifice than Cain, through which he obtained witness that he was righteous, God testifying of his gifts; and through it he, being dead, still speaks.

5 By faith Enoch was taken away so that he did not see death, "and was not found, because God had taken him"; for before he was taken he had this testimony, that he pleased God.

6 But without faith it is impossible to please Him, for he who comes to God must believe that He is, and that He is a rewarder of those who diligently seek Him.

7 By faith Noah, being divinely warned of things not yet seen, moved with godly fear, prepared an ark for the saving of his household, by which he condemned the world and became heir of the righteousness which is according to faith.

8 By faith Abraham obeyed when he was called to go out to the place which he would receive as an inheritance. And he went out, not knowing where he was going.

9 By faith he dwelt in the land of promise as in a foreign country, dwelling in tents with Isaac and Jacob, the heirs with him of the same promise;

10 for he waited for the city which has foundations, whose builder and maker is God.

11 By faith Sarah herself also received strength to conceive seed, and she bore a child when she was past the age, because she judged Him faithful who had promised.

12 Therefore from one man, and him as good as dead, were born as many as the stars of the sky in multitude--innumerable as the sand which is by the seashore.

13 These all died in faith, not having received the promises, but having seen them afar off were assured of them, embraced them and confessed that they were strangers and pilgrims on the earth.

14 For those who say such things declare plainly that they seek a homeland.

15 And truly if they had called to mind that country from which they had come out, they would have had opportunity to return.

16 But now they desire a better, that is, a heavenly country. Therefore God is not ashamed to be called their God, for He has prepared a city for them.

17 By faith Abraham, when he was tested, offered up Isaac, and he who had received the promises offered up his only begotten son,

18 of whom it was said, "In Isaac your seed shall be called,"

19 concluding that God was able to raise him up, even from the dead, from which he also received him in a figurative sense.

20 By faith Isaac blessed Jacob and Esau concerning things to come.

21 By faith Jacob, when he was dying, blessed each of the sons of Joseph, and worshiped, leaning on the top of his staff.

22 By faith Joseph, when he was dying, made mention of the departure of the children of Israel, and gave instructions concerning his bones.

23 By faith Moses, when he was born, was hidden three months by his parents, because they saw he was a beautiful child; and they were not afraid of the king's command.

24 By faith Moses, when he became of age, refused to be called the son of Pharaoh's daughter,

25 choosing rather to suffer affliction with the people of God than to enjoy the passing pleasures of sin,

26 esteeming the reproach of Christ greater riches than the treasures in Egypt; for he looked to the reward.

27 By faith he forsook Egypt, not fearing the wrath of the king; for he endured as seeing Him who is invisible.

28 By faith he kept the Passover and the sprinkling of blood, lest he who destroyed the firstborn should touch them.

29 By faith they passed through the Red Sea as by dry land, whereas the Egyptians, attempting to do so, were drowned.

30 By faith the walls of Jericho fell down after they were encircled for seven days.

31 By faith the harlot Rahab did not perish with those who did not believe, when she had received the spies with peace.

32 And what more shall I say? For the time would fail me to tell of Gideon and Barak and Samson and Jephthah, also of David and Samuel and the prophets:

33 who through faith subdued kingdoms, worked righteousness, obtained promises, stopped the mouths of lions,

34 quenched the violence of fire, escaped the edge of the sword, out of weakness were made strong, became valiant in battle, turned to flight the armies of the aliens.

35 Women received their dead raised to life again. And others were tortured, not accepting deliverance, that they might obtain a better resurrection.

36 Still others had trial of mockings and scourgings, yes, and of chains and imprisonment.

37 They were stoned, they were sawn in two, were tempted, were slain with the sword. They wandered about in sheepskins and goatskins, being destitute, afflicted, tormented--

38 of whom the world was not worthy. They wandered in deserts and mountains, in dens and caves of the earth.

39 And all these, having obtained a good testimony through faith, did not receive the promise,

40 God having provided something better for us, that they should not be made perfect apart from us.

After the exhortations and warnings found in chapter 10, in which the writer closes with a clarion call to live by faith, he then proceeds in chapter 11 to parade "so great a cloud of witnesses" (12:1), to illustrate how believers by faith may patiently endure. He introduces this great theme by showing the connection between faith and endurance.

1. The product of faith (11:1).

In this familiar introduction, the writer is not attempting to define faith per se, but rather is showing the connection between faith and patient endurance. This verse is intimately connected with 10:35–39. Specifically, the word *faith* looks back to verses 38–39. The writer had pointed out the need for endurance (10:35) by quoting from Habakkuk 2:3–4. In so doing, he assumes that faith involves endurance. He then moves on in 11:1 to show that faith looks forward to the future, to things anticipated and hoped for. Since the future with all of its hopes are not yet realized, endurance is involved. Thus the author is not attempting to *define* faith, for that concept is far too well-known to his readers to need definition here. Instead, the writer is showing that the one who lives by faith will patiently endure.

Since the word *faith* is used without the article, it refers to faith as a principle, not just the Christian faith. It shows that faith deals with what is future, the things expected but as yet unrealized. The word *substance*, in Greek literature, was used for a title deed. While the deed itself has no value, it is a guarantee of ownership. The reality of the possession is not established by the title deed, but the title deed does certify ownership. In the same way, faith does not establish the reality of what is anticipated, but it does rec-ognize that which is hoped for. We must be careful not to understand this use of the word to mean that the objective reality depends on one's faith, for this is not true. While some would assert that "believing will make it so," this is not what the author suggests. It is best to understand the word *substance* to mean assurance, confidence, or certainty (cf. 2 Cor. 9:4; 11:17; Heb. 3:14). Faith, then, is that which gives assurance or confidence concerning the things hoped for. The things hoped for include everything contained in the promises of 10:36–39.

In Scripture, *hope* is never a wish, a dream, a fantasy. Hope is that settled assurance that comes to the child of God who by faith lays hold of the promises of God and claims them for himself.

The Christian cliché about being "so heavenly minded that you're no earthly good" perhaps doesn't hold water. According to this passage, our ability to be any "earthy good" for the cause of Christ is based entirely on what we know in our minds to be true about our "heavenly" position. Based on what is true from a heavenly perspective, we can live victoriously in this earthly realm.

Hope must have a foundation, and in Scripture the foundation of hope is always that which God has promised. The word *evidence* includes the idea of conviction, a settled feeling of certainty. This certainty concerns things that as yet are in the future, for they are "not seen." If by faith we have assurance, confidence, and conviction, we will of necessity patiently endure until we realize that which we confidently expect.

2. Faith illustrated (11:2–3).

In verse 2 the author makes a summary statement that will be demonstrated through the remainder of this chapter. The writer is using the word *elders* as a synonym for the Jewish forefathers. Old Testament history testifies that the readers' ancestors received a promise from God, by faith claimed that promise, and then patiently endured until the promise was fulfilled. On no other basis was promise ever realized. He is not saying that their fathers bore witness to the life of faith, but

rather that the life that they lived by faith was observed by others.

It is as necessary for faith to operate concerning things in the past as it is concerning things that are yet future. There were no human witnesses present at the time of creation. Therefore it is necessary for us to place our faith in the Creator's testimony concerning how the worlds were framed. This is vividly seen in God's discourse with Job when He asked, "Where were you when I laid the foundations of the earth?" (Job. 38:4). The angelic hosts evidently witnessed the work of creation, since "the morning stars" and "the sons of God" in Job 38:7 seem clearly to refer to the angels as witnesses of creation. But the angels never conveyed to men what they witnessed, so we are not called on to put our faith in the word of angels. But throughout Scripture God has provided testimony that all that exists came into existence by His command. This is a fact we are called upon to believe. The credibility of the word we are asked to believe concerning creation is based on the Person making the revelation. In the natural realm, something cannot come out of nothing. But the God whose word we are asked to believe is a God who could call all that exists into being from nothing. A God of such power is worthy to be believed.

If faith suffices for things that are past, it certainly is sufficient for things that are future. While "no one has seen God at any time" (John 1:18), by that which He has created we believe He exists, so that the very existence of creation continues to bear witness to the existence of the infinite Person who authored it. Without having seen God, by faith we know He exists.

3. Faith exemplified (11:4–40).

a. Faith in the prepatriarchal period (11:4–7).

The first example of faith the author cites is that of Abel. Abel was not the first to exercise faith, for Adam believed the promise of God when he gave his wife the name Eve, "because she was the mother of all living" (Gen. 3:20). But one event is singled out in the life of Abel—the sacrifice he brought to God (Gen. 4:4). The sacrifice is described as "more excellent," which would indicate the quality of his sacrifice. Or the word could signify "more abundant," which would emphasize the quantity of his sacrifice. The sacrifices of both Cain and Abel seem to have been offered as acts of worship. Both recognized an

Again the Bible makes a direct connection between the fact that God created all things as recorded in Genesis 1 and the believer's faith in the credibility of God. Professing Christians who want to make light of the Genesis record, or compromise their belief in it, are in fact compromising their belief in the credibility of God and His Word. This should not be taken lightly.

obligation on the part of the creature to the Creator. Later in the Levitical Law, one could worship God through the sacrifice of an animal (the burnt offering of Leviticus 1 or the peace offering of Leviticus 3), or through the grain offering (Lev. 2). Either an animal sacrifice or the grain sacrifice was perfectly acceptable to God as an act of worship. Thus when Cain offered his sacrifice—which had cost a great deal more effort than Abel's sacrifice—it could have been accepted. However, Cain's offering was offered out of obligation *without faith,* whereas Abel's sacrifice, while recognizing an obligation, was offered *in faith.* Thus the writer of Hebrews is stressing the fact that Abel's obligation was discharged by faith (Heb. 11:4). It was not through the sacrifice that Abel obtained righteousness, but through faith that produced obedience. And it was declared righteous. God saw his sacrifice as an evidence of his faith. Even though this event took place long ago, Abel still bears witness that faith produces obedience, and that worship offered to God in faith is acceptable to Him.

Enoch is the next who bears witness to the life of faith (11:5–6). By faith Enoch walked in fellowship with God, and his faith produced a righteousness that pleased God. Although he lived in a corrupt age that was headed for judgment by flood, Enoch did not conform to the standards of the age in which he lived, but walked in accordance with the standards of God's righteousness. Faith produced a life so pleasing to God that God translated him into His presence without physical death. Enoch did not preach a message that called men to walk by faith, but witness was borne by others to the fact that Enoch by faith had produced a walk that pleased God. The writer is careful to make it clear that the only way one could possibly walk so as to please God was to walk by faith. The word *but* in verse 6 introduces the concept that "without faith it is impossible to please Him." One who would walk to please God must first of all believe that He exists, and then believe that God will fellowship with those who by faith seek to please Him. Without these two basic concepts, no one would seek to walk by faith.

Noah is the next person in the period prior to the patriarchs to whom our attention is directed. God had said to him, "The end of all flesh has come before Me, for the earth is filled with violence through them; and behold, I will destroy them with the earth" (Gen. 6:13). Noah believed God even though that which God promised was yet a long way off. The cause of his reverential respect for God was his faith. He demonstrated his faith in God by his obedience as he proceeded to build the ark according to the plan God revealed to him (Gen. 6:14-22). Noah's obedience was seen in his undertaking of construction of the ark, which passed judgment on his disobedient generation. His obedience condemned their disobedience. It was not his obedience that caused him to inherit righteousness; rather, his faith in the God who announced judgment produced righteousness, which God imputed to him by faith.

Thus in the prepatriarchal period, the faith of Abel was demonstrated through recognizing his obligation to the Creator; the faith of Enoch was demonstrated through his fellowship with God; and the faith of Noah was manifested through his obedience to God's command.

b. Faith exemplified in the patriarchal period (11:8-22).

Now incidents from Abraham's (Abram) life are pre-

The Genesis flood and Noah's part in it is another episode from Genesis 1–11 that is taken literally and without question by the writer of Hebrews. Interestingly, the credibility of Genesis 1–11 is perpetually under fire from the world, while the Bible uses the same crucial section as a basis for much of what it teaches about God's nature and the believer's trust in Him.

sented to show that Abraham's faith produced obedience to the God who gave him promises. God had appeared to a pagan who lived in a pagan household in a pagan land (Josh. 24:2). God enticed Abraham to follow Him by faith. Stephen tells us that the God of glory appeared to Abraham when he was dwelling in his home land (Acts 7:2). The promises God gave were not themselves sufficient to move Abraham to begin a long journey when he did not know where he was going; but the revelation of glory that belonged to the God who gave promises was sufficient to bring Abraham to faith in Him. And that faith produced immediate obedience. Coupled with that obedience was patient endurance, for before Abraham entered the promised land, he had to undergo a journey that covered countless miles and spanned many years. Abraham's faith was not a blind faith, even though he did not know where he was going; for Abraham's faith was not in the land, but in the God who had promised

land and descendants to him. Since his faith was placed in such a glorious Person, it could not be called blind faith. Abraham's journey was a journey of faith that took him from Ur along the Euphrates past Haran, until eventually he came into the land of Canaan, which God identified as the land He had promised (Gen. 12:6–7).

Though the Canaanites dwelt in cities, Abraham was content to dwell in tents (Heb. 11:9). The city dweller considers himself a permanent resident, while one dwelling in a tent considers himself a temporary resident. While the land of Canaan was given to Abraham by God's decree, he considered himself a foreigner in a foreign land. While this might seem to indicate Abraham's unbelief concerning God's assignment of this land to him, it actually reveals that there was something inherent in God's promise that Abraham had claimed and was looking forward to by faith. This is explained to us in that Abraham "waited for the city which has foundations, whose builder and maker is God" (11:10). The city God had promised Abraham would not be built in the land of Canaan that God had given Abraham, but rather would be a heavenly city in which Abraham would eventually dwell together with the God whose promises Abraham believed (Heb. 12:22–24). Because that heavenly city was to be Abraham's final destiny, he considered himself only a temporary resident in the land of Canaan. That land was the land through which he would pass on his way to that which God had promised. Thus we see that Abraham's faith in God produced immediate obedience. That obedience entailed patient endurance, for the journey was long. And even when he settled in the land of promise, he was called on by faith to patiently endure, for that land was not his ultimate destiny. By faith he would await the fulfillment of all God had promised.

Interestingly, the writer did not direct our attention to that great example of Abraham's faith recorded in Genesis 15, where in response to God's promise that Abraham would father a son, he "believed in the Lord, and He accounted it to him for righteousness" (Gen. 15:6). Had the writer been addressing unbelievers to bring them to saving faith in Christ, he could hardly have ignored that outworking of Abraham's faith that provided a basis upon which God could publicly proclaim him righteous (that is, acceptable to Himself). But since the writer is

Our faith is often tested most when our present circumstances seem completely contrary to what God has revealed to us through His Word. That is precisely the situation Abraham faced, and yet he did not succumb to "doubting in the dark what God told him in the light." Instead, he lived his life in accordance with what God had said. This essentially is the lesson of Hebrews 11.

addressing believers and wants to call their attention to obedience and the patient endurance Abraham's faith produced, he directs their attention to the particular incidents in which Abraham's faith and obedience are most clearly seen.

Next, Sarah is presented as one whose faith in the promise of God produced patient endurance. At the very inception of His dealing with Abraham, God had promised that He would make Abraham a great nation. This meant that Abraham must father a son. This promise remained uppermost in the mind of Abraham (Gen. 15:1–4). When Sarah, who had been barren through her life (Gen. 16:1), realized she did not have the ability to provide Abraham with the son through whom God's promise would be fulfilled, and believing the promise *must* be fulfilled, she offered Abraham her servant as a concubine. It was Sarah's belief in the promise that led to this incorrect solution, and from this union Ishmael was born. At this time Abraham was

eighty-six years old (Gen. 16:16). It was some thirteen years later, when Abraham was ninety-nine (Gen. 17:1), that God reiterated His covenant with Abraham (Gen. 17:4–8) and reaffirmed the promise that by Sarah Abraham would father the child of promise (Gen. 17:15–16).

From a human standpoint, such a birth would have been impossible. If Sarah had conceived immediately, Abraham would have been one hundred years old and Sarah would have been ninety when the child would be born (Gen. 17:17). From a physical viewpoint, such a birth would have been impossible. When Abraham offered Ishmael as one through whom the original promise might be fulfilled, God rejected Ishmael and affirmed that the child of promise would come through Sarah (Gen. 17:19). And He revealed the specific time when the appointed child of promise would be born (Gen. 17:21). It seems that even though Sarah knew the original promise and had a knowledge of God's revelation that she would mother the child of promise, her barrenness (Gen. 16:1) and her age (Gen. 18:11-12) caused her faith to waver. To strengthen her faith, God sent angelic messengers to reaffirm what God had previously revealed to her through Abraham. The promise was given that "Sarah your wife shall have a son" (Gen. 18:10). Sarah heard the message and responded with laughter. Abraham's laughter at God's message (Gen. 17:17) was the laughter of joy because Abraham believed the message from God. Sarah's laughter, however, was the laughter of unbelief, for she considered only her barrenness and age. She did not look beyond those circumstances to God's power that was sufficient to fulfill what He had promised (Gen. 18:14). At this point Sarah was certainly not responding in faith to the promise of God. Abraham and Sarah together would have to believe the message, so it became necessary to strengthen that wavering faith.

In delivering the message concerning the birth of Isaac, the angels also announced judgment on Sodom and Gomorrah. Then the angels left Abraham and Sarah and proceeded on to Sodom and Gomorrah to destroy those wicked cities (Gen. 19:13). Since Lot was given no time to prepare to flee those cities (Gen. 19:15), we can conclude that judgment on Sodom and Gomorrah took place within a few days. Moreover, Abraham and Sarah would be able

---

Does God honor right motives but wrong methods? Apparently He does, though He may allow the wrong methods to run their course and produce unfortunate results. If you have found yourself in the wrong, even though your genuine desire was to please God and serve Him in obedience, don't lose heart. Sarah's faith in the promise of God, though misapplied in the incident with Hagar, was significant enough for God to include in this "Hall of Faith."

to witness the destruction of those cities (Gen. 19:27–28). Thus there were two parts of the angelic message to Abraham and Sarah. First, Sarah would conceive and bear a son; and second, Sodom and Gomorrah would be destroyed. The point, then, is that if God fulfilled one portion of His promise literally, He could be trusted to fulfill the other portion of His promise in the same way. Thus the cities' destruction supported and strengthened Sarah's faith in God's promise.

The writer of Hebrews makes it very clear that the birth of Isaac was the result of Sarah's faith, and that God caused her to look beyond the impossible circumstances to the God who had given the promises. Thus Sarah was brought to the place where "she judged Him faithful who had promised" (Heb. 11:11). It is obvious that there was an extended period of time from the original promise of a son (Gen. 12:2) until that son eventually was born (Gen. 21). There was also an extended period of time between God's

reaffirmation of the promise (Gen. 17:15–19) and the actual birth of the son. Thus the faith of Abraham and Sarah was tested, and they demonstrated patient endurance while they waited for the fulfillment of the promise during that time of testing.

The descendants of Abraham to whom the author was writing were part of the fulfillment of the promise. God promised Abraham that his descendants would be as innumerable as the sand upon the seashore or as the stars in the heaven (Gen. 13:16; 15:5; 22:17; 26:4). But the author makes it clear that the faith of Abraham and Sarah looked beyond the birth of Isaac, because his birth did not fulfill all God had promised to them. Until the birth of Isaac, they continued to live according to the rule of faith, or under the influence of and according to the principle of faith. To the end of their days there was more in the promise to which they continued to look forward. It is evident that faith produced a continuing patient endurance.

As the writer previously

said, they "waited for the city which has foundations, whose builder and maker is God (Heb. 11:10). Even though they had not entered that promised city, they were assured of its existence and of their participation in it. That assurance was the product of their faith, and it changed their attitude toward the land in which they lived. That land had been given to them as their permanent possession (Gen. 12:7), yet they considered themselves "strangers and pilgrims" (Heb. 11:13). They acknowledged they were in a foreign land, for that promised city was their permanent possession. As sojourners they had no permanent possession of the land in which they were living, and they had no rights of citizenship there, for their citizenship was in that promised heavenly city (cf. Phil. 3:20). They did not view Mesopotamia as their homeland, even though no obstacle prevented them from returning there. By faith they were content to dwell as strangers and pilgrims in Canaan, awaiting the ultimate fulfillment of what God had promised them. By faith they expected its fulfillment and patiently endured.

Because of their faith, God so identified Himself with Abraham that in dealing with Abraham's descendants throughout the book of Exodus He identified Himself as "the God of *Abraham*, of Isaac, and of Jacob" (Ex. 3:16). Proof of God's identification with those who walked by faith is seen in the explanation, "For He has prepared a

This should be an encouragement for those who understand the encouraging, motivating results of studying biblical prophecy. God's revelation concerning that "city which has foundations, whose builder and maker is God" is far more complete now than it was in Abraham's day; thus we can draw the same kind of assurance and hope from our study of future things as did those two saints.

city for them" (11:16). In response to their faith, God has prepared a city in which He will identify them with Himself in that place (Heb. 12:22–24).

While awaiting the ultimate fulfillment of God's promise, Abraham demonstrated the patient endurance of faith by obeying God's command to offer that promised son as a sacrifice. This clearly demonstrated the obedience of Abraham's faith. God had made it very clear that the covenant He had made with Abraham could be fulfilled only through Isaac (Gen. 17:19). It therefore must have seemed very strange to Abraham when God commanded him, "Take now your son, your only son Isaac, whom you love, and go to the land of Moriah, and offer him there as a burnt offering on one of the mountains of which I shall tell you" (Gen. 22:2). Though Abraham did not realize it, this was designed as a test not only of his faith, but of his obedience by faith. The test was not so much whether he would obey God, it was a test whether he would believe that

God would fulfill His promises in spite of the death of the only one through whom they could be fulfilled.

Abraham's faith was unwavering and his obedience was immediate. He could believe that the promise would be fulfilled through Isaac because he was "accounting that God was able to raise him up, even from the dead" (Heb. 11:19). Since Isaac was set apart to be a burnt offering (Lev. 1:1–17), he was being offered not in atonement for some sin, but as an act of worship to God. And the obedience of Abraham was itself acceptable worship. Thus, based on the life of Abraham, the writer desires that his readers should "imitate those who through faith and patience inherit the promises" (Heb. 6:12) and show the same patient endurance and obedience that their faith ought to produce.

The covenant given to Abraham was reaffirmed to Isaac (Gen. 26:1–5). Isaac designated Jacob as the appointed heir of the promises and conferred blessing upon him (Gen. 27:26–29), and even though

Esau was to be subservient to Jacob, Isaac also blessed him (Gen. 27:38–40). Likewise, Jacob designated Joseph as his heir (Gen. 37:3) and, before his death pronounced blessing upon his sons (Gen. 48:10–22). In each of these historical instances, God's original promise and covenant with Abraham is reiterated, recalling that God gave the land of Canaan to Abraham and Abraham's descendants as their possession unconditionally and eternally. Each patriarch who conferred blessing on the next generation did so by faith, anticipating the eventual fulfillment of God's covenant. Thus faith produced patient endurance.

Just before he died, Joseph reiterated his faith in the promise of God saying, "God will surely visit you, and bring you out of this land to the land of which He swore to Abraham, to Isaac, and to Jacob" (Gen. 50:24). Because of his faith in God, he was certain of the eventual restoration of Jacob's descendants to the land of promise that he made the Israelites promise with an oath that when the return came his bones would be carried from Egypt to the promised land (Gen. 50:25).

Thus all of those in the patriarchal period who play a significant role in Israel's history demonstrated their faith by their patient endurance and obedience. This is what the writer of Hebrews desires that his readers emulate.

While "God has no grandchildren" in terms of personal decision for Christ, the story of the Hebrew patriarchs reveals a continuation of saving faith from generation to generation through careful instruction and admonition. While some descendants chose to reject that instruction, others continued to look for the fulfillment of God's promises because they already knew what they were. Let us never neglect our great responsibility to instruct the next generation in the wonderful things of God!

c. Faith exemplified in the life of Moses (11:23–29).

The faith in God exemplified by Moses was first seen in his parents. Pharaoh had issued a decree that all male Hebrews were to be drowned at birth (Ex. 1:22). But faith in God's promise concerning the future of Abraham's descendants was greater than their fear of reprisal from Pharaoh. They sought a means whereby the life of this heir of promise might be spared (Ex. 2:3). Moses' parents lived in a time of great adversity. Yet their faith operated even in the midst of their circumstances. This certainly should have had a bearing on the experience of the readers who were being called upon to live by faith in their present sufferings. We see how God honored the faith of Moses' parents.

History strongly suggests that Moses was saved from Pharaoh's intended fate by Hatshepsut, the young daughter of Thothmes I (who had ordered the destruction of the Hebrew male babies—Ex. 2:5–10). Moses then became her adopted son (Acts 7:21).

Scholars tell us that this Pharaoh had a son, who because he was physically and mentally handicapped, was considered incapable of assuming the royal prerogatives to which he had been born. When he ascended the throne as Thothmes II, his sister Hatshepsut became regent and actually ruled the country. Thothmes II eventually died without a legitimate heir, but because both his father and sister had foreseen this lack of a successor, they probably had determined long beforehand that Moses would be the eventual heir. So from earliest years Moses had been educated with this in mind, as Stephen declares: "Moses was learned in all the wisdom of the Egyptians, and was mighty in words and deeds" (Acts 7:22).

When her brother died, it appears that Hatshepsut retained supreme authority as regent in Egypt and indicated her intention of placing Moses, her adopted son, on the throne as her successor. To legitimize this, she had planned to marry Moses to her elder daughter, Nepherus.

Moses, however, apparently refused both the throne and the bride, and thus sacrificed his position in the kingdom and the honor and the wealth that went with it.

At this point in his life Moses demonstrated his faith in the God who had given promises to his ancestors. God's program was not to be fulfilled through Egypt's throne, but through a throne which God would establish with Abraham's descendants. The word *refused* (11:24) shows that Moses made a knowledgeable decision, and that his decision was prompted by his faith. The phrase "the son of Pharaoh's daughter" emphasizes the royal position Moses knowingly forfeited, together with all the privileges such a position entailed. Moses was not exchanging one privileged position for another privileged position. Rather, he was giving up the royal position "to suffer affliction." He is disassociating himself with the royal family to identify himself with a race that had been reduced to abject slavery (Ex. 1:8–14). There was no prospect of privilege in the decision Moses made by faith. His decision clearly demonstrated that faith will choose adversity over disobedience. The sin Moses might have enjoyed (Heb. 11:25) was the sin of disobedience—staying in the royal court when the blessings of the promise could

What would it take for you to choose the world's offerings over continued close fellowship with God? Wealth enough to guarantee your security? A relationship seemingly better than the one you're in? Sensual pleasure at will? Material possessions beyond your wildest dreams? To some believers, these things would not be the least bit tempting, just as they weren't to Moses. But to others, a price tag may still hang on their commitment to Christ. If that is your case, settle the issue today. Recognize that there is nothing that can equal the privilege of serving Christ.

only be found by leaving that position. That disobedience would have left him in the place where he could have experienced the benefits of his princely state, but he would not have been viewing the enslaved Hebrew people as "the people of God." But by faith Moses could see that nation as the heirs of God's promise and covenant.

The basis for Moses' choice is revealed in verse 26. With patient endurance Moses was looking forward to the fulfillment of what God had promised His people. The phrase "the reproach of Christ" (11:26) can be understood in several ways. It can refer to the reproach Christ would bear which, though it was yet future in Moses' day, was a historic fact from the standpoint of the readers (cf. Rom. 15:3). Or it can be understood as the reproach Moses bore because of his relationship to the promised and anticipated Messiah who would come in fulfillment of the covenants. This was the object of his faith.

The author's point is that all Moses anticipated by faith

was not present, but future. Yet Moses was so assured of what God had promised that on the basis of that confidence he could separate himself from all the privileges of the royal court. While the record in Exodus seems to indicate that Moses fled Egypt because of fear of reprisal from Pharaoh after murdering an Egyptian, the author of Hebrews indicates in verse 27 that his departure from Egypt was the result of his faith. Had he remained in Egypt, he might have been forced to assume the crown and throne for which he had been prepared. To refuse this would have subjected him to the wrath of Pharaoh. The only way to disassociate himself from that which had been planned for him was to leave Egypt. This he did because of his faith in a God he had not even seen (11:27). He believed that "he who comes to God must believe that He is, and that He is a rewarder of those who diligently seek Him" (11:6).

Moses' faith is demonstrated further in that he kept the Passover. The Passover was the means by which God provided protection for the firstborn in Egypt who had come under the sentence of death (Ex. 12). As God had instructed, those who desired to escape the plague of death passed upon the firstborn should sacrifice an animal, which would have been done in the courtyard of the home. That animal's blood was then applied to the two doorposts and the lintel of the house. As the members of the household entered through blood into the house, they found safety in keeping with the promise of God: "For the Lord will pass through to strike the Egyptians; and when He sees the blood on the lintel and on the two doorposts, the Lord will pass over the door and not allow the destroyer to come into your houses to strike you" (Ex. 12:23).

The words translated "pass over" in that text literally means "to hover over." The picture is that when the Lord saw the blood, He would position Himself over the door to protect all those who had sought refuge through blood by faith, and He would turn aside the destroyer who had come to execute the judgment. No such example of deliverance from death had ever been seen before. Therefore those to whom this provision was given had to exercise faith in the God who promised He would be their protector from the judgment of death. Moses was one who exercised faith in God's provision and found deliverance from judgment. The implication for the readers should have been very clear: If by faith they availed themselves of God's promises, they—like Moses—would be delivered when the forthcoming judgment fell on that generation.

The final example of Moses' faith is when in obedience to the command of God he "passed through the Red Sea" (Heb. 11:29). For the children of Israel to pass through the Red Sea was an act of faith, for they had no such previous experience upon which to rely. Rather, they had to emulate the faith of Moses and cross the Red Sea in obedience to God's command. The implication should have been clear that if the children of Israel could find deliverance from bondage through their faith in God and obedience to their leader, the readers also by faith in God and obedience to their leaders might find deliverance from the circumstances pressing in on them.

d. Faith exemplified in the time of conquest (11:30–31).

The report brought by the ten spies after their survey of the land occupied by the Canaanites (Num. 13:28–33) made it very clear that the children of Israel were incapable of conquering the land, subjecting the people, and occupying that land themselves. Joshua and Caleb exhorted the people to occupy the land by faith in the promises of God and in obedience to the command of God. They said, "If the Lord delights in us, then He will

bring us into this land and give it to us, a land which flows with milk and honey" (Num. 14:8). But instead of proceeding by faith, the people rebelled against God and through unbelief disobeyed the commandment of God to occupy the land. They forfeited the promised blessings in the promised land.

A generation later, a new generation under the leadership of Joshua proceeded by faith, and in obedience to the commands of God entered and occupied the land God had given to Abraham and his descendants as their possession. God responded to their faith by opening the way through the floodtide of Jordan so that they might enter the land (Josh. 3:14–17). By faith they approached the fortified stronghold of Jericho that had been built to protect

There is no doubt that our trust in God faces its toughest tests when we suddenly find ourselves in unchartered territory, facing circumstances we have never before had to face. During those times we can look back to Moses, who, in a desperately unfamiliar situation, obeyed God and moved forward in confident trust.

the land from invasion from the east. Jericho seemed impregnable. But by faith in God and obedience to His commands, that fortified citadel fell (Josh. 6:1–21).

Rahab is an illustration of the fact that even a Gentile of such questionable character could be delivered by faith from the judgment decreed upon the inhabitants of Jericho. The men Joshua had sent to spy Jericho (Josh. 2:1) discovered that in some unknown way the knowledge of the true and living God had been brought to Rahab, for she confessed "the Lord your God, He is God in heaven above and on earth beneath" (Josh. 2:11). She also believed that the God whom she had come to revere was about to bring judgment on her city through its overthrow. Therefore she pled that her life and the life of her family might be spared (Josh. 2:12–13). Joshua gave the commandment that when the city fell, Rahab and her family were to be spared (Josh. 6:17).

The genuineness of Rahab's faith had been demonstrated by the protection she provided for the spies, and it was because of her faith that she was spared when Jericho fell. It was not Rahab's works that delivered her from judgment, but rather it was her faith in the God who brought judgment that provided deliverance when her city fell. Rahab, a stranger to the covenants, received blessing on the same basis as those mentioned earlier by the author; that is, by faith. Rahab believed in God and believed that the land would be given to Israel according to His promise. That same witness had been given to the people of Jericho, but unlike Rahab they "did not believe" (Heb. 11:31). They did not have faith, and so they were delivered over to judgment. What is recorded here shows that faith operates for anyone, whether those under covenant or those outside of the covenant. It also demonstrates that a lack of faith is the basis of judgment.

e. Faith exemplified in trials (11:32–38).

Having taken his readers through the period of patriarchs and the time of the conquest of the land, the author now moves through the era of the judges, the kings, and the prophets to show that the faith principle has extended over Israel's entire history.

Gideon's victory over the Midianites is another example of the sufficiency of faith in the midst of conflict. When Gideon was appointed by the Lord to deliver Israel from the Midianites (Judg. 6:14), he assumed that it would be necessary to assemble a large army to defeat the enemy. But if this army numbering in thousands had been successful in defeating the Midianites, Israel would have taken credit for their victory (Judg. 7:2). Therefore the army was reduced until only three hundred remained (Judg. 7:8). In the face of overwhelming odds Gideon exercised faith in God (Judg. 7:15) and proceeded into the conflict. His unwavering faith produced an obedience that led to victory.

When Sisera, captain of the host of Jabin, king of Canaan, threatened Israel, God gave Deborah a promise, "I will deliver him into your hand" (Judg. 4:7). By faith—faith in God who had given the promise, "this is the day in which the Lord has delivered Sisera into your hand. Has not the Lord gone out before you?" (Judg. 4:14)—Barak led ten thousand men of the tribes of Naphtali and Zebulun against Sisera. God honored the faith of Deborah and Barak and "routed Sisera and all his chariots and all his army with the edge of the sword before Barak" (Judg. 4:15). Once again faith triumphed in the midst of adversity.

When the Philistines occupied Judah and threatened its existence (Judg. 15:9), Samson attacked the forces of the Philistines with nothing more than a fresh jawbone of a donkey (Judg. 15:15) and killed a

In our experience of continuing by faith in spite of the circumstances, we may find that God will not accomplish His purpose in the way we might have imagined. We may even go through a period of apparent loss before we arrive at His point of solution to our problems.

thousand men. Evidently the Spirit of the Lord was upon Samson in this conflict as it had been upon him previously when he faced the roaring lion (Judg. 14:5–6). The Spirit of the Lord will give victory to one who walks by faith and who wars by faith.

When the Ammonites made war with Israel (Judg. 11:4), the elders invited Jephthah to become their captain (Judg. 11:11). Empowered by the Spirit of the Lord (Judg. 11:29) Jephthah engaged the Ammonites in battle, "and the Lord delivered them into his hands. And he defeated them . . . with a very great slaughter. Thus the people of Ammon were subdued before the children of Israel" (Judg. 11:32–33).

David is another example of the patient endurance faith produces. Samuel was commanded by the Lord to anoint David to be king (1 Sam. 16:12–13). It was not until years later that David was anointed king over Judah (2 Sam. 2:4), and then anointed king over all the tribes of Israel (2 Sam 5:3). Thus David was called upon to exercise

patient endurance while he awaited fulfillment of what God had promised. David's reign involved much conflict. There was conflict within the family. There was conflict within the nation. There was conflict with the nations that surrounded Israel. Consequently David was compelled to assemble a large army and to engage his enemies in battle (2 Sam. 8). In all of these conflicts David was sustained by faith and triumphed through faith.

Until the appointment of Samuel to be God's prophet (1 Sam. 3:20–21), the Levitical priests had been the mediator between God and man. The priest was God's spokesman to Israel. But with the appointment of Samuel to the office of prophet, God channeled his revelation to the nation through those who held that office. Samuel was also appointed as a judge in Israel (1 Sam. 7:15–17). Samuel's role as prophet/judge was marked by his ready obedience to the will of God as it was revealed to him. This obedience was the product of his faith. Samuel's faith produced a righteousness in his life so that none in Israel could find fault with him (1 Sam. 12:1–5). As an intercessor before God on behalf of the nation, Samuel had recognized the need to be faithful as a mediator, and he considered it a sin not to pray continually for them. In representing God before men Samuel had become their teacher (1 Sam. 12:23). Thus we see that faith produced faithfulness and righteousness in this one God had set apart as a prophet.

The faithfulness that characterized the first prophet Samuel, the writer says, also characterized those who in years to follow occupied the office of prophet. In Hebrews 11:33–38 the writer, without citing specific references, shows us what faith produced in those who are undergoing severe afflictions, adversity, and trials. In listing these experiences, the writer emphasizes that trials should not nullify faith, but rather should strengthen faith. Faith is not only tested by trials, it is strengthened by them. The author undoubtedly has in mind his readers' experiences. He desires that their faith be strengthened by the adversity they experience, in the same way that faith brought military victories to Israel.

Faith has always produced a righteous life that pleases God. Many by faith had experienced the fulfillment of God's promises. Faith delivered from physical harm. Lions' mouths were stopped. Faith delivered believers from harm by fire or by sword. By faith weakness was turned to strength. There were even those who voluntarily submitted to torture rather than try to find a way of escape. This torture might have been emotional as they were subjected to mockery, or it might have been physical as they were subjected to scourging or even imprisonment.

This is precisely the point of James 1:2–4. It is a difficult perspective to maintain in the midst of trials, but it is true nonetheless.

There were those who by faith witnessed the resurrection of the dead (1 Kings 17:17ff.; 2 Kings 4:17ff.; Luke 7:11–15; John 11; Acts 9:36–41). Resurrection miracles in Scripture were the highest pinnacle in what was accomplished by faith, as faith triumphs over death for those who in faith accepted death (Heb. 11:37). Others through faith were ostracized from their community. They wandered about and were reduced to poverty. They were homeless and lived in isolation in dens and caves.

As he wrote, the author must have seen many parallels between that to which he had made reference and the experiences of his readers. Many of them had been ostracized from society, had forfeited employment, and were reduced to poverty. Many who had been wealthy were now destitute. They had been subject to mockery and imprisonment. But they had not yet sacrificed their lives because of their faith in Christ.

f. The victory of faith (11:32–38).

The writer has run the gamut of human experiences to show that faith can triumph in any circumstance. Those who passed through such experiences were called upon to demonstrate patient endurance, for they "did not receive the promise" (11:39). During those experiences in which their faith was tested, they anticipated what God had promised to them. That destiny God promised Abraham (11:10) supported him in the midst of his sufferings. And the readers of this letter were partakers of that same

---

The issue of "blending in" is a good one with which to challenge believers of the younger generation. Many young people are eager to hear that it is normal to be teased, ridiculed, even physically abused for their faith in Christ. Knowing that persecution is something that will help move them on to maturity will more often motivate them rather than discourage them.

promise. Therefore the writer encouraged them to lay hold of that promise by faith and to demonstrate patient endurance. For if that expectation could sustain those who had suffered, as the writer had described in verses 33–38, that expectation could certainly sustain them in their present conflicts. The trials their ancestors endured did not cause them to surrender their faith nor to turn from walking by faith. Rather, they lived by faith and demonstrated patient endurance, anticipating the fulfillment of God's promise.

In the same way the recipients must have patience in their sufferings until they receive the fulfillment of God's promise. If their ancestors had already received that for which they were looking so that the promise had been exhausted, there would be nothing for the recipients to look forward to. But since the ancestors had not yet received it, the readers should emulate their patient endurance. The unity of God's program demands that all His people inherit together. By faith we and they together await the consummation of the promise. And while the original recipients of this letter were indeed suffering, their sufferings did not equal the sufferings of those who had gone before. If faith sustained their ancestors, it certainly would sustain them—and will sustain us.

E. Exhortation to patient endurance (12:1–29).

1 Therefore we also, since we are surrounded by so great a cloud of witnesses, let us lay aside every weight, and the sin which so easily ensnares us, and let us run with endurance the race that is set before us,

2 looking unto Jesus, the author and finisher of our faith, who for the joy that was set before Him endured the cross, despising the shame, and has sat down at the right hand of the throne of God.

3 For consider Him who endured such hostility from sinners against Himself, lest you become weary and discouraged in your souls.

4 You have not yet resisted to bloodshed, striving against sin.

5 And you have forgotten the exhortation which speaks to you as

to sons: "My son, do not despise the chastening of the Lord, nor be discouraged when you are rebuked by Him;

6 For whom the Lord loves He chastens, and scourges every son whom He receives."

7 If you endure chastening, God deals with you as with sons; for what son is there whom a father does not chasten?

8 But if you are without chastening, of which all have become partakers, then you are illegitimate and not sons.

9 Furthermore, we have had human fathers who corrected us, and we paid them respect. Shall we not much more readily be in subjection to the Father of spirits and live?

10 For they indeed for a few days chastened us as seemed best to them, but He for our profit, that we may be partakers of His holiness.

11 Now no chastening seems to be joyful for the present, but painful; nevertheless, afterward it yields the peaceable fruit of righteousness to those who have been trained by it.

12 Therefore strengthen the hands which hang down, and the feeble knees,

13 and make straight paths for your feet, so that what is lame may not be dislocated, but rather be healed.

14 Pursue peace with all people, and holiness, without which no one will see the Lord:

15 looking carefully lest anyone fall short of the grace of God; lest any root of bitterness springing up cause trouble, and by this many become defiled;

16 lest there be any fornicator or profane person like Esau, who for one morsel of food sold his birthright.

17 For you know that afterward, when he wanted to inherit the blessing, he was rejected, for he found no place for repentance, though he sought it diligently with tears.

18 For you have not come to the mountain that may be touched and that burned with fire, and to blackness and darkness and tempest,

19 and the sound of a trumpet and the voice of words, so that those who heard it begged that the word should not be spoken to them anymore.

20 (For they could not endure what was commanded: "And if so much as a beast touches the mountain, it shall be stoned or shot with an arrow."

21 And so terrifying was the sight that Moses said, "I am exceedingly afraid and trembling.")

22 But you have come to Mount Zion and to the city of the living God, the heavenly Jerusalem, to an innumerable company of angels,

23 to the general assembly and church of the firstborn who are registered in heaven, to God the Judge of all, to the spirits of just men made perfect,

24 to Jesus the Mediator of the new covenant, and to the blood of sprinkling that speaks better things than that of Abel.

25 See that you do not refuse Him who speaks. For if they did not escape who refused Him who spoke on earth, much more shall we not escape if we turn away from Him who speaks from heaven,

26 whose voice then shook the earth; but now He has promised, saying, "Yet once more I shake not only the earth, but also heaven."

27 Now this, "Yet once more," indicates the removal of those things that are being shaken, as of things that are made, that the things which cannot be shaken may remain.

28 Therefore, since we are receiving a kingdom which cannot be shaken, let us have grace, by which we may serve God acceptably with reverence and godly fear.

29 For our God is a consuming fire.

1. The exhortation (12:1).

The writer now will pointedly apply the truth presented in chapter 11 to those to whom he is writing. The word *therefore* (12:1) introduces the application. The basis for his appeal is in the fact that "we are surrounded by so great a cloud of witnesses." Here the author envisions all believers as engaged in a marathon. The race has begun, but it has not yet been completed. What motivates the runner is that "we are surrounded by so great a cloud of witnesses." These are not spectators watching to see how we run the race, nor to see if we endure to the end. Rather, they are witnesses *to us* concerning the life of faith. The witnesses are all who have been presented in the previous chapter. They bear witness to the sufficiency of faith, and they demonstrate that faith will produce patient endurance, will result in obedience, and will accept trials without wavering. No further evidence is needed to show that faith will support the runner through the course of the race until he reaches the final goal. On this basis, then, the author gives three exhortations.

First, readers are exhorted to "lay aside every weight." For a runner, weight can be either excess body fat or a burdensome load. The words *lay aside* convey the idea of taking off a robe. If one is to reach the goal in the race that had been begun, it is necessary to lay aside any encumbrance. Thus the contestant will train down to a desired weight and lay aside any garments that might impede his progress.

The second exhortation is to lay aside "the sin which so easily ensnares us." While it is true that any sin will impede the contestant's progress, the fact that he refers specifically to "the sin" suggests that the writer has in mind the sin of unbelief (10:38–39). The word translated "ensnares" is a compound that literally means to "stand around us." Just as the runner is surrounded by a multitude who bear witness to the validity of faith, so unbelief also surrounds us and entices us to abandon faith. The moment the contestant loses his assurance that he will complete the race, he begins to doubt that he will be able to finish. And he can easily give up.

The third exhortation is to "run with endurance the race that is set before us." Faith gives assurance to the one who runs the race that he will complete the race and reach the goal, which is maturity (Heb. 6:1). The race is not a sprint to a goal that can be reached in a short period of time. Rather, it is an extended marathon that spans one's

---

While there is no real practical application of Scripture without first knowing what it really says, neither should we study the Word of God without exploring the effects it should have in our lives. This is not an "either/or" but a "both/and" proposition. It is the perfect marriage between the way we should be at work in the Word of God and the way the Word of God should be at work in us.

life. Thus, the author does not exhort that we run with faith, but that we run with patient endurance by faith.

2. The example of Christ (12:2–4).

In the phrase "looking unto Jesus," the author is presenting the continuing attitude with which they are to run. Since every runner presses toward a goal, some have suggested that Jesus Himself is the goal and since we are pressing on to maturity, and maturity is found in Christ, that would seem reasonable. However, the author goes on to point to Jesus as one who exemplified patient endurance in all that He suffered. We, therefore, are to follow His example. Significantly, the author uses the name "Jesus," which emphasizes the true humanity of the One to whom we are to look as we run our race. Because the author had referred to so many Old Testament saints who ran with patient endurance, readers might be tempted to use them as ideal examples. However, almost all of those cited as witnesses to the life of faith also had failures, so that they would not be perfect examples. Jesus perfectly exemplified patient endurance and obedience. The word translated "looking" here has the idea of turning away from something else, so that we do not look to these as our example, but rather to Jesus. Thus we would conclude that all those saints previously cited were not to be considered examples of faith, but rather as witnesses to the patient endurance that faith produces. The fact

---

If you like to jog, play tennis, or participate in another kind of sport, try this experiment. The next time you take part in the game wear a pack full of books on your back (don't try this if you are a swimmer). Then, every time you are conscious of that backpack's hindrance to your performance, remind yourself, "This is the effect sin has on my Christian life."

that Jesus is referred to as both the initiator of faith and the one who brings faith to its fullest expression emphasizes the perfect example of the One to whom believers are exhorted to look.

There is no greater example of patient endurance in suffering than Jesus, both in His trial and in his crucifixion. The prophet Isaiah said of Him, "He was oppressed and He was afflicted, yet He opened not His mouth; He was led as a lamb to the slaughter, and as a sheep before its shearers is silent, so He opened not His mouth" (Isa. 53:7). Peter testified to the patient endurance of Christ in His sufferings when he said, "Christ also suffered for us, leaving us an example,

that you should follow His steps: 'Who committed no sin, nor was guile found in His mouth'; who, when He was reviled, did not revile in return; when He suffered, He did not threaten, but committed Himself to Him who judges righteously" (1 Pet. 2:21–23).

That which motivated Jesus in His suffering was "the joy that was set before Him." His great joy was that of submitting unreservedly to the will of His Father. His joy sprang from His obedience. Paul referred to this when he wrote, "He humbled Himself and became obedient to the point of death, even the death of the cross" (Phil. 2:8). Christ's petition that He

---

One of the most dangerous mistakes a deckhand on a commercial fishing vessel can commit is to let his foot or ankle get tangled in the rope-like cable as it is dragged overboard with the massive nets. To become so entangled can instantly result in injury or death. The effects of becoming entangled in sin are no less serious in our spiritual lives. If you are becoming slowly wrapped up in sinful practices, tendencies, or relationships, forsake them now. The temporary unpleasantness will be far better than the long-term consequences of continuing.

might be restored to the glory which He had with the Father from all eternity past (John 17:5) was answered because of His submission to the will of God. God honored the obedience and the patient endurance of His Son by enthroning Him at His own right hand. Paul says that the consequence of Jesus' obedience was that "God also has highly exalted Him and given Him the name which is above every name, that at the name of Jesus every knee should bow, of those in heaven, and of those on earth, and of those under the earth, and that every tongue should confess that Jesus Christ is Lord, to the glory of God the Father" (Phil 2:9–11). The cross, which was an emblem of shame among people, became the source of incomparable joy to the Son of God.

In order for Jesus to demonstrate patient endurance, it was necessary for Him to enter into spiritual and physical death to provide salvation for sinners. The author points out that as strenuous as oppressed believers may consider their afflictions to be, they have not been called upon to suffer in the will of God as Jesus was called upon to suffer (12:3–4). While it is true that some believers such as Stephen and James had suffered physical death, they belonged to a previous generation. This infers that the sufferings of the church's second generation were not as severe as those experienced by the first generation, and certainly not as severe as the sufferings Jesus experienced. Thus they were to look to His patient endurance as their example.

Though many positional benefits of the Christian life are "instant," the Bible repeatedly refers to the Christian experience as a long, steady process requiring "endurance." Be wary of any group that promises "instant" spirituality through some practice or experience, and instead gird your heart and mind for the long haul. It is worth the trip.

3. The explanation of discipline (12:5–11).

In verses 5–11 the writer now shows the benefits that will come to these believers if they endure their sufferings patiently. When the writer charges them, "do not despise the chastenings of the Lord," he is inferring that they are in fact despising the Lord's correction, an attitude he wants to discourage. The word *despise* has in it the idea of regarding lightly or making of little account. This implies that they saw no benefit in the experiences they were undergoing. In contrast, by quoting Proverbs 3:11–12, the writer asks these sufferers to view their afflictions as evidence of a father's love for his children. Rather than despising His chastening or being discouraged when sufferings come, they should welcome them as assurance that they are the sons of God, for God will chasten only those who are His own children.

Here it is important to distinguish between punishment and chastening. Punishment is retribution for evil that has been done. God never punishes His children for their iniquities, because all punishment for sin was borne by Jesus Christ on the cross: "There is therefore now no condemnation to those who are in Christ Jesus" (Rom. 8:1). So no child of God needs fear punishment from God.

Chastening or discipline, on the other hand, has moral training in view. It is an instructive device by which a child is conformed to the standards or expectations of his father. And just as it is the responsibility of earthly fathers to discipline their children, so God as our Father disciplines us, His children. The absence of any discipline would indicate that we are not sons of God. Therefore

There is an undeniable relationship between joy and obedience in the Christian life. If your joy is lacking, start first by taking inventory of your obedience to Him.

correction or discipline should be viewed as an evidence of our sonship. Further, these disciplines are an evidence of the Father's love. There may be degrees in discipline, as suggested in the contrast between chastening and scourging (12:6). These do not differ in kind, but rather in degree or intensity. God may begin the discipline process very gently, and then increase the intensity of the discipline only if the one being disciplined resists it. When that which brought the discipline is removed, or when the discipline has accomplished its desired purpose, then the discipline will be lifted. If the child of God is perpetually unresponsive, God's ultimate discipline may be to remove that individual from life here on earth and transfer him into glory where the process of perfection will be completed (1 John 5:16).

The earthly child who is disciplined will respect and honor the father who is faithful to his responsibilities and disciplines his child. Thus the application is obvious: "Shall we not much more readily be in subjection to the Father of spirits and live?" (Heb. 12:9). This emphasizes the spirit in which any discipline should be received. If this attitude characterizes those who are suffering, they will profit by their present experiences. Disciplines from an earthly father are temporal and brief. But the author makes no reference to the temporal aspect of God's discipline, because it may continue until it accom-

---

Responding to God's discipline with thankfulness rather than bitterness is a tough challenge. That's why we are admonished to look at it from the viewpoint of God's love for us, just like a parent who disciplines a child to keep him out of the street or to help him learn obedience. In answer to the question, "Why do I undergo God's discipline, yet the unrighteous don't seem to suffer at all," God does not even bother to discipline those who are not His.

plishes its desired end. Therefore the sooner one submits to God's discipline and learns from it, the sooner he may expect that discipline to end. God's discipline may indeed be grievous, but it may be endured with patience because of its intended purpose.

Divine discipline is not an evidence of God's anger, but is designed "for our profit" (12:10). The author makes two significant statements that show the result of suffering if endured patiently. First, "we may be partakers of His holiness" (12:10) and second, "it yields the peaceable fruit of righteousness" (12:11). Holiness has to do with the essential character of the individual, while righteousness is the external manifestation of that character. To be a partaker of His holiness and to manifest the peaceable fruit of righteousness is to manifest the perfection or maturity that was the goal set before us (12:1). Thus it appears that suffering is a necessary prerequisite to maturity.

In referring to "those who have been trained by it," the writer uses the same word as in 5:14 where he wrote, "Solid food belongs to those who are of full age, that is, those who by reason of use have their senses exercised to discern both good and evil." The word *exercised* and the word *trained* are the same New Testament word, suggesting that the discipline is designed to bring us to maturity.

4. The believer's obligation (12:12–17).

Discipline is a basis for one's assurance of sonship, for the heavenly Father disci-

Even though not a popular or often-taught concept today, the Bible is clear that God may choose to remove a perpetually disobedient child from life on earth. More than scaring us into conformity, this should motivate us to be among His obedient, responsive, responsible children who bring glory to His name.

plines only His own sons. All discipline is administered, not in anger, but in love. Discipline received in the right attitude will make us partakers of His holiness and produce in us the peaceable fruit of righteousness. Thus a specific obligation rests on all believers. The word *therefore* in verse 12 introduces that obligation.

First, the apostle points out the obligation of those who are practicing patient endurance toward those who are being overwhelmed by their experiences. The metaphor of a marathon contestant discussed in 12:1 is still a strong image here. In the race are those contestants who have become so weary their hands are hanging at their side. They have become so weak they can scarcely stand. It is

therefore the privilege and obligation of those who are running with patience to so identify with the weak that their strength will be imparted to them. In making "straight paths," the one who is patiently enduring will keep the exhausted one from veering off course. It also has in it the idea of removing any obstacle that would cause the runner to dislocate a joint. Either the weakness or the dislocation of a joint would eliminate the contestant from the race. The writer uses the illustration of the body to show the responsibility of one member to another. This is in perfect harmony with Paul's teaching in 1 Corinthians 12:12–31. The exhausted physical posture depicted in verse 12 suggests the present experience for some who are

Again holiness and righteousness are inextricably united with the process of spiritual maturity. Since this is the true process of spiritual growth, we are genuinely hurting rather than helping ourselves any time we compromise the holiness of God in the way we live. This would include the "big things"—like infidelity or criminal activity—as well as the "little things," like gossip, lying, or dishonesty.

in the race, while making "straight paths" anticipates what may be ahead for a fellow contestant. One who is pursuing the goal of maturity will render assistance to another who is in danger of falling short of the goal.

Next, the author shows one's obligation to himself while running with patience. He is not to become so preoccupied with the weakness of another that he loses sight of the goal set before him. In facing adversity, there is a temptation to become antagonistic toward one's adversaries. However, this attitude makes it impossible to fulfill the biblical injunction, "Do not avenge yourselves, . . . if your enemy hungers, feed him; if he thirsts, give him a drink; for in so doing you will heap coals of fire on his head; do

not be overcome by evil, but overcome evil with good" (Rom. 12:19–21). Christ commanded, "Love your enemies, bless those who curse you, do good to those who hate you, and pray for those who spitefully use you and persecute you, that you may be the sons of your Father in heaven" (Matt. 5:44–45). God is holy, and His holiness is manifested by loving those who are His enemies. God's child will be demonstrating that he is a partaker of God's holiness if he loves his enemies, and manifesting these character qualities is evidence that one is advancing toward maturity.

But now the apostle sounds a warning. Someone who has patiently endured suffering still might "fall short of the grace of God." The writer sees three dangers confronting

Scripture makes clear that the church should not be an "army that shoots its wounded." The lengthy discussion on Christian maturity here in Hebrews indicates that one of the most visible, most important, and most immediate results of that maturity will be Christians helping other Christians who are struggling. Not criticizing, not condemning, not belittling—but helping.

believers. The first is a failure to continue progressing toward maturity. He previously said, "Let us therefore come boldly to the throne of grace, that we may obtain mercy and find grace to help in time of need" (4:16). That grace is the promise of divine enablement to meet every circumstance. But there is a danger that a believer might become so preoccupied with circumstances that he will not take refuge in God's grace to enable him to endure that adversity.

Thus a believer might face a second danger; that is, he may become embittered. This would be a failure to "pursue peace with all men, and holiness" (12:14). A slow process might begin that would gradually grow and develop so that this attitude of bitterness characterizes the individual. And his attitude would not

only affect himself, it would influence many others to become embittered as well.

This would lead to a third danger, best illustrated by the experience of Esau (Gen. 25:27–34). To satisfy his physical appetite, Esau voluntarily surrendered every privilege and blessing to which he was heir as a son of the covenant. Esau was called a "fornicator" not because he was immoral, but because he lived to gratify his fleshly appetite. The physical gratification from the food he received from Jacob was very brief, whereas the benefits he would have received had he held on to the promised blessings would have been eternal. Later he realized what he had forfeited and pled for the covenanted blessings "with an exceedingly great and bitter cry" (Gen. 27:34). But because Isaac had already blessed Jacob, Esau's

Often we gauge our spiritual progress by comparing ourselves to other Christians—particularly those who are not doing as well as we seem to be doing. The true standard of comparison, however, should be Jesus Christ, and how we are conforming to His image.

tears were in vain. While Esau changed his mind, it was impossible for Isaac to withdraw the benediction on Jacob and give the blessing to Esau. So Esau "found no place for repentance" in Isaac. The decision he had made to exchange God's covenanted blessings for physical gratification determined Esau's future.

Application to all readers of Hebrews is very clear. If we do not avail ourselves of God's gracious provision of strength for conflict, and if we become embittered because of circumstances, exchanging spiritual blessings for momentary relief from physical sufferings, we will—as the readers have already been warned in chapter 6—lapse into a state of immaturity. And this imma-ture state may well be one from which it will be impossible to be restored to the same blessings enjoyed by those who, through patient endurance, progress toward maturity.

5. A refuge for those who are tested (12:18–24).

Those who were experiencing intense persecution needed a refuge to which they could flee. Some felt that their refuge was to return to the external forms of Judaism, so that those who had persecuted them following their public baptism would forget that they had severed their relationship to the old system. The Law given to Israel at Sinai was a manifestation of the glorious holiness that belonged to the God who there revealed Himself to His covenant people. But by

We live in a culture of ever-increasing hate and bitterness. Everyone has an axe to grind, a complaint to make, a hardship to blame on someone else. But the Bible teaches that the mature Christian recognizes God's hand in all things and is not embittered toward Him on account of even the most trying circumstances. This perspective offers true freedom and a foundation for lasting joy.

directing their thoughts back to Exodus 20:18–19, the writer reminds his readers that at the time the Law was given, the people were overwhelmed with fear because of the fire, blackness, darkness, tempest, and trumpet sound that caused them to flee from His presence. They did not experience quietness, rest, and peace, but rather an overwhelming fear. So unapproachable was the God who revealed Himself at Sinai that instructions had been given that if an animal touched the mountain, it was to be put to death (Ex. 19:12–13). The people were so afraid of such a God that they begged that His voice might be stilled (Ex. 20:18–19). Such was the response not only of the people, but even of Moses himself—in spite of all God had previously revealed of Himself (Heb. 12:21). the author's point is that if one were to seek refuge again in the Law, he will not find the peace and rest he desires, but like Moses would experience only an overwhelming fear.

The word *but* in 12:22 contrasts the refuge provided for believers. They do not come to an earthly Sinai but to a heavenly Mount Zion. They do not come to a city that is the pride of the people, but to the city of the living God. They do not come to an earthly Jerusalem founded by David as the capital of his kingdom, but rather to the heavenly Jerusalem. The earthly Jerusalem—with its temple to which some were tempted to return—was inhabited by multitudes who by their rejection of Christ had declared themselves to be His enemies. But the inhabitants of this heavenly city are quite different. This city is inhabited by "an innumerable company of angels," referring to the vast multitude of unfallen angelic beings.

Moreover, this city is the dwelling place of "the general assembly and church of the firstborn who are registered in heaven." This refers to all believers of this present age, which had its beginning on the day of Pentecost and will continue until the translation of the saints out of this world into glory (1 Thess. 4:13–17).

Included in that city will be "the spirits of just men made perfect." This refers to all the Old Testament saints, together with the Tribulation saints who will be resurrected and translated there at the Second Advent of Christ to earth (Isa. 26:19–20; Dan. 12:12; Rev. 20:6).

All of these are in the presence of "God the Judge of all" and are together with "Jesus, the Mediator of the new covenant." This city is the place our Lord referred to as "My Father's house" (John 14:2). This is the place believers will share with Christ (John 14:3). John describes "the holy city, New Jerusalem" (Rev. 21:1–8) as the eternal dwelling place of all the redeemed of all the ages. This is the city to which Abraham looked forward (Heb. 11:10), in which "the tabernacle of God is with men, and He will dwell with them, and they shall be His people, and God Himself will be with them and be their God" (Rev.21:3).

Christ declared, "I am the way, the truth, and the life. No one comes to the Father except through Me" (John 14:6). Thus the writer of Hebrews reminds us that believers will enter this city on the basis of New Covenant blood (13:24). Abel offered an acceptable sacrifice of the blood of an animal, but Jesus Christ offers better blood that becomes the foundation of a better refuge, because He offered His own blood. This blood does not, like the revelation of God at Sinai, produce fear and a desire to flee. This blood of the New Covenant brings rest and peace.

In light of this brief look ahead at our future dwelling place together with all believers, many of our petty complaints against one another should seem very small. Certainly, the holding of grudges or longstanding anger should cause us embarrassment, knowing we will all be together with Him in that eternal city!

6. Warning and encouragement (12:25–29).

In light of the refuge provided for us, the writer sounds a word of warning. The word *see* (12:25) emphasizes the obligation resting on those who have such a hope set before them. While God spoke at Sinai, the writer views God as still speaking from heaven (12:25). God's revelation was given to the apostles, who by inspiration recorded what had been revealed to them. That revelation—coming through an apostle, recorded by inspiration—is as authoritative as the revelation given to Israel through Moses. And just as Israel is accountable for the word God spoke to them, the recipients of this letter are accountable for the revelation given to them through the apostle. Israel could not escape discipline if they disobeyed or neglected the revelation given to them. Likewise, the recipients of this epistle cannot expect to escape severe discipline if they do not heed its warnings and the apostle's exhortations as God's authoritative word

for them in their present circumstances.

When the Law was given at Sinai, the word from God "shook the earth" (12:26). This word suggests a violent convulsion of nature. The giving of the Law instituted a new order, and the authority of the One instituting that order was seen in nature's response to that revelation. What happened at the institution of the Law will happen in a greater degree at the institution of a new order. Anticipating the coming of the covenanted messianic age, the prophet Haggai said that before the institution of that age, "thus says the Lord of hosts: " 'Once more (it is a little while) I will shake heaven and earth, the sea and dry land; and I will shake all nations, and they shall come to the Desire of All Nations, and I will fill this temple with glory,' says the Lord of hosts" (Hag. 2:6–7). The prophet's prediction of the coming new age associated with the shaking of the earth again signifies that the old order established with a shaking of the earth will be done away. Although anticipating a final, future shaking prior to the second advent of Christ, the writer also seemed to anticipate the predicted shaking of Jerusalem by Titus, which was drawing near. Haggai's prophecy gave notice that the existing Levitical order was a temporary arrangement which ultimately would be terminated so that a permanent and unshakable order may be instituted. The implication the writer is made was that if his readers attempt to revert to Judaism to find refuge from affliction, they will be returning to that which would be done away. They can find no permanent rest or peace in a temporary system. Those who are suffering because of their identification with Christ have the promise of "a kingdom which cannot be shaken" (12:28). They are already "registered in heaven" (12:23). And because of that the writer can exhort, "Let us have grace." They have access to the throne of grace where they "may obtain mercy and find grace to help in time of need" (4:16). Their particular need here is for patient endurance; by receiving the gift of God's grace they "may serve God acceptably with reverence and godly fear" (12:28).

This service will be offered out of reverential respect for God. And it will be offered in fear lest, in spite of all God has provided to enable people to live by faith and to evidence patient endurance, they might fall short of that which God has promised and fail to progress toward maturity. As a consuming fire, God purifies all that is unworthy and unacceptable in those who serve Him and all that is unfit to abide in His presence.

While our neglect of these admonitions may not result in consequences as severe as those faced by the original recipients of this letter, we should realize that neglect of God's Word—especially when we clearly understand what it is saying—can bring less than desirable consequences, as James 1:23–25 confirms.

Therefore do not attempt to serve God in that which is outdated and no longer acceptable to Him. Serve Him instead in that which is pleasing and acceptable.

F. Concluding exhortations (13:1–19).

1 Let brotherly love continue.

2 Do not forget to entertain strangers, for by so doing some have unwittingly entertained angels.

3 Remember the prisoners as if chained with them--those who are mistreated--since you yourselves are in the body also.

4 Marriage is honorable among all, and the bed undefiled; but fornicators and adulterers God will judge.

5 Let your conduct be without covetousness; be content with such things as you have. For He Himself has said, "I will never leave you nor forsake you."

6 So we may boldly say: "The Lord is my helper; I will not fear. What can man do to me?"

7 Remember those who rule over you, who have spoken the word of God to you, whose faith follow, considering the outcome of their conduct.

8 Jesus Christ is the same yesterday, today, and forever.

9 Do not be carried about with various and strange doctrines. For it is good that the heart be established by grace, not with foods which have not profited those who have been occupied with them.

10 We have an altar from which those who serve the tabernacle have no right to eat.

11 For the bodies of those animals, whose blood is brought into the sanctuary by the high priest for sin, are burned outside the camp.

12 Therefore Jesus also, that He might sanctify the people with His own blood, suffered outside the gate.

13 Therefore let us go forth to Him, outside the camp, bearing His reproach.

14 For here we have no continuing city, but we seek the one to come.

15 Therefore by Him let us continually offer the sacrifice of praise to God, that is, the fruit of our lips, giving thanks to His name.

16 But do not forget to do good and to share, for with such sacrifices God is well pleased.

17 Obey those who rule over you, and be submissive, for they watch out for your souls, as those who must give account. Let them do so with joy and not with grief, for that would be unprofitable for you.

18 Pray for us; for we are confi-

dent that we have a good conscience, in all things desiring to live honorably.

19 But I especially urge you to do this, that I may be restored to you the sooner.

Throughout this epistle, the writer presents many important doctrinal truths that become the basis of his exhortations to live by faith and to let faith produce the fruit of patient endurance. Now the writer gives exhortation to apply truth to specific circumstances in which the readers might find themselves. No doctrine is without its practical application, and the doctrine of the superiority of Christ is so forcefully presented in this letter that it will certainly affect the practical conduct of believers.

1. Exhortations in the moral realm (13:1–6).

The first exhortation concerns the relationship of believers to each other. This is a reiteration of the obligation the writer stated in 12:12–13. The term *brotherly love* refers to the relation of Christians one to another because of their mutual relationship to the Lord. While the love a Jew had was national (Deut. 23:19), the love a believer has is universal. This is why John commanded his spiritual children, "By this we know love, because He laid down His life for us. And we also ought to lay down our lives for the brethren. But whoever has this world's goods, and sees his brother in need, and shuts up his heart from him, how does the love of God abide in him? My little children, let us not love in word or in tongue, but in deed and in truth" (1 John 3:16–18).

When the author says this love is to continue, he implies that his readers had been demonstrating such love one for another, but that bond was in danger of being severed. Such love, on the other hand, would fulfill the command of Christ (John 13:34–35).

His second exhortation has to do with showing hospitality, which itself is a manifestation of the universal love believers should demonstrate. The writer evidently has in mind the experience of Abraham as recorded in Genesis 18. Those Abraham entertained were God's messengers. This passage does not suggest that we may expect special revelation from God through angelic beings as Abraham experienced, but rather that if we show hospitality, the one we entertain may prove to be a messenger from God to bring encouragement, strength, or assurance.

The third exhortation encourages believers to identify with those who are actually imprisoned for their faith, or who are suffering because they live in the midst of those who are hostile to Christ. These believers would be in desperate need of another's help. Paul wrote, "If one member suffers, all the members suffer with it" (1 Cor. 12:26). Those who are not persecuted should identify themselves with those who are, because they are part of the same body.

The fourth exhortation has to do with marriage and the marital relationship. Paul taught (1 Cor. 7:25–38) that in order that one might devote himself completely to the ser-

vice of the Lord, and in view of the persecutions he could foresee coming upon believers, it would be better to remain single. These believers might have drawn the conclusion that it would be wrong for a believer to marry. Or if a believer married, it would be better to live in celibacy. So the writer reaffirms marriage as a divine arrangement. The relationship between husband and wife in marriage was designed to satisfy God-given appetites (1 Cor. 7:9). Because of the prevalence of divorce among the Jews, as sanctioned by their teachers (Matt. 19:3–12), some might resort to some form of immorality to escape the pressures of persecution. Thus the writer guards against anything that would lower the dignity of marriage or violate its sacredness.

A fifth exhortation is given in light of the many believers who had forfeited all their worldly possessions for Christ's sake. It would be easy for these believers to be covetous and discontented with their lot in life. Therefore they are exhorted to bring their attitudes into conformity with the mind of Christ so that they will not be covetous, but be content with what they have. The writer shows them (13:5b–6) that their security is not found in material possessions, but in a Person who promised, "I will never leave you nor forsake you" (Deut. 31:6) Their confidence that the Lord can supply their every need will sustain them even in their destitution. Such was the attitude of the apostle Paul when, as a prisoner in Rome, he wrote, "My God shall supply all your need according to His riches in glory by Christ Jesus" (Phil. 4:19). The God who could sustain Paul in his material losses and supply his every need is sufficient for them as well.

Here the word *leave* communicates the idea of loosing a hold, withdrawing the support rendered by a sustaining grasp. The word *forsake* includes the idea of abandoning, deserting, or leaving one alone either in a battle or in an athletic contest. The one forsaken, then, would have no companion to stand beside him. God has promised that He will neither withdraw His sustaining grasp that supports us, nor will He abandon us in the conflict.

2. Exhortations in the religious realm (13:7–17).

The writer next directs his readers' attention to the example of "those who rule over you." The word *remember* means to observe carefully or to consider something in meticulous detail. Believers therefore are seen as God's flock committed to the careful oversight of shepherds. Peter writes of the responsibility of the shepherds of the flock, "The elders who are among you I exhort, I who am a fellow elder and a witness of the sufferings of Christ, and also a partaker of the glory that will be revealed: shepherd the flock of God which is among you, serving as overseers, not by constraint but willingly, not for dishonest gain but eagerly; nor as being lords over those entrusted to you, but being examples to the flock" (1 Pet. 5:1–3).

These shepherds had by faith borne a good witness to

the life of faith and of the patient endurance faith produces. It was the responsibility of shepherds to exercise a God-given authority over the flock, to guard the flock, to guide the flock, to teach the flock, to discipline the flock, but above all to be an example to the flock of the life of faith. The writer views these shepherds as having been faithful to their trust; therefore the members of the flock are exhorted to follow their example (Heb. 6:12). Some may have been persecuted and may even have lost their lives in the discharge of their oversight. Yet faith triumphed even in those circumstances, and their example—if followed—would enable those who are suffering to be victorious. This is based on the fact that "Jesus Christ is the same yesterday, today, and forever" (13:8). The One who brought their shepherds to

victory would certainly bring them to victory as well.

The writer now sounds a warning concerning false doctrines to which these believers had been exposed, fearing that they might be "carried about" with these teachings. The contrast here is between the doctrine that had been taught in this epistle and the doctrine of the Judaizers, who taught that through external ordinances they could obtain favor from God and enjoy intimate fellowship with Him. But the author reminds them that such sacrifices in the Old Testament were ineffectual and did not bring the offerers to maturity. All progress comes through that which grace provides and faith appropriates.

The writer previously stated, "The law made nothing perfect; on the other hand, there is the bringing in of a better hope, through which

---

Recent changes in church leadership styles have led to unfortunate abuses by some of those entrusted with the care of God's flock. We would do well, therefore, to remember that God's model of leadership is that of a shepherd, not an overlord.

we draw near to God" (Heb. 7:19). Faith will provide a foundation so that the one living by faith might enter into rest and peace even in the midst of conflict.

Evidently some false teachers were stating that if Christians abandoned the sacrifices, they would be leaving that which God had provided for their nourishment, their strength, and their fellowship with God. It is true in the Old Testament that those who offered the sacrifices were nourished by them. All who observed the Passover ate the flesh of the sacrificial lamb and were sustained by it. The priests who ministered at the altar were able to eat of the flesh of the sacrifices and of the bread that was offered in the tabernacle. The priests and their families were nourished and sustained by those sacrifices. But the writer sug-

gests that it is better to be nourished or established by that which God's grace provides rather than to seek nourishment from those sacrifices which became the food of the worshipers in the old order.

Believers who left those rituals were not forfeiting, but gaining; for as believer/priests they had access to the presence of God in a better tabernacle (Heb. 9:11–12). Those serving under the old order had no access to that tabernacle from which we draw our strength and support. While the priests could eat of the sacrifices they offered on behalf of the people, they were not permitted to eat the flesh of that which was sacrificed as a sin offering. God commanded that after the blood of the bullock had been placed on the altar of incense, and the remainder of the blood poured

The apostle's careful attention to counter false doctrine shows us that it is a responsibility of all Christians to carefully examine all teaching alongside the Word of God and to reject what is false. Being wary of false teaching is not "unloving"; it is an essential practice for those who want to go on to maturity.

out at the brazen altar, the carcass of that sacrifice was to be carried outside of the city and there it was to be burned (Lev. 4:1–35). While that sacrifice satisfied the demands of God's holiness and justice concerning the guilt of sin, it made no provision for the physical needs of those who offered it. The author views the death of Jesus as a sin offering, because Jesus was crucified outside the gate (Mark 15:20). Christ, by offering Himself as a sin offering, granted cleansing from defilement and freedom from the guilt of sin.

By crucifying Christ outside the city, the religious leaders caused Him to be a sin offering; but they were unable to receive any benefit from His death. However, believers who separate themselves from that system and identify themselves with Him find that He provides all they need for nourishment, strength, and fellowship. We have a privilege denied to the Old Testament priests—to receive benefit from the sin offering through our identification with Him by faith.

The word *for* (13:14) gives the reason they are to go outside the camp and thus separate themselves from the temple and all of its useless rituals. They have the assurance of a permanent city that takes the place of that earthly Jerusalem. This is the city Abraham anticipated (11:9–10), which they are encouraged likewise to anticipate by faith (Heb. 12:22–24). They are in the process of "receiving a kingdom which cannot be shaken" (12:28), and on the basis of that expectation, they are to patiently endure.

For the Jews, Jerusalem was viewed as their permanent city. Little did they realize that it had been devoted to destruction (Matt. 23:37–24:2; Luke 21:24). That which they viewed as permanent was only temporary, while that which these believers anticipated, although as yet unrealized, is eternal.

If these believers had been deceived by false teachers into thinking that without animal sacrifices they had nothing to offer to God and no acceptable worship to present to Him, the writer reminds them that there are sacrifices they may offer which will be acceptable to God. These are sacrifices they can offer continually, not just on certain stated occasions, as under the Mosaic system.

The first of these is the sacrifice of praise to God, which is further explained as "the fruit of our *lips*, giving thanks to His name" (Heb. 13:15). The first three offerings of Leviticus 1–6 were sacrifices of thanksgiving for blessings received. Even though these sacrifices have been done away because of the sacrifice of Christ, thanksgiving may still be offered to God. Praise has a Person in view and is occupied with the perfections of the character of that Person. Thanksgiving focuses attention on the gifts that One has given. The person who is so occupied will respond in worship, and that worship is an acceptable sacrifice to God.

The next sacrifice is doing good and sharing. While the praise and the giving of thanks is directed toward God, sharing is directed

toward other men. This is a manifestation of the brotherly love the writer previously spoke of (13:1). According to their ability, believers are to share with those in need. This sharing benefits a brother or sister in Christ and is an acceptable sacrifice to God.

The final exhortation is to give obedience and submission to those who rule over you (13:17). Believers are viewed as a flock over whom God has placed shepherds responsible to safeguard the sheep. Because the sheep are under the authority of the shepherds, the shepherds cannot fulfill their ministry to the flock unless the sheep submit to them. The shepherds are not without responsibility in their guidance, their teaching, or their discipline, for they realize they will be called to give an account to the great Shepherd. If the shepherds see that some of the sheep are growing weak because of conflicts, if some are entertaining false doctrine taught by false teachers, if some are being enticed to return to the old forms abolished by the sacrifice of

Christ, the shepherds are responsible to so teach, guide, and discipline so that they will not stray. If the shepherds fail to do this, they will be held accountable before "that great Shepherd of the sheep" (13:20).

Discipline by their rulers may not be pleasant, but they are to submit to it. And if guidance is given by those rulers, they are to obey it. Such faithfulness by the undershepherds to the Great Shepherd of the sheep will result in joy for them and profit for the flock.

3. Personal exhortations (13:18–19).

The writer now requests prayer for himself and evidently for Timothy with whom he is associated in the ministry. If the readers rejected oversight from those who had been appointed to rule over them, they might well reject oversight from him as well. Since this epistle is really a manifestation of spiritual oversight exercised by an apostle, he wants them to profit by it. He assures them that all he has written to them has come from a good conscience and consequently is worthy to be believed and obeyed. It is the writer's expectation that through their prayer he might be restored to them quickly. This implies that he had been with them previously but had been separated from them and now expects to visit them. His visit would put their obedience to his exhortation to the test.

This same motivation to obedience was used by the apostle Paul when he wrote to Philemon. After exhorting him to accept a wayward

---

In several places the Bible teaches that those who are entrusted with leadership over God's people will be strictly accountable to Him for that stewardship. While this should not frighten us away from serving Him in this way, it should make us as leaders that much more diligent and careful in all that we say, do, and teach.

slave back into fellowship, he concluded by saying, "Prepare a guest room for me, for I trust that through your prayers I shall be granted to you" (Philem. 22). The uncertainty of the time of the apostle's arrival demands immediate obedience, lest he arrive and find them in disobedience.

G. The benediction (13:20–25).

20 Now may the God of peace who brought up our Lord Jesus from the dead, that great Shepherd of the sheep, through the blood of the everlasting covenant,

21 make you complete in every good work to do His will, working in you what is well pleasing in His sight, through Jesus Christ, to whom be glory forever and ever. Amen.

22 And I appeal to you, brethren, bear with the word of exhortation, for I have written to you in few words.

23 Know that our brother Timothy has been set free, with whom I shall see you if he comes shortly.

24 Greet all those who rule over you, and all the saints. Those from Italy greet you.

25 Grace be with you all. Amen.

After asking for their prayers in his behalf, the author pours out his heart on their behalf. In this prayer he reaffirms his confidence that the God of peace is able to meet their every need in their present trials. This reference to God as a God of peace is significant. We might expect that he would refer to God as the God of power or as the Lord of the armies of heaven who was able to overthrow all their adversaries. But their greatest need in these circumstances is for the peace of God. The assurance he gives them is the same that Paul gave to the persecuted Philippians when he said, "The peace of God, which surpasses all understanding, will guard your hearts and minds through Christ Jesus" (Phil. 4:7).

The God who is able to grant them peace is the very God "who brought up our Lord Jesus from the dead." While the creation of the universe stands as an example of the power of God, that power is exemplified to a greater degree in the redemption of Israel from bondage in Egypt.

But the climactic demonstration of the exceeding greatness of God's power is the resurrection of the Lord Jesus from the dead (Eph. 1:19–20). The words *brought up* emphasize the attaining of a glorious victory after suffering the defeat of death. He was brought up to become "that great Shepherd of the sheep." All believers are in His flock. He is a faithful Shepherd, exercising protective care over the flock to guard, to guide, to instruct, to supply every need they might have.

His work as a shepherd is to "make you complete in every good work to do His will." His will as revealed in this letter is to bring these believers to perfection, or spiritual maturity. And God is at work in them, even through their sufferings, to accomplish that very purpose. His goal for believers will be realized through the shepherding work of Jesus Christ. He who is introduced to us as the One who "sat down at the right hand of the Majesty on high" in glory (Heb. 1:3) is the same One who now is being glorified as believers progress toward maturity. Thus the theme of the perfection or the maturity of believers which has been woven into this epistle becomes the subject of the closing prayer of the apostle.

Response to any exhortation is not obligatory; it is optional. So the writer closes with a very strong appeal that those who have received this "word of exhortation" will not ignore it, dismiss it, or reject it; but that they will embrace it so that God—who is at work in their experiences to conform them to Christ—might accomplish His will in them.

The author is careful to respect the authority of those who have been made rulers over them. He does not want to appear to usurp their authority, and so he sends greetings to them as an equal. The writer sends greetings from "those from Italy." While some have suggested that this epistle was written from Italy, this may actually suggest that there were many who had fled from Italy and were then in company with the writer. Because of the persecution of the Jews in Rome under Claudius (Acts 18:2), many such as Aquila and Priscilla had fled from Rome and had settled in other parts of the empire. The point the writer was making in referring to those from Italy is that there were other believers in other places who were undergoing severe persecutions, but had not compromised their testimony to escape persecution, and for Christ's sake had left Rome to settle elsewhere. The faithfulness of those from Italy under persecution was an example to the recipients of the letter.

The apostle closes with the benediction, "Grace be with you all." The grace was that to which the writer referred when he invited the believers to "come boldly to the throne of grace, that we may obtain mercy and find grace to help in time of need" (4:16). God's grace is sufficient for every need. God's grace is available, and all believers are free to draw upon His grace to enable them to stand in the face of persecution, and to progress steadily toward maturity with patient endurance.

Therefore, let us cultivate in ourselves and encourage others to strive for a faith that endures by His Spirit.

Throughout this letter we have seen that the ultimate responsibility for bringing believers to maturity rests on Jesus Christ and His ability to do what He has promised. The Christian's responsibility is to forsake those things that would stand in the way of maturity and to willfully submit to Him. The two-fold formula is simple: Our responsibility to is submit to Him in faith; His responsibility is to take us on to maturity.

Note to the Reader

The publisher invites you to share your response to the message of this book by writing Discovery House Publishers, P. O. Box 3566, Grand Rapids, MI 49501, U.S.A. or by calling 1-800-653-8333. For information about other Discovery House publications, contact us at the same address and phone number.